Miladyp Vangelatos
3/6/91

SYSTEMS DESIGN
UNDER
CICS®
COMMAND
AND
VSAM®

To My Wife Marie and to My Children
Mary and George

SYSTEMS DESIGN
UNDER
CICS®
COMMAND
AND
VSAM®

ALEX VARSEGI

TAB Professional and Reference Books

Division of TAB BOOKS Inc.
P.O. Box 40, Blue Ridge Summit, PA 17214

FIRST EDITION
FIRST PRINTING

Copyright © 1987 by TAB BOOKS Inc.
Printed in the United States of America

Reproduction or publication of the content in any manner, without express permission of the publisher, is prohibited. No liability is assumed with respect to the use of the information herein.

Library of Congress Cataloging in Publication Data

Varsegi, Alex.
Systems design under CICS Command and VSAM.

Includes index.
1. System design. 2. CICS (Computer system)
3. Virtual computer systems. I. Title.
QA76.9.S88V36 1986   005.4′2   86-23129
ISBN 0-8306-2843-6

Contents

Acknowledgment	viii
Introduction	ix
1 The Workings of Interactive Systems	**1**
1.1 On-Line Versus Batch Processing 1	
1.2 Response Time 2	
1.3 On-Line Data Entry 3	
1.4 Suspense File Concept 3	
1.5 Generic Search 4	
1.6 Design Consideration Using the Menu Concept 4	
1.7 Inquiry and Fourth Generation Languages 7	
2 The CICS Environment	**11**
2.1 Overview 11	
2.2 Data Communications 14	
2.3 Data Management Functions 16	
2.4 Applications Program Services 19	
2.5 Systems Services 20	
2.6 Monitoring Functions 22	
2.7 CICS Table Entries 22	

3 Introduction to CICS Command 29
3.1 Overview 29
3.2 Command Statement Structure 30
3.3 Restrictions 31
3.4 Logical Relations: The LINK, XCTL, and RETURN Commands 32

4 The Handle Commands and the Com Area 37
4.1 HANDLE CONDITION
4.2 HANDLE AID (Handle Attention Identifier) 39
4.3 The Communications (COM) Area 46

5 Maps and Mapsets 51
5.1 Overview 51
5.2 Attribute Bytes 52
5.3 Map Generation 57
5.4 Screen Definition Facility (SDF) 62

6 The Terminal Control Commands 93
6.1 The SEND MAP Command 93
6.2 The Converse Command 96
6.3 Miscellaneous Terminal Control Commands 98
6.4 The RECEIVE MAP Command 98

7 File Control Commands 103
7.1 Overview 103
7.2 The READ Command 104
7.3 The WRITE Command 108
7.4 The REWRITE Command 109
7.5 The DELETE Command 110
7.6 The File BROWSE Commands 112
    7.6.1 The STARTBR or Start Browse 112
    7.6.2 The READNEXT Command 113
    7.6.3 The READPREV Command 114
    7.6.4 The ENDBR Command 116
    7.6.5 The RESETBR Command 117

8 Case Study I 119

9 Temporary Storage 127
9.1 Overview 127
9.2 Temporary Storage Queues 127
9.3 The WRITEQ TS Command 128
9.4 The READQ TS Command 130
9.5 The DELETEQ TS Command 132

10 Case Study 2 135
10.1 Overview 135

11 Transient Data Control 149
11.1 Overview 149
11.2 Automatic Task Initiation (ATI) 151
11.3 The Destination Control Table 151
11.4 The WRITEQ TD Command 152

11.5 The READQ TD Command 155
11,6 The DELETE Command 157

12 Interval Control — 159

12.1 Overview 159
12.2 The Asktime Command L159
12.3 The Delay Command 160
12.4 The Post Command 160
12.5 The Wait Command 161
12.6 The Start Command 162
12.7 The Retrieve Command 164
12.8 The Cancel Command 165

13 Systems Design Under CICS Command: Part 1 — 169

13.1 Overview 169
13.2 The Menu Concept 171
13.3 Table-Drive Systems 176
13.4 The Help Screen 178

14 Systems Design Under CICS Command: Part 2 — 183

14.1 Message Prompting 183
14.2 Creating Paths 186
14.3 Locating Data 187
14.4 Add, Delete, and Change Mechanisms 188

15 Introduction to VSAM — 191

15.1 Overview 191
15.2 Access Methods Services 194
15.3 Security and Protection 195
15.4 Cluster Definition 196
15.5 Alternate Indexes 199

16 Establishing Addressability — 203

16.1 Overview 203
16.2 Common Work Area (CWA) 203
16.3 Miscellaneous Storage Techniques 204
16.4 The Getmain/Freemain Commands 204
16.5 The Load/Release Commands 208
16.6 Locate Versus Move Mode 209

17 Recovery and Debugging — 211

17.1 Overview 211
17.2 The Abend Command 211
17.3 The Execute Diagnostics Facility (EDF)
17.4 Command Level Interpreter (CECI) 224
17.5 Master Terminal Commands 243
17.6 Journal Control 246

Glossary — 251

Index — 259

Acknowledgment

I wish to express my appreciation to Jeff Mueller for his support and knowledge on a number of topics presented here.

Introduction

When CICS, or Customer Information Control System, was first introduced by IBM, it was a well-anticipated response to a changing technology. Although the introduction of CICS was triggered by certain user groups whose need for up-to-the-minute information was simply a matter of business survival, what really allowed CICS to grow was the fact that computer hardware was becoming less expensive by the hour. Can you imagine the airline reservation business not having the ability to respond to a customer request until the following day?

The first releases of CICS were done in what is called a total *macro-based* environment. That is to say, if you had been an application programmer in those days, you had to know Basic Assembler inside and out, and you were expected to be quite knowledgeable about CICS internals. Consequently, rather than focusing on a particular application, you had to use both software engineering and application programming. Because of the complexity of macro-based CICS, long and extensive sessions were dedicated to training and education, because a technician had to have a thorough understanding of areas well beyond the area of application programming.

With the introduction of command language, however, the overall use of this telecommunications monitor was drastically simplified. A high-level language such as ANS COBOL or PL/I became the focal point for using command language procedures.

Knowledge of CICS command language today is probably the most attractive skill that an applications programmer can have at his command, and it is quite rewarding in the financial sense. Knowing CICS command is the most practical and marketable tool, even in a relatively tough market situation, enabling you to find work quite easily. This book is geared toward the technician, the beginner, who is in the process of learning CICS, the programmer analyst who wishes to enhance his skills, and the experienced programmer who needs to refer to certain topics. This book is organized in the following manner:

Chapter 1 deals with a number of basic functions characteristic of an on-line environment. Among these functions are the suspense file concept, the use of menu screens, and fourth generation inquiry languages.

In Chapters 2 and 3, attention is focused on the architecture of CICS with regard to the operating system and the internal workings of the CICS telecommunications monitor. At the end of Chapter 3 you should have a fairly good understanding of some of the background information, such as what the nucleus is, what kinds of access methods are available, and what is meant by logical relations.

I recommend that you review these chapters before concentrating on the coding requirements presented in Chapter 4. I also recommend that you review the summary section presented at the end of each chapter and see if you can answer those questions. You may check your answers in the back of the book.

Chapter 5 is unique in the sense that I have dedicated an entire chapter to the discussion of the screen painting procedures IBM refers to as the *Screen Development Facility* software package, or *SDF*. This package is an interactive basic mapping tool used in place of more conventional macro-based coding methods.

Chapters 6 through 11 concentrate on the various options available under CICS. You should take time to understand the instructions coded in the program exhibits and the logic used, and you should review the related flowcharts.

Chapters 13 and 14 deal with the design aspect under this monitor, highlighting a number of topics that are important, but often overlooked during the design of a system.

Chapter 15 reviews the *Virtual Storage Access Method*, or *VSAM*, in detail. If your installation is not currently under VSAM, you may skip this chapter. However, I'd like to recommend that you read this chapter in order to understand some of the CICS commands that relate strictly to VSAM.

Chapter 16 acquaints you with the use of storage facilities outside the boundaries of your application program and tells you how to establish addressability through the *Base Locator for Linkage*, or *BLL*, cells.

Chapter 17 deals primarily with a new technique in interactively debugging your application program through the use of the *Execute Diagnostics Facility* package, or *EDF*.

This book should be used quite similar to a textbook where the technical complexities and the overall intensity of the material gradually increase chapter by chapter.

1
The Workings of Interactive Systems

HIGHLIGHTS
- On-Line Versus Batch Processing
- Response Time
- On-line Data Entry
- Suspense File Concept
- Generic Search
- Design Consideration Using the Menu Concept
- Inquiry and Fourth-Generation Languages

1.1 ON-LINE VERSUS BATCH PROCESSING

Even ten years ago on-line systems were considered somewhat luxurious by most medium sized firms. However, successive breakthroughs both in software and hardware products, and competitive pressure to acquire and utilize the most up-to-date systems caused business to take a hard look at the emerging technology.

One of the greatest drawbacks of batch systems is the lack of timeliness of information. In a typical batch environment it may take as long as 24 hours to satisfy a user request. Once a report is generated, errors may still be prevalent, and additional time is then required to resolve these problems. What does that do to the timeliness of information? How would you like to read the Tuesday edition of the Chicago *Tribune* on the following Friday?

In an on-line real-time environment on the other hand, processing may be virtually instantaneous, and it is normally triggered outside the computer room, typically by the user himself. Through a telecommunications monitor, such as CICS, on-line systems are able to access, review, and update information on a second's notice. For example, if your bank is still operating in a completely batch environment (which may be quite difficult to visualize in this day and age), and if you were to deposit some money to cover your check, your deposit may not be posted until the following day or even a couple of days afterward depending on the circumstances. There is a chance that your check may bounce due to insufficient funds, even though you have more than enough money to cover your outstanding obligations.

While on-line systems allow you to maintain an up-to-the-second database, batch systems have the tendency to lag far behind, reflecting an obsolete state of affairs.

In reality today, a typical computer environment contains both on-line and batch functions, although there is a trend toward the paperless flow of information allowed by an on-line environment.

1.2 RESPONSE TIME

Response time refers to the time interval the system requires to process a transaction. To put it simply, when a terminal operator inquires about an employee by entering his or her social security number, the response time is the amount of time the system requires before displaying the appropriate screen showing the employee's salary history or demographic profile.

The quickness or the sluggishness of the response time essentially depends on a number of conditions, such as the size of a given file, the access method, the number of people utilizing the system at the moment, competition by other concurrent systems for the same type of resources, and the physical hardware configuration of the overall system.

Figure 1-1 illustrates the concept of response time. Step 1 refers to the

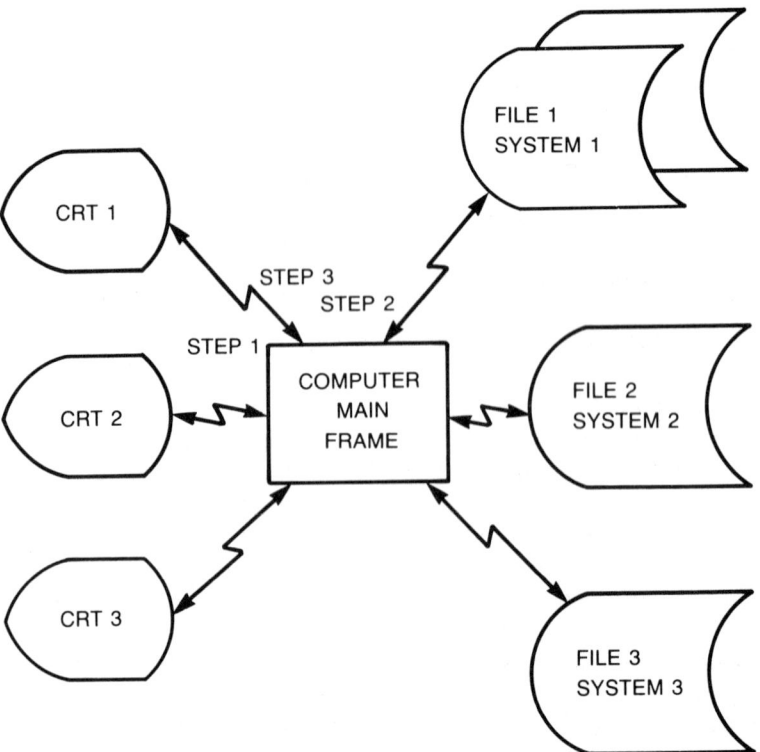

Fig. 1-1. Response time refers to the amount of time required by the system to respond to a user request.

terminal operator's request for computer processing. Step 2 reflects the time it requires for the computer system to interrogate a file or data set. Step 3 refers to the system's response to the initial request following a successful or unsuccessful interrogation of the required data set.

1.3 ON-LINE DATA ENTRY

Editing data online is both efficient and time saving. It gives the terminal operator a chance to visually verify the data entered and monitor the system's response. For example, he can review and correct a host of errors, such as the following:

A social security number containing nonnumeric characters
A job classification code that does not exist
A job classification code containing the wrong salary range
A missing name
An incorrect or nonexistent insurance code
Conflicting information between two files

Instead of waiting for lengthy and time consuming printouts, the terminal operator can clean up the majority of the problems on the spot and in the matter of seconds.

In order to bring existing problems to the attention of the terminal operator, the application programmer may utilize a number of programming techniques, most of which are related to the manipulation of the *attribute bytes*. He may *intensify* the field(s) in error, display it in red, or even underscore it until the problem is resolved. (For a comprehensive review on attribute bytes and field intensification, please turn to Chapter 5, "Maps and Mapsets.")

A particular file may be accessed for one of two purposes:

1. to delete, update, or add to its contents.
2. to inquire about its contents.

CICS and the operating system, such as MVS, provide sufficient security safeguards and password protection for the file and the screen, and even provide protection on the individual data element level. However, I must stress that setting up a comprehensive password scheme and determining who has access to what information is an organizational, not a data processing, decision.

1.4 SUSPENSE FILE CONCEPT

Systems analysts often monitor change through the use of on-line *suspense* files. For example, assume that three weeks from now an employee will be reclassified with a corresponding pay raise, as illustrated in Fig. 1-2.

```
Suspense File                           Payroll Master

Current Date: August 12                 Activate Date:   August 31
Pete Smith                              Pete Smith
Start :          August 31      ———→
Class Code:      SW25463TR12    ———→
HR Rate:         $10.27         ———→
Ins.Code:        W172437Z       ———→
```

Fig. 1-2. Pete Smith's data, entered August 12, will be activated and transferred from the suspense file on August 31.

Also assume that the terminal operator has sufficient time at present to start entering available data on the suspense file.

Every time a preliminary payroll is initiated, using, for instance, the front-end edit cycle, the on-line system will *browse* through the suspense file in order to equate the current date with one on the suspense file. Once the desired date is reached, the employee's record may be activated and transferred to the permanent payroll master. His current status on the suspense file would be simultaneously flagged and disabled.

As we mentioned before, on-line systems enable you to add, change or delete a particular record. There may be additional functions such as the ability to browse through the file using, for example, a generic or even a phonetic key.

1.5 GENERIC SEARCH

Generic search is a method to locate an individual based on a partially defined key. In order to find Johnston on the file, assuming that one of the VSAM keys is set up in last and first name sequence, we may specify the entire or partial last name.

Suppose we are trying to find a person on the payroll master file because we need to know his or her social security number. All we happened to know, however, is that the person's last name starts with the characters Rob. We also know that he or she lives on Maple Street in Oak Park. When an inquiry based on the three letters Rob is initiated, the system may respond with the display shown in Fig. 1-3.

1.6 DESIGN CONSIDERATION USING THE MENU CONCEPT

When we talk about a system being menu driven, we are in fact referring to a major-function directory as well as components of that directory broken down in terms of submenus. A *menu screen* provides the user with a method of selecting a specific task from among a number of alternatives and then performing such a task within an established path.

When you look at the menu selection at a restaurant, for example, you

```
Rob,John          1202 Mozart      Chicago,Il    60212    122-22-1876
Robacek,Steve     1172 Vincent     Chicago,Ill   60164    546-32-9755
Robe,Betty        2333 W 14th St   Harvey,Il     60411    766-13-4855
Robertsen,Alex    32 Park Ave      Elmhurst,Il   60126    134-66-7123
Robertson,Kay     302 Maple        Oak Park,Il   60211    298-44-8721
Sandberg,Dan      34 Wrigley St    Chicago,Il    60612    333-94-1735
```
Fig. 1-3. A display block including the name of Kay Robertson.

probably want to look at the entire entree section at first. Once you have glanced at it you may wish to look at the sea food selections (the submenu). Then you may decide on swordfish or stuffed flounder depending on your preference, the price, or even the recommendation of your waiter. As you can see, the menu concept in computing refers to a set of choices or alternatives that resembles a menu that you'd use in a restaurant.

Figure 1-4 shows a major function screen, which the terminal operator may have to refer to at least once a day. (At this point, we assume he is in charge of handling a number of activities within the entire human resources systems.) By entering an A, for example, the terminal operator is ready to do payroll processing. Note that only A, B, C, and D are valid codes, and an error message is generated should any other code be entered. Option D will enable the operator to sign off whenever he is ready to do so.

The display in Fig. 1-5 is triggered by the main menu (Fig. 1-4). At this time the terminal operator is already performing the initial stages of the payroll cycle while reviewing and evaluating the alternatives.

By entering the code 7 as a selection, he will be able to sign off at the submenu level rather than having to branch back to the major functions menu (Fig. 1-4). If he were to enter an 8, he would immediately be sent back to the initial menu screen. Notice that only functions 1 through 8 will be tolerated by the system; if any other key is pressed, an error message will be displayed.

If he chooses function 1, the terminal operator will be able to perform maintenance on the payroll database, as shown in Fig. 1-6. Function 2 from

```
              CONSOLIDATED AMERICAN CO.


        (A)    PAYROLL PROCESSING
        (B)    PERSONNEL SYSTEMS
        (C)    POSITION CONTROL
        (D)    SIGN OFF


         _     INPUT DESIRED CODE HERE THEN DEPRESS THE ENTER KEY


        ERROR MESSAGES...............
```
Fig. 1-4. The main menu screen, offering four possible alternatives.

```
                CONSOLIDATED AMRERICAN CO.

        (1)     FILE MAINTENANCE
        (2)     PAYROLL REVERSALS
        (3)     INSURANCE RELATED SCREENS
        (4)     FEDERAL, STATE AND LOCAL TAXES
        (5)     RETROACTIVE PAY
        (6)     SUSPENSE FILE TRANSFERS
        (7)     SIGN OFF
        (8)     RETURN TO MAIN MENU

         _      INPUT CODE HERE THEN DEPRESS ENTER

                ERROR MESSAGES.........
```
Fig. 1-5. Consolidated American's submenu selection.

this submenu will enable him to update certain employee records. At this point the employee profile can be accessed and the information concerning that employee can be altered as shown in Fig. 1-7. Once the task is done, and the record is updated, it will not be necessary for the operator to return to any of the submenus to process another employee. He can simply clear the current employee profile display and continue with the next employee. If the validation or the changes are successfully entered into the system, a message will be displayed at the bottom of the screen advising the terminal operator that the file is ready for update. At this point, the operator may update the file merely by depressing the assigned function key (function key 2 in this particular instance), which will invoke the code that will complete the task. Afterward, the cursor can be positioned at the first entry field, which is the employee's social security number.

Note that at any point during the processing cycle of the transaction, a help screen may be triggered (Fig. 1-8). An entire set of help screens, can be made available, should the operator require guidelines or specifics

```
                CONSOLIDATED AMERICAN

                  MAINTENANCE MENU

        (1)     ADD A NEW RECORD TO PAY MASTER
        (2)     UPDATE PAYROLL RECORDS
        (3)     DELETE RECORD FROM FILE
        (4)     INQUIRY MODE
        (5)     TASK MENU
        (6)     RETURN TO MAIN MENU
        (7)     SIGN OFF

         _      ENTER SELECTION HERE

                ERROR MESSAGE(S).........
```
Fig. 1-6. A submenu showing the maintenance tasks.

```
                CONSOLIDATED AMERICAN

                EMPLOYEE PAYROLL PROFILE

    SOCIAL SECURITY NUMBER    112-34-3714
    EMPLOYEE NAME             GEORGE B AARON
    CLASSIFICATION            AS77FTY9942

    PAY RATE   10.123         DEPENDENTS 04
    MARITAL STATUS            MARRIED

    ADDRESS       33 W ROOSEVELT RD
    CITY/STATE    CAROL STREAM, IL.
    ZIP CODE      60395
    TELEPHONE     (312) 786-7644

    USE PF KEY 1 TO SIGN OFF
        PF KEY 2 UPDATE FILE
        PF KEY 3 TO RETURN TO THE MAIN MENU
        PF KEY 4 TO ACCESS THE TASK MENU
        PF KEY 5 TO ACCESS THE SUB_MENU

        ERROR MESSAGES...
```
Fig. 1-7. The display of an employee's payroll profile.

concerning his task. Help screens can also be accessed through the use of a command key (more on this in following chapters).

1.7 INQUIRY AND FOURTH GENERATION LANGUAGES

The term *fourth generation language* is a vendor-supplied term that refers to an interactive, on-line, real-time oriented language rather meager in its total performance or overall capabilities.

Fourth-generation languages are nonprocedural languages geared to both the user and the analyst. By *nonprocedural*, I mean that they are languages that can trigger and perform a number of automatic functions, such as formatting, totalling, and prototyping, utilizing a relatively few lines of code.

```
            HELP SCREEN SEQUENCES

    EMPLOYEE PAYROLL PROFILE SCREEN

    PAY RATE MUST BE IN 99.999 FORMAT CONSISTING
    OF TWO INTIGERS AND THREE DECIMALS FOR ACCURACY.

    *** THIS FIELD MUST BE A NUMERIC FIELD AND
        SHOULD NOT BE LEFT BLANK AT ANY TIME ***
```
Fig. 1-8. Pay rate instructions on one of a number of help screens, which are available as systems tools for quick problem solving.

```
LIST ALL EMPLOYEES IN FILE PERSONFL AS FOLLOWS:

SEX='F' AND ETHNIC='H' AND
START LESS THAN 19801102 AND EDUC='BS ', OR 'BA ', OR
'MBA', OR 'MS ' AND SALARY=25000 AND STATUS=100%,
THEN, PRINT HEADING; NAME/START/SALARY,
DETAIL=PNAME,PSTART,PSALARY
RUN JOB
```

Fig. 1-9. An example of a fourth-generation inquiry language.

The important thing is that we recognize not so much what these languages are capable of doing at the present, but what their potential is in the years ahead.

Let's assume that the personnel director, whose job is to monitor certain affirmative action related events, wants to search through the personnel database for all employees who meet the following criteria:

- Is a female
- Has a Hispanic background
- Has been with the organization for at least five years
- Has a bachlor's degree or preferably an MBA
- Earns a salary of at least $25,000 a year
- Is a full time employee.

Using a fourth-generation inquiry language, the personnel director can enter a program statement like the one shown in Fig. 1-9 on the screen and press the Enter key. The code is checked quickly for any syntax errors. If there are no errors, a list of all eligible employees will be displayed on the screen beneath the program statement, as shown in Fig. 1-10.

The fields SEX, RACE, START, EDUC, are predefined in a data element glossary or dictionary, which is part of the overall software.

LIST, PRINT, and RUN JOB are action words that resemble ANS COBOL reserved words; they trigger an action by the software.

HEADING, and DETAIL essentially describe to the program whether constants or variable data are to be printed.

NAME	START	SALARY
CONCEPTION, R	11-12-79	26,240
GONZALES, C	01-05-75	25,900
JESUS, M	08-17-76	27,900
ROJAS, R	10-09-79	25,100

Fig. 1-10. The results of the inquiry program.

Please note that Fig. 1-9 does not show any specific fourth-generation language, but rather a composite of a number of languages with similar features.

SUMMARY

In an on-line-real-time environment, processing, as requested by the terminal operator, is instantaneous. Response time refers to the time the system requires to process a transaction. The quickness or the sluggishness of such a response depends on a number of conditions, such as the size of a given file, the access method used, the number of people utilizing the system at the moment, competition by other computer systems for the same type of resources, and last but not least, the physical hardware configuration of the overall system.

A terminal operator may access a file either in an update or in an inquiry mode. Update mode means that the contents of the file may be modified or a record may be completely deleted. In inquiry mode, the terminal operator can display the information but cannot change it.

Systems analysts often monitor change through the use of an on-line suspense file. Such a file is used to trigger a transaction at some time in the future that activates an entire record or a single element.

Generic search is a method to locate an individual record or an item based on a partially defined key.

Menu screens provide the user with a method of selecting a specific task from among a number of alternatives and then proceeding in a predefined path.

Fourth generation languages are nonprocedural in nature and geared to the user and the analyst. They have the ability to perform a number of automatic functions such as totalling, formatting, and prototyping, utilizing relatively few lines of code.

QUESTIONS

1. In what ways do on-line application programs differ from their batch counterpart? Describe these differences.
2. What factors contribute to the quickness or the sluggishness of response time?
3. Describe the advantages of using an on-line suspense file.
4. In what specific application would you utilize a generic search?
5. True or false: menu screens are only adaptable to certain large applications each containing at least a hundred or more programs?
6. True or false: although HELP screens are extremely useful as tutoring tools, they tend to substantially increase the overall cost of a system.

2

The CICS Environment

HIGHLIGHTS
- Overview
- Data Communications
- Data Management Functions
- Applications Program Services
- Systems Services
- Monitoring Functions
- CICS Table Entries

2.1 OVERVIEW

CICS, or Customer Information Control System, is a general-purpose data communications monitor. You may think of CICS as an operating system responsible for supporting your on-line application programs. Some view it as an operating system that is within the framework of an even larger operating system and has a multilevel interface. That is to say that CICS interfaces with the operating system (such as OS/VS1, OS/MVS), while the operating system, in turn, interfaces with the computer.

Historically, CICS was first introduced almost 15 years ago. Since then, it has undergone successive enhancements, and with the introduction of CICS Command Language, it has been vastly improved and its use greatly simplified.

CICS is currently supported by the IBM System/370, 4331, 4341, 303X, and 308X computers. It is compatible with VSE, as CICS/DOS/VS, or with OS/VS1, MVS, or MVS/XA, as CICS/OS/VS. Either of the above versions can run in a real machine or in a VM/370 virtual machine environment.

In Fig. 2-1 I have segregated CICS into two major areas. These are the nucleus and the dynamic area. The dynamic area contains the storage facilities required for the processing of a transaction as well as the storage of the corresponding application programs. The nucleus is made up of eight additional modules. The discussion of some of these will overlap into the subsequent presentation of major CICS functions.

1. The Program Control program that establishes a hierarchical path during transaction processing is essentially responsible for transferring con-

```
PROGRAM   TASK      TERMINAL  FILE      JOURNAL   TRACE     TRANSI.
CNTRL     CNTRL     CNTRL     CNTRL     CNTRL     CNTRL     CNTRL
TABLE     TABLE     TABLE     TABLE     TABLE     TABLE     TABLE
```

```
PROGRAM   TASK      TERMINAL  FILE      JOURNAL   TRACE     TRANSI    TEMP.
CNTRL     CNTRL     CNTRL     CNTRL     CNTRL     CNTRL     CNTRL     CNTRL
PROG.     PROG.     PROG.     PROG.     PROG.     PROG.     PROG.     PROG.
```

```
       Common Systems Area.....
              Common Work Area.....
                              .....Terminal Control Area...
                              ....Execute Interface Bloc..
                              .....Transaction Work Area....
              APPLICATION PROGRAM.......   APPLICATION PROGRAM
       APPLICATION PROGRAM.........
                                           APPLICATION PROGRAM
```

Fig. 2-1. An overview of the nucleus, which contains a number of internal table and control programs.

trol between the application programs through the XCTL, LINK and RETURN commands.

2. The Task Control program is a module whose functions are based on a priority scheme.
3. The Terminal Control program provides the communication link between your application program and the terminal. This is accomplished through one of a number of access methods, such as:

- BTAM, or Basic Telecommunications Access Method
- VTAM, or Virtual Telecommunications Access Method
- TCAM, or Telecommunications Access Method.

Please note that the application programmer does not really have to be familiar with the internal workings of the above access methods. They are mentioned to bring you up to date on some of the technical terms used.

The File Control program basically provides the application programmer with the ability to access a particular file specified in his program. This is done via an access method that allows the programmer to access and retrieve the required records from his file. CICS supports three access methods. These are:

- ISAM or Indexed Sequential Access Method
- VSAM or Virtual Storage Access Method
- DAM or Direct Access Method.

Unlike the access methods mentioned relative to the Terminal Control

Program, the method of file access should be understood by the application programmer. While in most installations he's not expected to know the internals of the access method, (like the method of building VSAM clusters or alternate indexes), it is important that he have at least some understanding of the basic concept and know what he can or cannot do when using the system. For example, there are many commands under VSAM that are simply unavailable under ISAM or DAM.

4. The Journal Control Module is used when the user needs to reconstruct the file as the result of some major disaster. Journal Control utilizes a sequential data set, such as a tape or a sequential disk file. As shown in Fig. 2-2, Journal Control places the data into the buffer area, and then, through the Journal Control program, it transfers all that to a sequential Journal File. This is necessary in case the task abnormally terminates, and the user needs to reconstruct the file the way it looked prior to that *abend*.
5. The CICS Trace Control Program is a debugging tool available for the application programmer. This program relies on a Trace Table that is in main storage and is triggered by the Trace Control command.
6. Transient Data Control, which functions through the Destination Control Table, provides input to non-CICS batch programs. Through this function you may also activate a remote printer and print sequential data through CICS.
7. Finally, temporary storage allows the user to have access to additional main or auxiliary storage facilities. Through this the programmer may build the pages of the display screen, moving forward and backward at will. This storage facility is created, maintained, and deleted by the application programmer and *requires* no corresponding CICS table entries.

Please note that all these topics will be extensively reviewed in subsequent chapters.

If I were to summarize and group all the major functions performed by CICS, I'd probably come up with at least five major areas. Although these areas represent an overwhelming array of topics, I *intent to present* them in a somewhat simplified manner. The five areas are as follows:

- Data communications functions
- Data management functions
- Application program services
- Operating systems services
- Monitoring functions

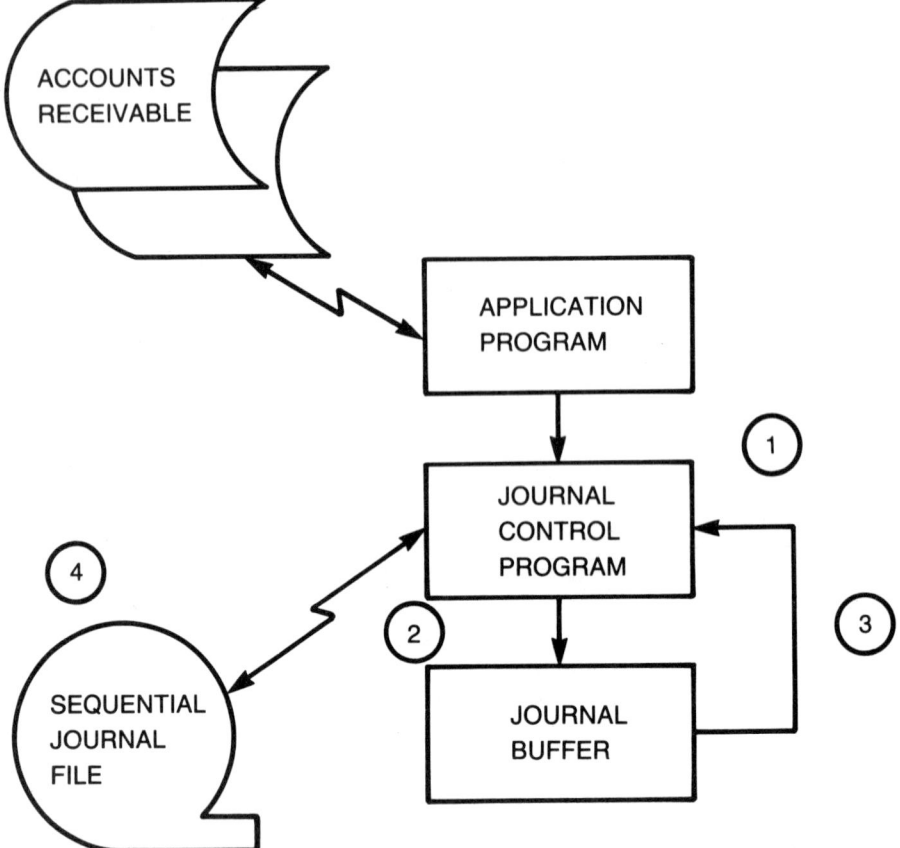

Fig. 2-2. The logical flow of recording a data set on a sequential journal file. The Journal Control program will record all the required information about the job (1) in the journal buffer (2). This buffer area and the Journal Control program (3) will monitor your job (3) in order to write it to a sequential data set (4), which in referred to as the journal file.

2.2　DATA COMMUNICATIONS

CICS, the telecommunications monitor, allows the applications programmer to concentrate his effort on developing application programs without having to get too involved with terminal connection facilities, telecommunications line protocol, and device dependencies (Fig. 2-3). In a typical CICS environment, it is the systems programmer who sets up the required control tables. Once these tables (such as the terminal control table or TCT) are set up, CICS will make sure that terminals defined in the TCT will be able to send and receive messages and otherwise properly interface with the system. The kind of terminals used in this process may require an additional interface with a teleprocessing access method such as BTAM or VTAM. (I briefly talked about this in section 2.1).

Basic Mapping Support, or *BMS*, comes into play between the applica-

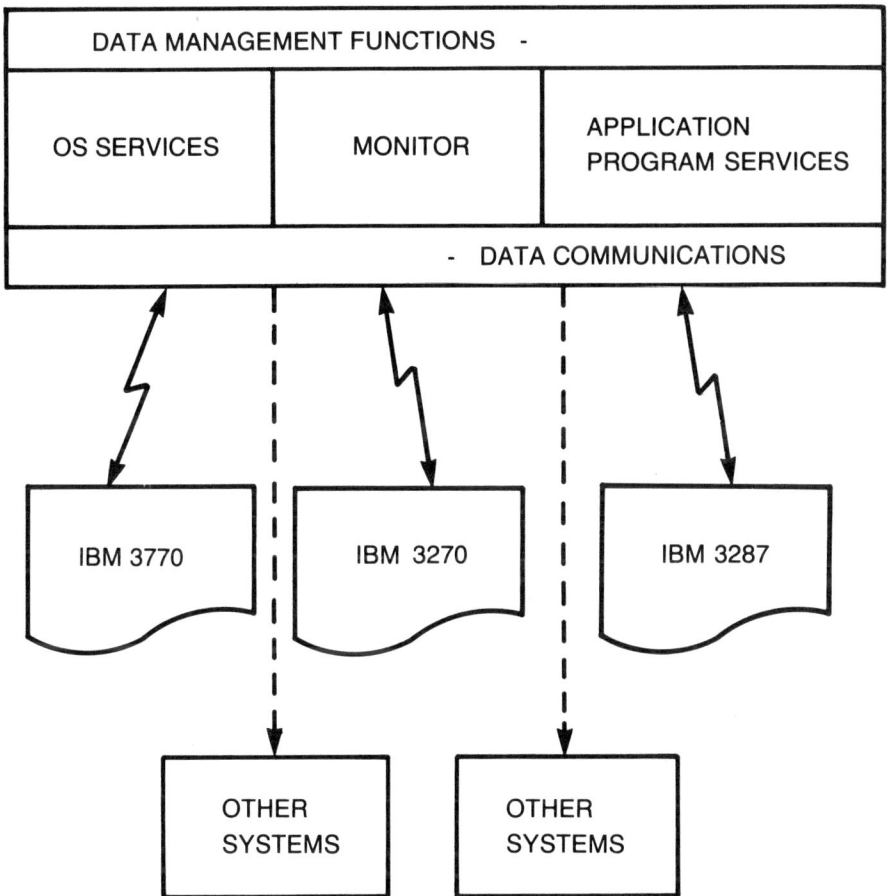

Fig. 2-3. Data management and communications provide the user with device independence and with the support of a number of devices, including on-line printers and CRT terminals.

tion program and the terminal control functions to provide device and format independence. BMS allows you to format or *map* your data on the screen as you'd format your printer layout in order to generate a report.

BMS provides a logical relationship between the data and the way you'd like to see it displayed on the terminal. The analyst can define the contents of the display screen via a CICS-supplied macro instruction (either BMS or an interactive technique referred to as CICS/SDF; we'll be talking about this method extensively in Chapter 5).

CICS allows communications between two CICS systems; it can also be used to interface a CICS system with other systems, such as IMS, (Information Management System, a hierarchical database software package with its own monitor) through what IBM refers to as *Systems Network Architecture*, or SNA. SNA will allow you to "talk" to other systems and use their files and databases with a minimum of effort: no additional hours need to be put into file and systems design (Fig. 2-4).

I should also point out at this time that through multiregion operation, you will be able to hook up one communications region with another. This means that your users will be able to access programs already in production mode, while you can test new application programs located in another region.

Also you may allocate different partitions to CICS applications based on their needs in terms of response time. For example, you may run a data entry application requiring quick response time in one of the higher priority regions. At the same time, jobs requiring extensive CPU time and only a few terminals may be placed in lower priority regions, so that they won't impede or degrade the response time for higher priority tasks.

2.3 DATA MANAGEMENT FUNCTIONS

CICS interfaces with the appropriate access method supported by the operating system. Among a number of functions, CICS file control provides browsing facilities as well as buffer and block management. In addition to conventional files, CICS often utilizes two other forms of storage facilities: temporary storage and transient data control. As shown in Fig. 2-5, transient data control provides an additional function: it creates queues of sequential data to be sent to an on-line printer, using the destination control's intra-and extrapartition mechanism. Transient data may also be used as input to non-CICS programs. (More on this in Chapter 11.)

Temporary storage may be used like the communications area (DFHCOMMAREA) for passing information between transactions, thus providing the user with an internal *scratch pad* facility.

Let's pause for a moment and review some of the important terminology we'll be using throughout this book. First of all, let's talk about what we mean by a *transaction*. A transaction is normally initiated by the terminal operator, who invokes one or more application programs. A transaction could easily be an update to your accounts receivable file, an addition to your payroll master, or a simple inquiry to display the location of your office equipment, which is part of your property inventory control master.

Another term requiring some brief introduction is *task*. We normally tell CICS the kind of transaction we require via the *transaction identifier* (TRANSID). CICS scans the Program Control Table in order to locate the particular transaction identifier that will point to the first program to be executed. CICS maintains a separate thread of control for each task. While one task is waiting for a file to be read or a map to be received from one of the terminals, CICS will give control to another task. Tasks are handled by the CICS Control Program. When a number of tasks are managed con-

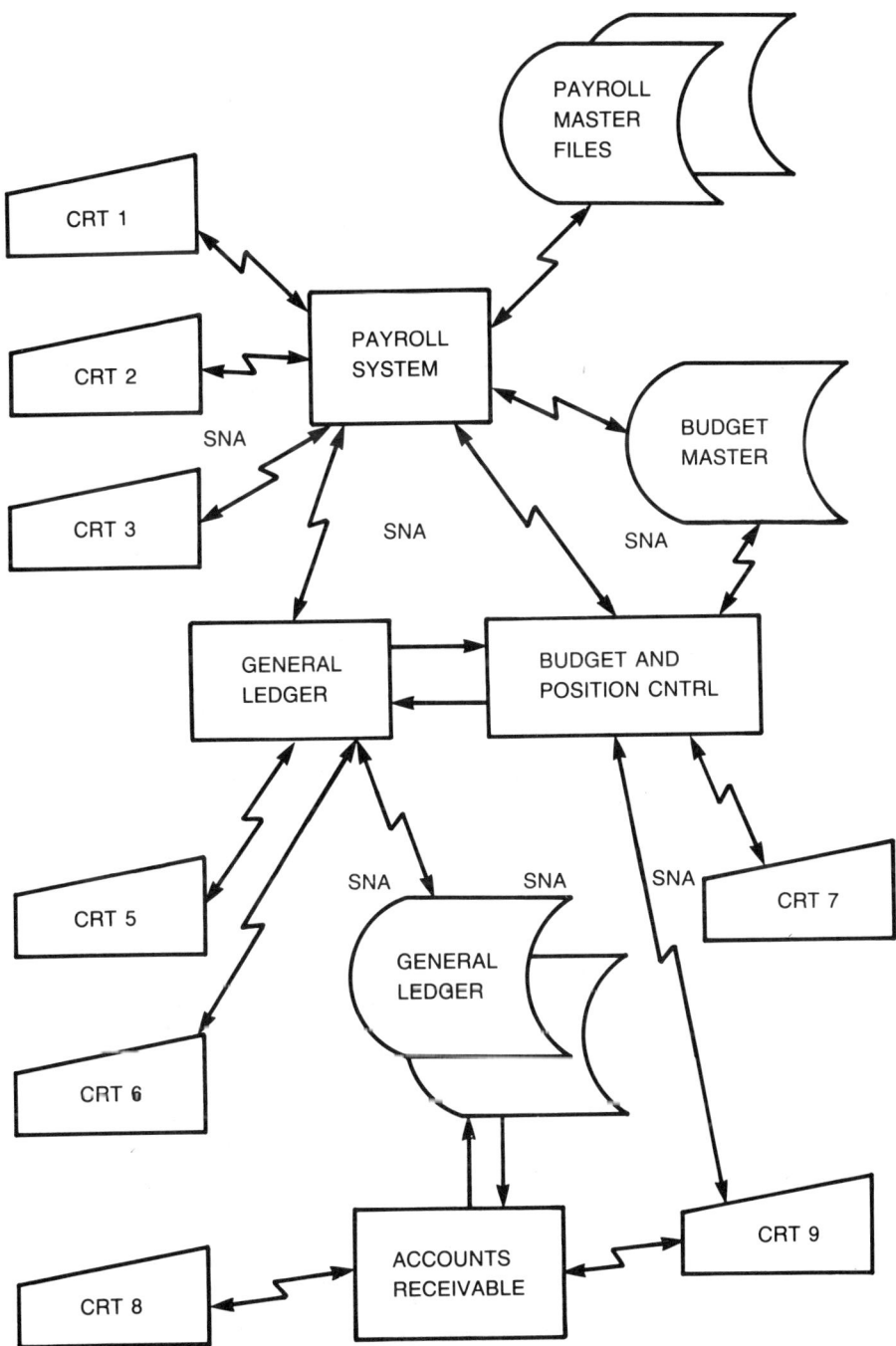

Fig. 2-4. An illustration of the extensive relationships among systems and file structures. SNA accomplishes total systems integration in an efficient manner.

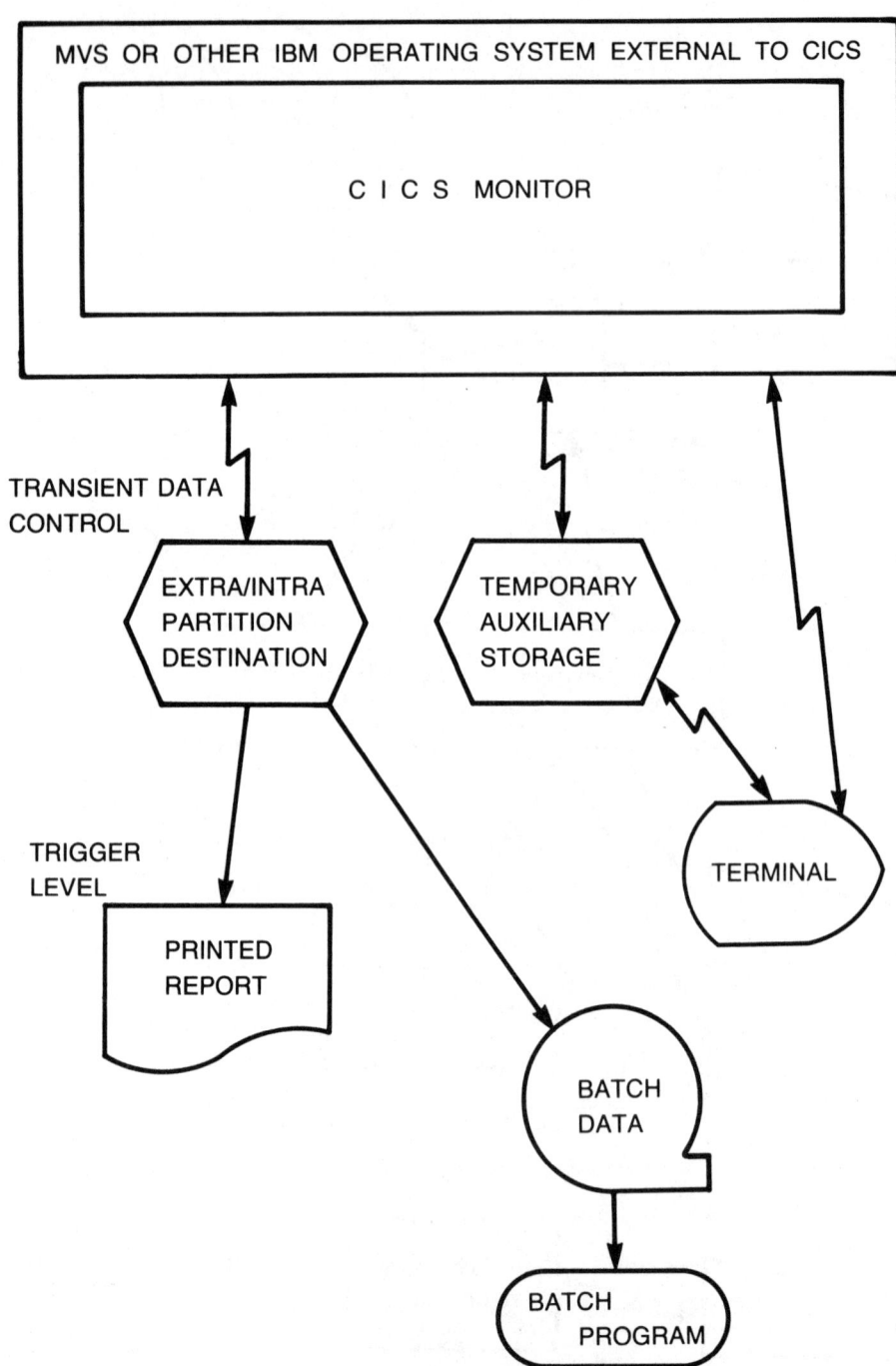

Fig. 2-5. CICS provides the user with limited batch facilities and sequential processing through transient data control.

currently, it is called *multitasking*.

One of the many functions CICS provides is data security. The most common phenomenon in a large scale CICS environment is that there are many users accessing the same file or database and continually making changes in its contents. To enable a user to successfully update a file, CICS will check to make sure that any previous task has already been completed. Also during the normal course of transaction processing, CICS saves information that's being changed by logging it into a dynamic area. These changes are available only if the task is unsuccessful. Once the task is completed, CICS will delete this log. This type of mechanism is referred to as *Dynamic Transaction Backout* or DTB. The Dynamic Transaction Backout is invoked by CICS upon the *abnormal termination* (*abend*) of a transaction, such as may result from a transmission error or the cancellation of a transaction by a terminal operator. At this point the Dynamic Transaction Backout will reverse everything to make it look like the transaction never took place. In an application program, you may specify *immediate synchronization points* or *synpoints*. This is done so that only the problem areas in your program may be backed out and not the entire application program. This may save you a great deal of time. Figure 2-6 shows transaction processing in light of syncpoints. If you have a long complex program with a great volume of incoming changes, you may want to split it into logically separate segments, called *logical units of work*. This can be easily accomplished via the syncpoint command. In the event of an abnormal system termination, syncpoint tells CICS that certain segments of the application program will have to be backed out. For example, as soon as your program abnormally terminates during the processing of Segment B, Segment A will have been completed already up to Syncpoint 1; thus only Segment B will have to be backed out.

It is the responsibility of the application programmer to issue syncpoints in his code, if they are indeed required. Syncpoints help speed up and simplify recovery procedures especially in a long running task. However, from the standpoint of sound coding conventions, tasks should be kept short and sweet; thus no syncpoint(s) in your program would be required. Note that Syncpoint 4 is automatically issued by CICS at the end of the task.

2.4 APPLICATIONS PROGRAM SERVICES

CICS Command supports two high-level languages: ANS COBOL and PL/I. RPG II is also supported, but only under VSE. CICS also provides an array of tools for the development of application programs. To mention a few, the command language translator runs very much like a batch program. It preprocesses CICS source code and generates call statements whenever they are required.

There is also an extensive diagnostic aid, the Execution Diagnostics Facility, or EDF, which allows the application programmer to scan through

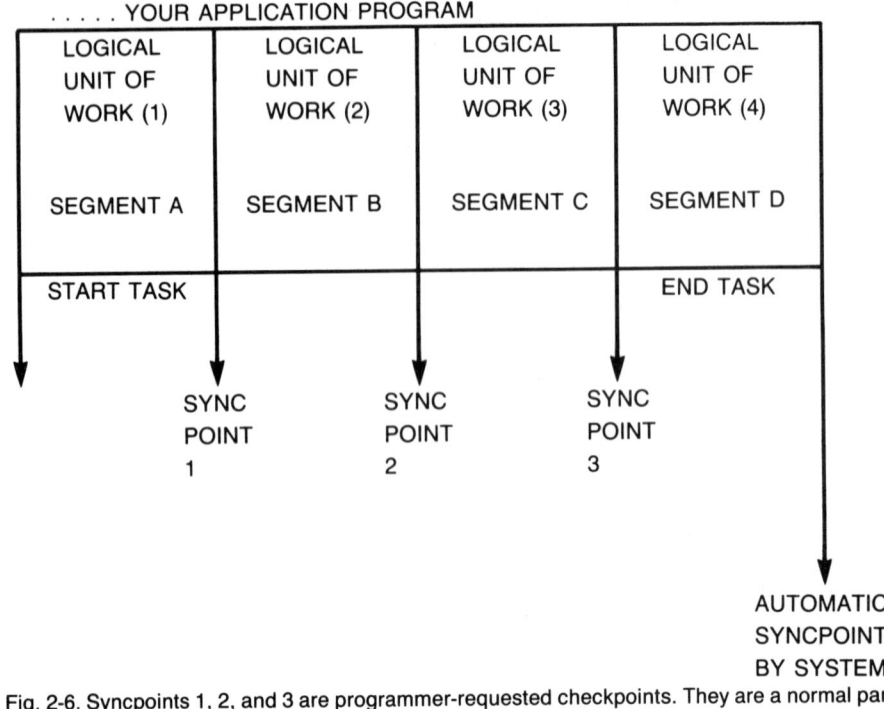

Fig. 2-6. Syncpoints 1, 2, and 3 are programmer-requested checkpoints. They are a normal part of a complex application program.

his logic and locate potential problem areas. This will be discussed in detail in Chapter 17.

The command Level Interpreter is another one of the facilities provided by CICS. Here the software will help you figure out the syntax of the command statement, defauls, and option values.

In addition to the Execution Diagnostics Facility module, you may also use the Trace Control program we have earlier reviewed.

Through the Dump Control Mechanism, you can record the contents of certain areas on a sequential dataset and then print that dataset. This is an automatic feature allowing you to generate either a formatted or an unformatted dump of the CICS region and partition.

Another IBM product that interfaces with CICS is the Screen Definition Facility, or SDF, software package. The advantage of this IBM product over the more conventional macro packages is that you will be able to define the format of your screen interactively and rather efficiently. You design your screen, change it, and modify it to your liking.

2.5 SYSTEMS SERVICES

CICS performs a number of control functions for handling and allocating resources in a given environment. The four major functions are:

- Task control
- Program control
- Storage control
- Interval control

These modules were briefly introduced in section 2.1; however, some additional explanation is now in order.

Task Control

Task control is responsible for the execution of a task within CICS. The term *multitasking* refers to the system's ability to run a number of tasks concurrently. Since there may be a number of users running jobs at the same time, task control checks all existing priorities in order to determine which tasks should be initiated first. Task control is also responsible for the continuous, uninterrupted processing of tasks in the most economical fashion. That is, when one task is in a wait mode (in anticipation of additional input or because of the temporary unavailability of a certain file, for example), another task may begin or resume execution.

Program Control

Once the task is initiated, Program control will associate the task with the appropriate application program. Since there is a likelihood that more than one user will be accessing the same application program for a given task, only a single copy of that program is loaded into the CICS partition. The advantage of this is that all users will be relying on the same physical copy throughout the processing, all utilizing the same version.

Storage Control

Storage control provides the application programmer with temporary work areas. The easiest way to acquire such storage facilities is through the WORKING-STORAGE section in your application program. The advantage of this is that CICS will eventually manage such storage facilities for you. Other storage facilities however, reside outside your program and to define or access them, you will have to use the Base Locator for Linkage (BLL) cell to establish pointers in your linkage section. (More on this in Chapter 16 under Establishing Addressability.)

Interval Control

Interval control functions provide the applications with an array of time-dependent activities such as the ability to specify to the system the expiration of a transaction or the ability to retrieve data stored and triggered at a specific time. You may also delay the processing of a task based on predetermined time intervals, as well as cancel an existing command. Requesting the current date and the time of the day from the system is also one of the functions of interval control.

2.6 MONITORING FUNCTIONS

CICS also provides the mechanism to monitor the operation of the entire system and supply you with relevant statistics. This function, for example, can tell you the number of times a given transaction was used, or how often paging was invoked. It can also tell you the maximum (peak) number of concurrent tasks running, and the number of times the application program has been referenced.

For each terminal, CICS will monitor the number of input and output messages that were sent and received, including the number of transactions and transaction errors.

In order to analyze your data, you can rely on available performance tools (you may also need to contact your friendly software department to have access to such tools).

Here are two of these performance tools:

- CICS Performance Analysis Reporting System (CICSPARS)
- Service Reporter II (SLRII).

The Performance Analysis Reporting System or CICSPARS (Fig. 2-7) is a comprehensive set of reports that provides you with important statistics about paging and the overall performance of this monitor. Among a number of things, CICSPARS keeps track of CPU as well as Wait time, and the utilization of the current storage facilities, both virtual and real.

The Service Level Reporter II reports on the transactions processed, processing time, overall performance, exception conditions, and so on.

2.7 CICS TABLE ENTRIES

CICS is a table-driven system software package. In order to enable certain functions to maintain independence from the application program, CICS utilizes a number of separate tables. Chapter 13 and 14 will review the concept of a table-driven system. For the time being, however, I'd like to emphasize the tremendous flexibility provided by these tables. The fact is that changes affecting numerous application programs, files, maps, and destinations can be accomplished in a centralized *directory* at a single location.

In this section, we will be specifically reviewing the use of three CICS tables. These are the File Control Table of FCT, the Program Control Table or PCT, and the Processing Program Table or PPT.

```
CICS PERFORMANCE ANALYSIS REPORTING SYSTEM.
MESSAGE COUNT VS SIZE GRAPHS.
------------------------------

TIME       VALUE    MESSAGES IN = *, MESSAGES OUT= /

HH.MM.SS            ___90__160__270__360__450__540__630__720__810__900


14.05.30   100      ***///
14.06.00   410      ************/////////////
14.06.30   625      *******************//////////////////
14.07.00   901      **************************///////////////////////////
14.07.31   970      ****************************/////////////////////////
14.08.00   790      **********************//////////////////////////
14.08.30   710      ******************///////////////////////
14.09.02   205      *****///////

TIME       VALUE         TOTAL MESSAGE SIZE

                    10,500   20,100   31,200   41,900   52,500

                    ----  ----  ----  ----  ----  ----  ----  ----  ----

HH.MM.SS

14.05.30   12000    ******/////
14.06.00   21400    ************/////////////
14.06.30   39800    *******************//////////////////
14.07.00   52100    **************************///////////////////////////
14.07.31   53000    ****************************/////////////////////////
14.08.00   44700    **********************//////////////////////////
14.08.30   42250    ******************///////////////////////
14.09.02   11200    *****///////
```

Fig. 2-7. The Performance Analysis report shows input and output messages, paging, and the total size of messages at a given time. (HH.MM.SS designates hours, minutes, and seconds.)

Let's first review the entries to the File Control Table. Figure 2-8 shows two entries necessary for CICS. The entries are segregated by an asterisk. Coding conventions here correspond to JCL (Job Control Language) requirements. Every line within a given definition, except for the last (RECFORM), must be continued with a comma. Also, column 72 must contain a nonblank character to further designate continuation.

Statement 1 defines the File Control Table through the DFHFCT macro. It then states TYPE = DATA. The actual name of the dataset PAYMAST, is specified in Statement 2.

Statement 3 specifies the access method (ACCMETH), which is key sequenced VSAM (Virtual Storage Access Method).

In Statement 4, the SERVREQ option specifies the type of operation permitted against the file (PAYMAST). These are browsing, deleting, adding, and updating.

Statement 5 indicates that the record is of fixed length and that it is blocked.

Statements:

```
1   DFHFCT    TYPE=DATASET,                              C
2   DATASET=PAYMAST,                                     C
3   ACCMETH=(VSAM,KSDS),                                 C
4   SERVREQ=(BROWSE,DELETE,NEWREC,UPDATE),               C
5   RECFORM=(FIXED,BLOCKED)
```

```
         *

    DFHPCT    TYPE=DATASET,                              C
    DATASET=POSCNTR,                                     C
    ACCMETH=(VSAM,KSDS),                                 C
    SERVREQ=(BROWSE,DELETE,UPDATE),                      C
    RECFORM=(FIXED,BLOCK)
```

Fig. 2-8. The required entries in the File Control Table for the datasets names PAYMAST and POSCNTR.

Figure 2-9 shows two entries made in the Processing Control Table designated by the DFHPCT macro. This table contains the DFHPCT macro and the TYPE = ENTRY option (Statement 1). Statement 2 shows the transaction identifier, or TRANSID, of the application program; the identifier is completed in Statement 3, which shows the actual name of the program in reference.

The Processing Program Table in Fig. 2-10 starts with the macro DFHPPT, including the TYPE = ENTRY. Statement 2 contains the program identifier and the programming language, which is ANS COBOL.

Finally, Statements 4 and 5 refer to a map specified under PROGRAM = MENU1. Note that no programming language is available under this entry.

Statements:
```
    1    DFHPCT    TYPE=ENTRY,           C
    2    TRANSID=C001,                   C
    3    PROGRAM=PGM0071
            *
         DFHPCT    TYPE=ENTRY,           C
         TRANSID=C002,                   C
         PROGRAM=PGM0072
```

Fig. 2-9. Two entries in the Processing Control Table. Each entry includes the program and transaction identifiers.

Statements:
```
    1    DFHPPT    TYPE=ENTRY,           C
    2    PROGRAM=PGM0071,                C
    3    PGMLANG=COBOL
            *
    4    DFHPPT    TYPE=ENTRY,           C
    5    PROGRAM=MENU1
```

Fig. 2-10. Two entries in the Processing Program Table, these are required for the definition of both programs and maps.

SUMMARY

The CICS telecommunications monitor is segregated into two major areas. These are the nucleus and the dynamic areas. The dynamic area contains the storage facilities required for the processing of a transaction as well as the storage and the corresponding programs. The nucleus is made up of eight additional modules. These are:

- The Program Control program
- The Task Control program
- The Terminal Control program
- The File Control program
- The Journal Control program
- The Trace Control program
- The Transient Control program
- The Temporary Control program

CICS performs the following major functions:

- Data communications
- Data management
- Application program services
- Operating systems services
- Monitoring functions

A *transaction* is normally triggerd by the terminal operator, who invokes a single or possibly a number of corresponding application programs.

Tasks are handled by the CICS Control program. When a number of CICS tasks are managed concurrently, it is called *multitasking*.

The Dynamic Transaction Backout (DTB) is invoked by CICS upon the abnormal termination of a transaction (ABEND). At this point the Dynamic Transaction Backout will reverse all pending updates to restore everything to make it appear as if the transaction never took place. *Syncpoints* are defined in the application program so that only the problem areas are backed out and not the entire program. This may save you a great deal of time.

CICS is a table-driven system by design. Some of these tables are the File Control Table (FCT), the Processing Control Table (PCT), the Processing Program Table (PPT), and the Destination Control Table (DCT).

Two of the performance tools mentioned in conjunction with efficiency are the CICS Performance Analysis Reporting System (CICSPARS) and the Service Reporter II (SLRII).

QUESTIONS

1. Briefly describe the nucleus and the dynamic areas.

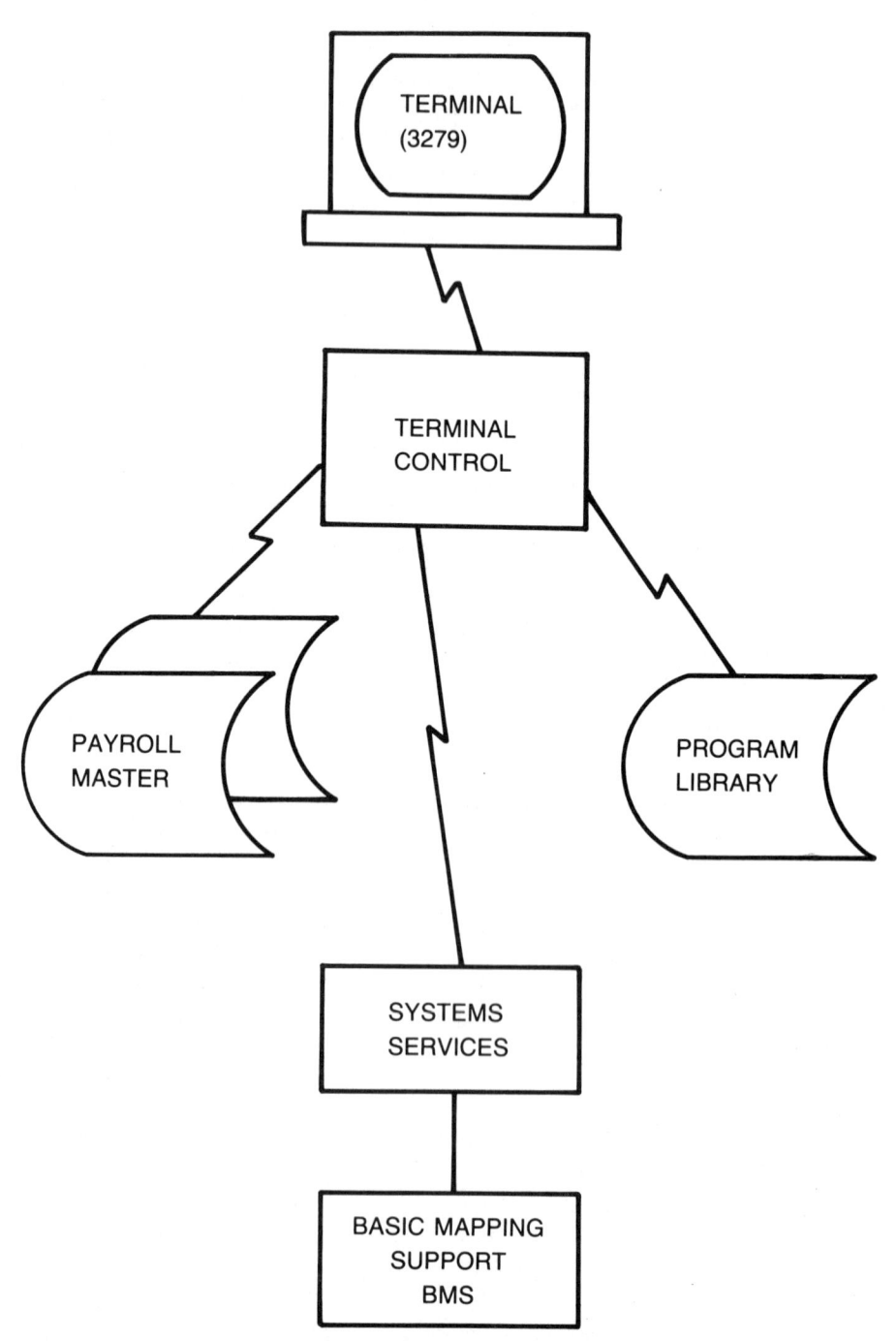

Fig. 2-11. A chart of the way Basic Mapping Support (BMS) functions.

26

2. Name the access methods utilized by the Terminal Control program.
3. Name the access methods utilized by the File Control program.
4. When do you use the Journal Control file?
5. Explain briefly the functions the Basic Mapping Support performs in CICS. Explain the chart presented in Fig. 2-11.
6. Briefly explain the difference between temporary storage queues and transient data control.
7. When should you utilize syncpoint(s) in your on-line application program?
8. Mention two performance tools available in CICS to monitor the overall performance of your system.

3
Introduction to CICS Command

HIGHLIGHTS
- **Overview**
- **Command Statement Structure**
- **Restrictions**
- **Logical Relations: the LINK, XCTL, RETURN COMMANDS**

3.1 OVERVIEW

CICS commands are coded and embedded throughout the source code of the application program. Once the source program is ready, it is executed via the CICS command language translator, which translates each command into valid COBOL statements and CALLs.

The Call statements invoke the *Execute Interface program*, which in turn will invoke one or possibly a number of CICS modules, depending on the type of services required.

Let's assume that you are to issue a SEND MAP command, which, using CICS command language would look something like this:

```
EXEC CICS SEND MAP('MAPO101') MAPSET ('MSET101') END EXEC.
```

This command will send a *MAP*, or screen display, to a terminal, such as the IBM 3279 type CRT, so that the operator may enter the required data into the system or do whatever is required at the time. The CICS translator will scan the above statement and the following set of commands will be generated internally:

```
MOVE MAPO101 TO DFHIV1
MOVE MSET101 TO DFHEIV2
CALL'DFHEIV1' using DFHEIV0 DFHEIV1 MAPO101 DFHEIV98 DFHEIV2 DFHEIV99 DFHEIV11.
```

Note that the application programmer doesn't have to know the mechanics of how instructions are translated into commands and calls; he need only to realize the fact that the translator dissects each relatively concise statement into a more task-oriented set of procedures, as shown in Fig. 3-1.

29

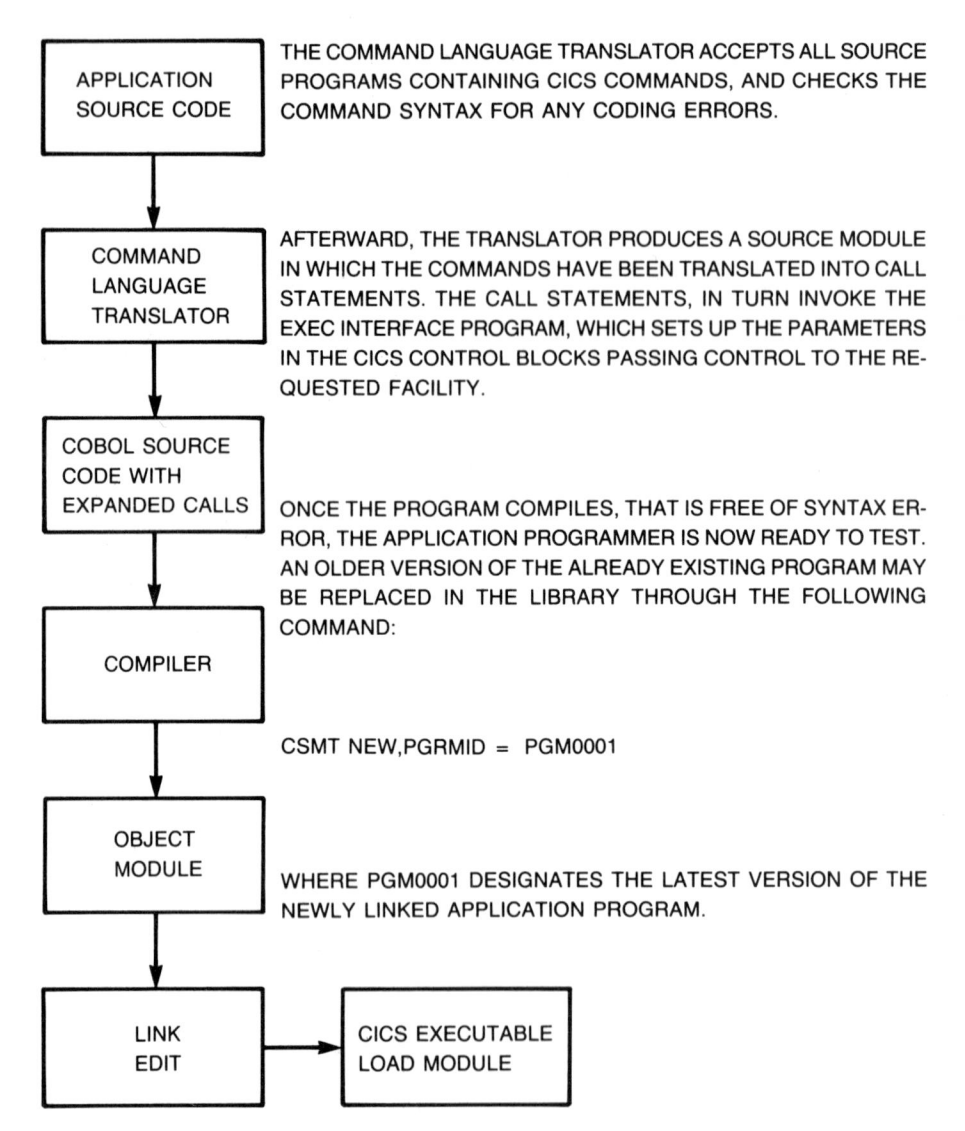

```
┌─────────────┐      THE COMMAND LANGUAGE TRANSLATOR ACCEPTS ALL SOURCE
│ APPLICATION │      PROGRAMS CONTAINING CICS COMMANDS, AND CHECKS THE
│ SOURCE CODE │      COMMAND SYNTAX FOR ANY CODING ERRORS.
└──────┬──────┘
       │
       ▼
┌─────────────┐      AFTERWARD, THE TRANSLATOR PRODUCES A SOURCE MODULE
│  COMMAND    │      IN WHICH THE COMMANDS HAVE BEEN TRANSLATED INTO CALL
│  LANGUAGE   │      STATEMENTS. THE CALL STATEMENTS, IN TURN INVOKE THE
│  TRANSLATOR │      EXEC INTERFACE PROGRAM, WHICH SETS UP THE PARAMETERS
└──────┬──────┘      IN THE CICS CONTROL BLOCKS PASSING CONTROL TO THE RE-
       │             QUESTED FACILITY.
       ▼
┌─────────────┐
│ COBOL SOURCE│
│ CODE WITH   │
│EXPANDED CALLS│     ONCE THE PROGRAM COMPILES, THAT IS FREE OF SYNTAX ER-
└──────┬──────┘     ROR, THE APPLICATION PROGRAMMER IS NOW READY TO TEST.
       │            AN OLDER VERSION OF THE ALREADY EXISTING PROGRAM MAY
       │            BE REPLACED IN THE LIBRARY THROUGH THE FOLLOWING
       ▼            COMMAND:
┌─────────────┐
│  COMPILER   │
└──────┬──────┘
       │            CSMT NEW,PGRMID = PGM0001
       ▼
┌─────────────┐
│   OBJECT    │
│   MODULE    │     WHERE PGM0001 DESIGNATES THE LATEST VERSION OF THE
└──────┬──────┘     NEWLY LINKED APPLICATION PROGRAM.
       │
       ▼
┌─────────────┐     ┌──────────────────┐
│    LINK     │────▶│  CICS EXECUTABLE │
│    EDIT     │     │   LOAD MODULE    │
└─────────────┘     └──────────────────┘
```

Fig. 3-1. A brief overview of how source statements are converted to call statements and then to CICS executable load modules.

3.2 COMMAND STATEMENT STRUCTURE

CICS command language conforms to a format with required and optional features. Regardless of the length or the complexity of any given statement, all CICS commands must begin with:

```
EXEC CICS
```

and end with the delimiter

END-EXEC.

Following the EXEC CICS command is the function to be requested. There may also be one or a number of options attached to the statement, including its logical arguments. Please note that these command statements are coded in a somewhat free format, depending on the preference of the application programmer. My recommendation is to keep all command statements to a minimum per line for easy visual review and correctability.

Figure 3-2 depicts a typical command structure used to read a file. This statement may be presented in a single line as long as coding is confined between positions 12 and 72:

```
EXEC CICS RETURN TRANSID('P001')
COMMAREA(WORK-STORAGE) LENGTH(8) END-EXEC.
```

Also note that with the exception of the initial CICS Command (EXEC-CICS) and the delimiter (END-EXEC.), there is no specific order in which components of these commands must be presented:

```
EXEC CICS READ DATASET('MSTRFLE') UPDATE
RIDFLD(REC-KEY) LENGTH(LNG) END-EXEC.
```

Regular COBOL statements need not be segregated from CICS command statements. Figure 3-3 shows an example of a mixture of CICS commands and ANS COBOL statements. To put these lines in plain English, if the given record identifier in the program equals either an "A" or a "B", then branch out of the current program into program PGM0001. Otherwise, send a map, including an error message, to alert the terminal operator of the possibility of erroneous codes. These statements will be explained in detail in a number of upcoming chapters. Figure 3-3 is merely an example of mixed statements.

3.3 RESTRICTIONS

There are substantial differences in the way ANS COBOL is structured

```
EXEC CICS
READ
DATASET('MSTRFLE')
UPDATE
RIDFLD(REC-KEY)
LENGTH(LNG)
END-EXEC.
```

Fig. 3-2. A typical command structure used to read a file.

```
If REC-ID = ('A' or 'B')
*** valid ANS COBOL statement ***

EXEC CICS XCTL PROGRAM('PGM0001') COMMAREA(WORK-AREA)
LENGTH(COMLEN1) END-EXEC.
*** valid CICS command statement ***

MOVE 'ERRONOUS RECORD TYPE' TO ERR-MSGO
*** valid ANS COBOL statement ***

EXEC CICS SEND MAP('PMM0002') MAPSET('PSET0002')
CURSOR DATAONLY END-EXEC.
*** valid CICS command statement ***
```

Fig. 3-3. A mixture of CICS command and ANS COBOL statements.

under CICS command as opposed to the way it is structured for conventional batch programming. Under CICS command, the ENVIRONMENT DIVISION contains no select clauses; in fact the entire division is of documentary nature. Furthermore, the DATA DIVISION has no FD, or FILE DESCRIPTION, section, since CICS is a table-driven system and all file-description related information is first defined and stored in the File Control Table (FCT). Where as in batch mode, there is no wide-spread use for the linkage section, under CICS command a great deal of communications pass through the DFHCOMMAREA. Both the DFHEIBLK and the DFHCOMMAREA modules are linkage section residents. Separate ANS COBOL programs may not be linked together, since CICS handles that option through the LINK, RETURN, and XCTL commands.

Certain reserved words are not available under CICS command. Some of these are:

SYMDMP	UNSTRING	SEGMENTATION	STXIT
DYNAN	ACCEPT	STATE	FILE SECTION
SYST	DISPLAY	ENDJOB	INSPECT
TEST	TRACE	READ	STMPDM
REPORT WRITER	EXHIBIT	OPEN	ALTER
SORT	FLOW	CLOSE	STOP RUN
STRING	COUNT		

Finally, I should caution application programmers about the perform statements. They must consider all the features not found in a typical batch environment. Under CICS command a perform statement may not be completed because of certain handle condition bypasses, exit control statements, and so on.

3.4 LOGICAL RELATIONS:
THE LINK, XCTL, AND RETURN COMMANDS

Under the control of CICS, various application programs follow a number of logical paths in the way they interact with each other. Although this topic will be reviewed shortly, it is imperative to understand the concept of this interdependency. To comprehend what happens when *linking* is used by program A to invoke program B (Fig. 3-4), visualize the relationship that exists when a procedure is invoked via a perform statement. When program A is linked to program B, the invoked program B, will execute until the termination of that module. Afterward control returns to the next executable instruction of the first program, which issued the link command.

Exit Control, or XCTL, may be equated to a *go to* statement, which is an unconditional branch. If the second program, which is invoked by the first, has no instruction to the contrary, control will remain with the invoked

PROGRAM A (THE INVOKING PROGRAM)

```
EXEC CICS LINK

PROGRAM ('PGMB')
COMMAREA (WORK-STORAGE)
LENGTH (8) END-EXEC.
```

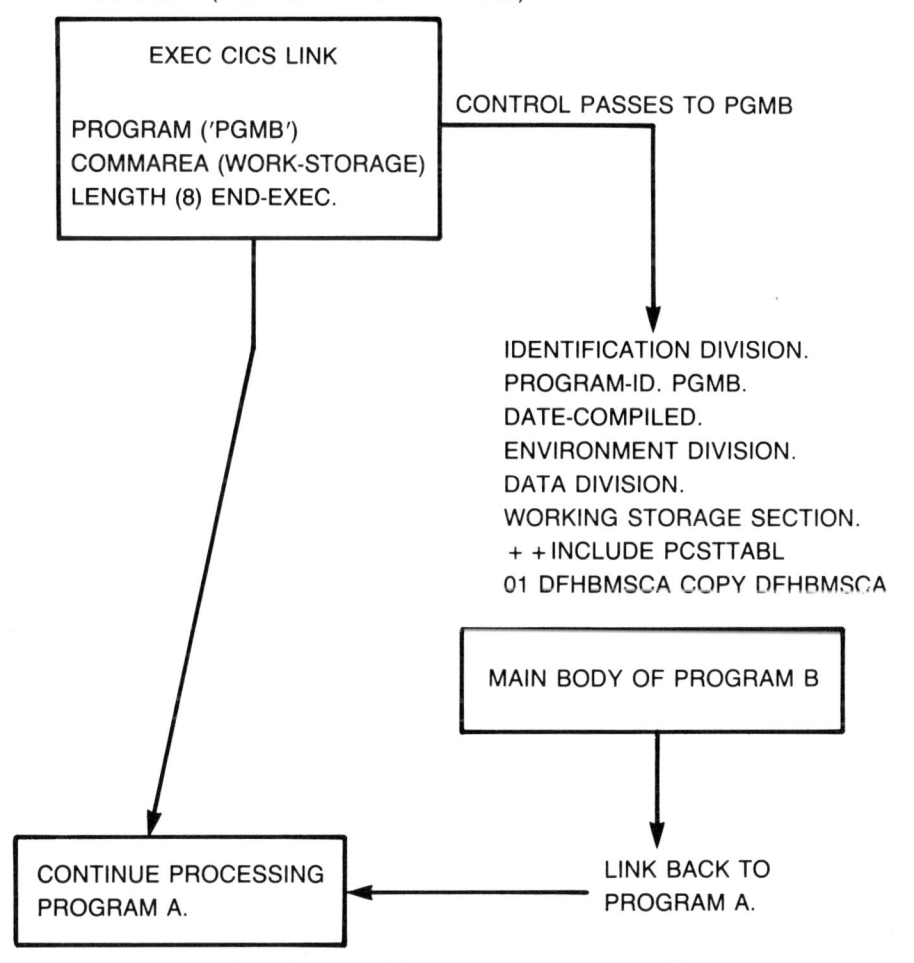

CONTROL PASSES TO PGMB

IDENTIFICATION DIVISION.
PROGRAM-ID. PGMB.
DATE-COMPILED.
ENVIRONMENT DIVISION.
DATA DIVISION.
WORKING STORAGE SECTION.
++INCLUDE PCSTTABL
01 DFHBMSCA COPY DFHBMSCA

MAIN BODY OF PROGRAM B

CONTINUE PROCESSING PROGRAM A.

LINK BACK TO PROGRAM A.

Fig. 3-4. An overview of the hierarchical functions invoked by the LINK statement.

(or second program) until the termination of that task, as shown below:

```
EXEC CICS XCTL
PROGRAM('PGMB')
COMMAREA(WORK-STORAGE)
LENGTH(8) END-EXEC.
```

Note that no logic should be coded past the XCTL instruction, since control will immediately pass to the next program module. Unlike the LINK command, when data is passed via the XCTL or the RETURN commands, it is copied and the copy's address is passed to the next program. RETURN is like XCTL in the sense that it too is unconditional.

In pseudo-conversational programming, it is a common practice that a returning program reinvoke itself via its own transaction identifier, as shown in the lines below. In such an environment, the programmer removes the application program from main storage while it is waiting for data from a terminal. If the program is not removed, it will continue to occupy valuable storage space needed by other application programs.

```
EXEC CICS READ UPDATE DATASET('MSTRFLE') LENGTH(LNG)
RIDFLD(REC-KEY) END-EXEC.
```

Reinvoking a transaction through the RETURN command means that you, in fact re-execute your program. It may be necessary in such environment to relay messages from one programming cycle to the next in order to inform the terminal operator about the status of the current transaction. This is done mainly via the Communications (COM) Area.

SUMMARY

CICS command statements are coded as part of the application program. Regardless of the length or complexity of a given statement, all CICS commands must begin with EXEC CICS and end with the delimiter END-EXEC. With the exception of these two statements, there is no specific order in which components of the commands must be presented.

There are substantial differences in the way ANS COBOL is structured under CICS command as compared to how it is structured in conventional batch programming. Under CICS command, the ENVIRONMENT DIVISION is of documentary nature. The DATA DIVISION has no FILE DESCRIPTION section, since CICS is a table-driven system.

Certain reserve words are also not allowed under CICS command. When linking is used to invoke another program, control will RETURN to the initial program upon the execution of the second, or invoked, program.

XCTL, or Exit Control, will cause an unconditional branch out of the current application program.

The RETURN command is used in order to utilize storage facilities in the most efficient way.

QUESTIONS

1. Every CICS command must start with _____ and end with an _____ statement.
2. True or false: the order in which CICS command statements are presented (with the exception of the first and the last mandatory statements) is important.
3. Describe the difference between a LINK and an XCTL statement.
4. Explain briefly the Command Language Translator.
5. True or false: it is not a good idea to mix CICS command level statements with a high-level language such as ANS COBOL, or PL/I, because it will eventually cause a great deal of difficulty when your program needs debugging.

4
The Handle Commands and the Com Area

HIGHLIGHTS
- Handle Condition
- Handle Aid (Handle Attention Identifier)
- The Communications (COM) Area

4.1 HANDLE CONDITION

Associated with most commands utilized by CICS are some exception conditions that can occur during the execution of a given set of commands. You may want to think of the HANDLE CONDITION as a contingency plan used when things don't work out the way you expect them to. Suppose you're looking for a specific record in order to update your file, but the record in question is not there. What, then, are the options at your disposal? Through a typical HANDLE CONDITION command, you can tell the system how to handle the unexpected. If you do not specify contingency plans, you will have to settle for the standard options or systems defaults, which tend to be all inclusive. For example, by specifying ERROR (GEN-ERR-CONDIT) in your HANDLE CONDITION statement, you are telling the system to branch to the GEN-ERR-CONDIT label or paragraph. Because of the lack of any specific distinction, it would be almost impossible to differentiate an out-of-space from a record-not-found condition.

The HANDLE CONDITION may appear in the beginning of your program, prior to any other commands. It is also possible to redefine the earlier criterion, by issuing a follow-up HANDLE CONDITION statement, as need arises.

A typical HANDLE CONDITION would look like this:

```
EXEC CICS HANDLE CONDITION
NOTFND(CHECK-RECORD)      ***1***
DUPREC(ERROR-HANDLE)      ***2***
NOSPACE(RETURN-TRID)      ***3***
ERROR(GEN-ERR-CONDIT)     ***4***
END EXEC.
```

1

In paragraph 1, you might want to notify the terminal operator that a particular record is not on file. If, for instance, the operator is in the process

37

of adding a new employee's record to the file, and therefore no such record exists prior to the add routine, the procedure should be specifically coded by the programmer.

2

A duplicate error situation occurs when you try to add a record to a file in which the same key already exists.

3

When the file has no space left for any subsequent maintenance operation, program logic, through the HANDLE CONDITION command, will branch to the RETURN-TRID paragraph. At that point you want to alert the terminal operator that the file size will be expanded shortly.

4

Any error condition other than NOTFND, DUPREC, and NOSPACE will cause the logic of the application program to branch unconditionally to the GEN-ERROR-CONDIT paragraph.

The HANDLE CONDITION has essentially the following format:

```
CONDITION 1    LABEL 1
CONDITION 2    LABEL 2
CONDITION 3    LABEL 3
```

The result of condition 1 is a branch to label 1. Likewise, conditions 2 and 3 cause branches to the corresponding labels or paragraphs. This is done mainly to relay to the application program certain processing requirements.

If two files are utilized in an application program, you might prefer to create two separate HANDLE CONDITION statements. The number of options that may be attached or processed through the HANDLE CONDITION routine is quite large, and the programmer usually uses only a small fraction of all that's available. Here are some examples.

DSIDERR	disk error occurred
DUPREC	duplicate record on file
ERROR	general exception condition
INVREQ	invalid request
IOERR	input/output error condition
ITEMERR	error using temporary storage facilities
NOSPACE	not enough file space to process
NOTFND	record sought not found
PGMIDERR	handling of abends.

Note the following rules that apply to the use of the HANDLE CONDITION command.

- Up to 12 conditions may be specified and handled in a single command. If you require more than 12, issue another HANDLE CONDITION statement.
- Any specific condition will take precedence over the general error condition.
- Once a HANDLE CONDITION has been requested, it remains in effect until the end of the program, or until such time as it is overridden by another HANDLE CONDITION of the same type.
- Any condition without a label will have a default value.

4.2 HANDLE AID (HANDLE ATTENTION IDENTIFIER)

The application programmer may have his hands full constantly checking the status of the keyboard in his program. Assume your business recently hired a new CRT operator who tends to activate the wrong function keys from time to time without realizing it. How can the programmer possibly build a logic into his program extensive enough to overcome such a seemingly major disaster and even recover from it? (Certainly, batch programmers wouldn't have to worry about all those mishaps.) That is one of a number of reasons why the HANDLE AID command was thought of.

The HANDLE AID or Attention Identifier (DFHAID) indicates which key on the terminal is used in order to initiate transmission. The IBM 3279 type CRT terminal has an Enter key and a Clear key, up to 24 function keys, and three attention keys. It may also have a selector pen and an operator identification card reader.

By copying the DFHAID block in Fig. 4-1 into your program, you may reference the entire keyboard in your application program. All you have to to is to say:

```
01   DFHAID COPY DFHAID.
```

the rest is generated by the system.
When you use the HANDLE AID command, please note the following:

- Function keys 1 through 24 (DFHPF1 through DFHPF24) may be utilized to initiate transactions from the terminal without entering a transaction identifier or TRANSID. (This is controlled by an entry made in the Program Control Table.) It is a lot easier to use a function key to trigger a transaction than to constantly enter a four-character long TRANSID, especially with frequently used transactions.
- There is no transmission of data when either the Clear key (DFHCLEAR)

39

or the PA keys (DFHPA1 through DFHPF3) are used. In fact the Clear key will completely erase the screen.

The HANDLE AID command will take precedence over the HANDLE CONDITION command.
The following options may be specified under the HANDLE AID command.

Clear or Enter keys
Program function keys (1 through 24)
Program attention keys (PA1, PA2, and PA3)
Light-pen
Operid (for the operator)
Anykey (Any PA or PF key or the Clear key, but not the Enter key.)

```
01   DFHAID.
     02   DFHNULL     PIC X   VALUE ' '.
     02   DFHENTER    PIC X   VALUE QUOTE.    ENTER KEY
     02   DFHCLEAR    PIC X   VALUE ' '.      CLEAR KEY
     02   DFHPEN      PIC X   VALUE '='.      LIGHT PEN.
     02   DFHOPID     PIC X   VALUE 'W'.      OPERATOR ID
     02   DFHMSRE     PIC X   VALUE 'X'.      MAG.STRIP
     02   DFHSTRE     PIC X   VALUE ' '.
     02   DFHTRIG     PIC X   VALUE '"'.      TRIGGER FLD
     02   DFHPA1      PIC X   VALUE '%'.      ATT KEY 1
     02   DFHPA2      PIC X   VALUE ' '.      ATT KEY 2
     02   DFHPA3      PIC X   VALUE ' '.      ATT KEY 3
     02   DFHPF1      PIC X   VALUE '1'.      PF KEY  1
     02   DFHPF2      PIC X   VALUE '2'.      PF KEY  2
     02   DFHPF3      PIC X   VALUE '3'.      PF KEY  3
     02   DFHPF4      PIC X   VALUE '4'.      PF KEY  4
     02   DFHPF5      PIC X   VALUE '5'.      PF KEY  5
     02   DFHPF6      PIC X   VALUE '6'.      PF KEY  6
     02   DFHPF7      PIC X   VALUE '7'.      PF KEY  7
     02   DFHPF8      PIC X   VALUE '8'.      PF KEY  8
     02   DFHPF9      PIC X   VALUE '9'.      PF KEY  9
     02   DFHPF10     PIC X   VALUE ':'.      PF KEY 10
     02   DFHPF11     PIC X   VALUE '#'.      PF KEY 11
     02   DFHPF12     PIC X   VALUE '@'.      PF KEY 12
     02   DFHPF13     PIC X   VALUE 'A'.      PF KEY 13
     02   DFHPF14     PIC X   VALUE 'B'.      PF KEY 14
     02   DFHPF15     PIC X   VALUE 'C'.      PF KEY 15
     02   DFHPF16     PIC X   VALUE 'D'.      PF KEY 16
     02   DFHPF17     PIC X   VALUE 'E'.      PF KEY 17
     02   DFHPF18     PIC X   VALUE 'F'.      PF KEY 18
     02   DFHPF19     PIC X   VALUE 'G'.      PF KEY 19
     02   DFHPF20     PIC X   VALUE 'H'.      PF KEY 20
     02   DFHPF21     PIC X   VALUE 'I'.      PF KEY 21
     02   DFHPF22     PIC X   VALUE ' '.      PF KEY 22
     02   DFHPF23     PIC X   VALUE '.'.      PF KEY 23
     02   DFHPF24     PIC X   VALUE ' '.      PF KEY 24
```

Fig. 4-1. Sowing key assignments for the application.

Figure 4-2 shows an application program highlighting HANDLE AID and HANDLE CONDITION related procedures. The HANDLE AID command defines the specific use of three command keys (3, 6, and 10) as well as the anykey option. When you press PF3 (9000-RETURN-TO-MAIN-MENU-RTN), your application program will branch unconditionally to the main menu. PF6 (2500-15-ATTRIBUTE-FILL-RTN) will reset the attribute bytes of each field on the map. A green color on IBM 3279 and compatible terminals will show that each data element has been set to an unprotected status. This will enable the system to accept new data entries from the terminal operator. When you press Command Key 10 (9990-LOGOFF-RTN), the system will return control to CICS, thus allowing you to sign off at your convenience.

The HANDLE CONDITION is initially defined in the first part of the PROCEDURE DIVISION. However, an additional routine is defined for records not found, as highlighted in paragraph 3000-05-READ-STUD-CRS-RTN. Notice that I have provided two error routines (quite similar in terms of execution) to handle general, as opposed to specific, error conditions dealing with *illogic*. Illogic normally occurs when a given file does not contain a single record for processing. A general error condition is defined under 9500-PROGRAM-ERR-RTN, causing an unconditional branch back to CICS. ILLOGIC (9501-ILLOGIC) will accomplish the same thing, but only after the message Check File Status is displayed on the screen.

Finally, a MAPFAIL condition, which may be triggered by a map that contains no data at the time of transmission (8500-RETURN-TO-CICS-RTN), is handled.

Figure 4-3 highlights the path taken by the HANDLE AID and the HANDLE CONDITION routines.

Figure 4-4 illustrates how the communications area may be utilized in a given application program. First an image of such area is defined in the WORKING-STORAGE SECTION under paragraph CA-PMP0040. Corresponding to that is the redefinition of the length of the communications area as +7, then +38, and finally as +2 bytes. This means that you may move the entire portion of that image once you have acquired it from the LINKAGE SECTION. As you can see, DFHCOMMAREA is initially defined as a 38 position record. When you are ready to retransmit such data, you may not have to deal with the entire 38 positions. An example of this is shown in paragraphs 8500-RETURN-TO-CICS-RTN and COM-AREA-LENGTH-ERROR.

Quite early in your program, you want to check the EIB BLOC by saying

```
IF EIBCALEN GREATER THAN ZERO, THEN...
```

to make sure that valid data has been passed on to the current transaction. If no valid message has been dispatched, through the communications area,

```
PROCEDURE DIVISION.

0000-MAIN-ROUTINE.
    EXEC CICS HANDLE AID
    ANYKEY (2500-10-ADV-TO-SCRN-RTN)
    PF3 (9000-RETURN-TO-MAIN-MENU-RTN)
    PF6 (2500-15-ATTRIBUTE-FILL-RTN)
    PF10 (9990-LOGOFF-RTN)
    END-EXEC.

    EXEC CICS HANDLE CONDITION
    MAPFAIL (8500-RETURN-TO-CICS-RTN)
    ILLOGIC (9501-ILLOGIC)
    ERROR (9500-PROGRAM-ERROR-RTN)
    END-EXEC.

2500-10-ADV-TO-SCRN-RTN.
    IF ATSL GREATER THAN ZERO
    IF (ATSL GREATER THAN ZERO) AND
        (ATSL LESS THAN 04)
    NEXT SENTENCE ELSE GO TO
    2500-15-ATTRIBUTE-FILL-RTN.
    IF ATSI = '01' MOVE 'PMP0010A' TO XCTL-PROG.
    IF ATSL = '02' MOVE 'PMP0020A' TO XCTL-PROG.
    IF ATSL = '03' MOVE 'PMP0030A' TO XCTL-PROG.
    IF ATSI NOT = ('01', OR '02', OR '03') go to ats-ERROR.
    MOVE 'Y' TO CA-FIRST-PASS-FLAG.
    EXEC CICS XCTL PROGRAM(XCTL-PROG)
    COMMAREA(CA-PMP0040)
    LENGTH(CA-LEN)
    END-EXEC.

2500-15-ATTRIBUTE-FILL-RTN.
    MOVE ATR-GREEN TO ATSA.
    TRLA, COLLEGEA, DEPTA, DISCA,
    SSNO1A, SSNO2A, SSNO3A, SELECTIONA,............
2500-20-UPDATE-CYCLE....................................

3000-05-READ-STUD-CRS-RTN.
    EXEC CICS HANDLE CONDITION
    NOTFND (9900-RECOR-NOT-FOUND)
    END-EXEC.

8500-RETURN-TO-CICS-RTN.
    IF ERROR-NOT-FOUND MOVE -1 TO TRLL.
    IF CA-FIRST-PASS
    MOVE 'N' TO CA-FIRST-PASS-FLAG
    EXEC CICS SEND MAP('PMM040A')
           MAPSET('PMS040A')
           ERASE
           END-EXEC
    ELSE
    EXEC CICS SEND MAP('PMM040A')
           MAPSET('PMS040A')
           FROM(PMM040AO)
           CURSOR
           DATAONLY
           END-EXEC.
```

Fig. 4-2. The use of the HANDLE AID and HANDLE CONDITION commands.

```
          EXEC CICS RETURN TRANSID('PC04')
              COMMAREA (CA-PMP0040)
              LENGTH(CA-LEN)
              END-EXEC.

     9000-RETURN-TO-MENU-RTN.
          MOVE +07 TO CA-LEN.
          MOVE 'Y" TO CA-FIRST-PASS-FLAG.
          EXEC CICS  XCTL PROGRAM('PMP0010A')
          COMMAREA(CA-PMP0040)
          LENGTH(CA-LEN)
          END-EXEC.

     9500-PROGRAM-ERROR-RTN.
          EXEC CICS SEND FROM(ERR-PROG)
          LENGTH(30)
          ERASE
          END-EXEC.
          EXEC CICS RETURN
              END-EXEC.
          GOBACK.

     9501-ILLOGIC.
          MOVE 'CHECK FILE STATUS'
          TO ERR-LINEO
          EXEC CICS SEND MAP('PMM040A')
          MAPSET('PMS040A')
          END-EXEC.
          EXEC CICS RETURN
          END-EXEC.
          GOBACK.
     9900-RECORD-NOT-FOUND.
          MOVE 'RECORD DOES NOT EXIST' TO ERROR-LINEO
          EXEC CICS SEND MAP('PMM040A')
          END-EXEC.
          EXEC CICS RETURN TRANSID('PC04')
          COMMAREA (CA-PMP0040)
          LENGTH(CA-LEN)
          END-EXEC.
     9990-LOGOFF-RTN.
          EXEC CICS RETURN
          END-EXEC.
          GOBACK.
```

then an error condition exists, perhaps caused by the lack of a specific password assignment or other equally important factors.

At this point you might want to rechannel your transaction into an error handler program (ERR-ROUTINE), utilizing the first seven positions (CA1-LEN) of the communications area to specify the problem to the receiving error handler program.

During the 8500-RETURN-TO-CICS-ROUTINE procedure the entire record is moved. However in a subsequent procedure only the first seven positions of such a migratory record is moved. (Note that you may also send

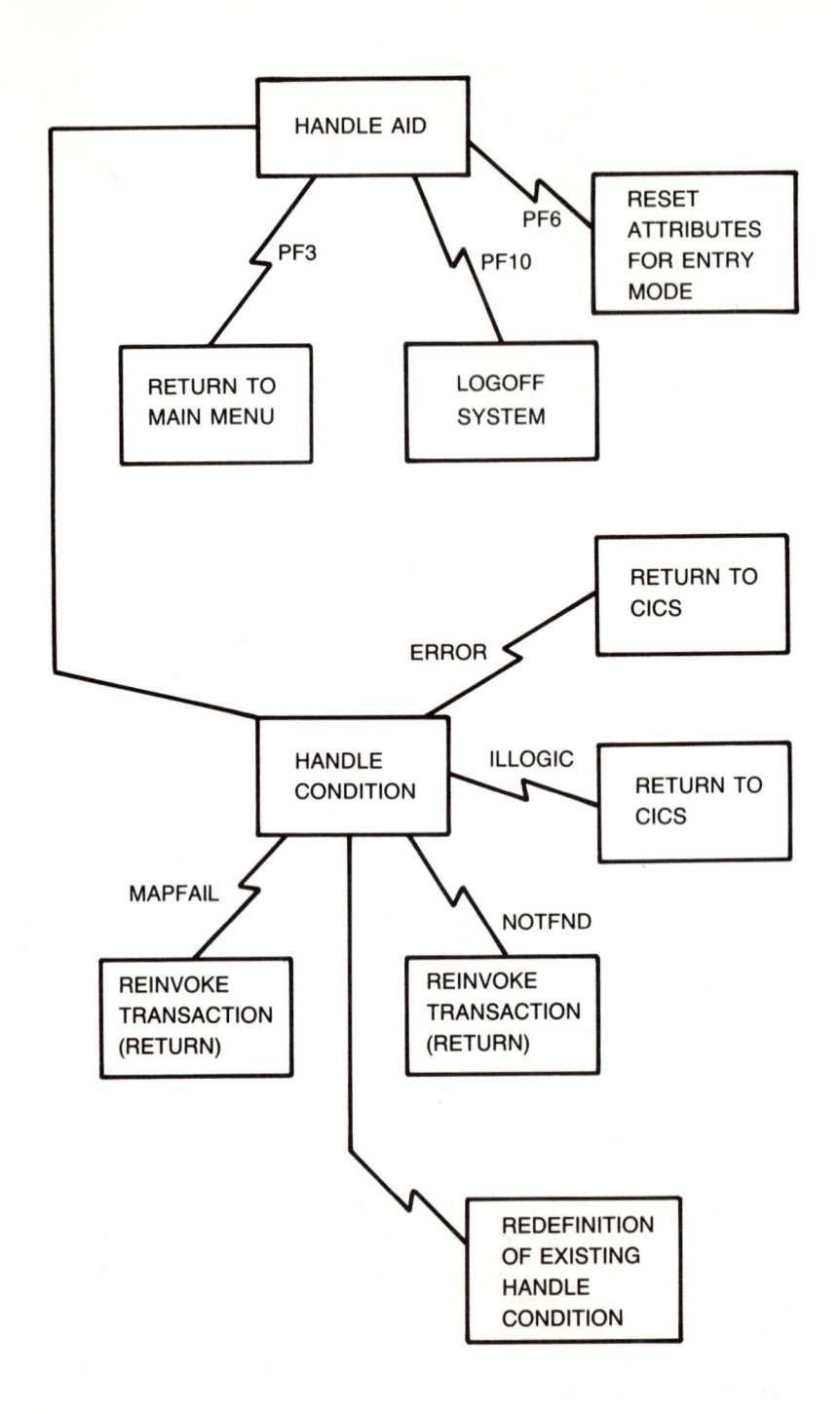

Fig. 4-3. The logical steps performed by both HANDLE commands in Fig. 4-2.

```
        IDENTIFICATION DIVISION.
        PROGRAM-ID. PMP0040A.
        DATE-COMPILED.
        ENVIRONMENT DIVISION.
        DATA DIVISION.
        WORKING-STORAGE SECTION.
        77  PAN-VALET      PIC X(28) VALUE '   PMP0040A    08/16/86 0944
        01  DFHBMSCA COPY DFHBMSCA.
        01  PMM999aI COPY PMS999A.
        01  ATTRIBUTE-LIST.
            05  ATR-GREEN  PIC X VALUE 'A'.
            05  ATR-RED    PIC X VALUE 'I'.
        ..............
        ..............
            ..............
        01  CA-PMP0040.
            05  CA-FIRST-PASS-FLAG   PIC X VALUE 'Y'.
                88  CA-FIRST-PASS          VALUE 'y'.
                88  CA-NOT-FIRST-PASS      VALUE 'N'.
            05  CA-PWRD.
                10  PWRD1            PIC X VALUE SPACES.
                88  CA-PWRD-ZZ1            VALUE 'C'.
                88  CA-PWRD-ZZ2            VALUE 'U'.
                88  CA-PWRD-ZZ3            VALUE 'G'.
                10  FILLER REDEFINES PWRD1.
                15  PWRD1-A          PIC X.
                10  FILLER           PIC X(04) VALUE SPACES.
                10  PWRD3            PIC X     VALUE SPACES.
            05  CA-REC-KEY           PIC X(31) VALUE SPACES.

        01  LENGTH-FIELDS.
            05  CA1-LEN              PIC S9(4) COMP VALUE +07.
            05  CA2-LEN              PIC S9(4) COMP VALUE +38.
            05  CA3-LEN              PIC S9(4) COMP VALUE +02.

        LINKAGE SECTION.

        01  DFHCOMMAREA.
            05  PASS-INFO            PIC X(38).
            EJECT.

        PROCEDURE DIVISION.
        ...............
            IF EIBCALEN GREATER THAN ZERO NEXT SENTENCE
            ELSE GO TO COM-AREA-LENGTH-ERROR.
            MOVE PASS-INFO TO CA-PMP0040.

            IF CA-NOT-FIRST-PASS NEXT SENTENCE ELSE
            GO TO 8500-RETURN-TO-CICS-RTN.
            ..............
                ..............
        8500-RETURN-TO-CICS-RTN.
            EXEC CICS RETURN TRANSID('AWWR')
            COMMAREA(CA-PMP0040)
            LENGTH(CA2-LEN)
            END-EXEC.
        COM-AREA-LENGTH-ERROR.
            EXEC CICS XCTL PROGRAM (ERR-ROUTINE)
            COMMAREA(CA-PMP0040)
            LENGTH(CA1-LEN)
            END-EXEC.
```

Fig. 4-4. Part of an application program, including the communications area.

45

the first two positions through the communications area through the CA3-LEN definition.)

Below is an example of the HANDLE AID command:

```
EXEC CICS HANDLE AID
PF1(MAIN-MENU)
PF2(UPDATE-FILE)
PF3(UPDATE-FIELD2)
PF10(SIGN-OFF)
ANYKEY(ERROR)
END-EXEC.
```

By pressing Function Key 1, a branch to the main menu will be triggered. That is, the program logic will branch to the MAIN-MENU paragraph, which at that point will exit (XCTL) the current transaction. PF2 will branch to the UPDATE-FILE1 routine where either a write (add) or a rewrite (update) routine will be activated.

PF10 will allow the user to sign off the system. Should any other key be used, a branch to the ERROR1 paragraph (an all purpose error handling routine) will occur.

Like with the HANDLE CONDITION statement, an option without the corresponding label or paragraph name will pass control to the next executable instruction. The ANYKEY option entails all keys except the OPERID, the light pen, and the Enter keys. Any specific option will override the general ANYKEY option.

Ignore Condition

The Ignore Condition command is used to specify that no action is to be taken if an exceptional condition occurs. It remains in effect until a subsequent HANDLE CONDITION for that particular command is encountered.

4.3 THE COMMUNICATIONS (COM) AREA

It is important that you have an early grasp on the workings of the communications (COM) area since messages are constantly sent and received through the COM area during the execution of a given task.

If you have been programming in the past in a typical batch environment and are somewhat familiar with the mechanics of setting condition codes in the JCL runstream, then equate the use of the communications area with condition codes you can utilize outside the boundaries of your application program. For example, if Program PGMAAA comes to a successful completion, you might want to set your condition code to 40, so that the JCL runstream can trigger the execution of the next program. If, however, PGMAAA (your current program) abnormally terminates and the files and data sets required by P6MBBB are not created, you want to be able to communicate that event so that the entire job can be flushed from the system.

As with the rather simplified batch environment, the communications area tends to both generate and utilize messages that survive the termination (both normal and abnormal) of a give task. Assume, for example, that your application program must be able to differentiate the way it handles a set of logic for the first time it receives communication from another program as opposed to subsequent processing. The first time around you might want to generate a message for the terminal operator in the form of a map, so that he may start entering data into the system. From the second time on, however, your program must be able to receive, or read, the data transmitted back to the application program by the terminal operator in order to edit and validate that information interactively. Finally, when the task of validation is complete, you might want to relay some of the information you have developed in your program to the next program to be invoked. When the communications area is used for relaying messages (as opposed to transient data queues or temporary storage facilities), data will become available in the DFHCOMMAREA in the LINKAGE SECTION of your application program. A PICTURE or PIC, clause attached to the DFHCOMMAREA, or to its 02 level equivalent, will reveal the intended size of the area. Thus, PIC X(20) means that communication up to 20 characters or bytes may be initialized by the program, provided that the length of the field is also defined as a 20 position data element.

```
01   COMLEN1   PIC S9(4) COMP VALUE +20.
```

The contents of the DFHCOMMARA can be easily modified through the redefinition of the length field. Thus, a program may receive a 20-byte message from a previous program, but relay only 10 bytes of it prior to the termination of the task.

Whenever a program receives communication from another application program or through revoking itself (a technique we will be discussing shortly), it must check the length of the communications area by testing the EIBCALEN field. If the EIBCALEN field is equal to zeros, then no valid form of communication has been received in the DFHCOMMAREA. You might want to provide a set of logic, just for this event. Note that the EIBCALEN is a four-position BINARY field, which is automatically generated in the program as part of the DFHEIBLK block (Fig. 4-5).

Let's review all this in the form of a simple case study. Remember that information flows in and out of the LINKAGE SECTION, but preferably work gets done in the WORKING-STORAGE section, provided that the EIBCALEN field is greater than zero. The final destination of the communication message is triggered through an EXEC CICS command in the PROCEDURE DIVISION.

Figure 4-6 shows how information may be stored, relayed, and modi-

```
01  DFHEIBLK.
    02  EIBTIME     PIC S9(7) COMP-3.   Time in OHHMMSS format
    02  EIBDATE     PIC S9(7) COMP-3.   Date in OOYYDDD formmat
    02  EIBTRNID    PIC X(4).           Transaction Identifier
    02  IEBTASKŃ    PIC X(4).           Task number
    02  EIBTRMID    PIC X(4).           Terminal Identifier
    02  DFHEIGDI    PIC S9(4) COMP.     Reserved bv the svstem
    02  EIBCPOSN    PIC S9(4) COMP.     Cursor Position
    ------------------------------------------------------------
    02  EIBCALEN    PIC S9(4) COMP.     Lenath of Commarea
    ------------------------------------------------------------
    02  EIBAID      PIC X.              Attention Identifier
    02  EIBFN       PIC X(2)            Function code
    02  EIBRCODE    PIC X(6).           Response code
    02  EIBDS       PIC X(6).           Dataset name
    02  EIBREOID    PIC X(8).           Reauest Identifier
    02  EIBRSRCE    PIC X(8).           Resource name
    02  EIBSYNC     PIC X.              Syncpoint reauired
    02  EIBFREE     PIC X.              Free terminal rea.
    02  EIBRECV     PIC X.              Data rec.reauired
    02  EIBSEND     PIC X.              Reserved bv svstem.
    02  EIBATT      PIC X.              Attached data exists
    02  EIBEOC      PIC X.              Rec.Data Complete
    02  EIBFMH      PIC X.              Rec.data has FMH
```

Fig. 4-5. The layout of the DFHEIBLK block in the data division. EIBCALEN is used for checking the COMMAREA.

fied, if necessary, in the communications area. Two cycles are normally differentiated in an on-line application program: the first time a transaction is invoked, and all subsequent cycles thereafter. During the first cycle, you want to make sure that all initial tasks are satisfied, verify the contents of the communications area in a predefined format, review the status of your map (whether you are about to send it or receive it), and verify the interaction between your application program and the terminal operator. This is accomplished in the application program in Fig. 4-6 by alternating an indicator with the predefined contents of ONE (first time send) and TWO (subsequent processing and reinvocation). The paragraph name UPDATE1 entails a number of edit criteria you might want to build within your own application programs under this label. Among these are the checking of a social security number for validity, the verification of a numeric field, and the verification that a search argument is within predefined table ranges. These edit checks are essentially batch functions. Should they fail, you will probably have to generate an error message to alert the terminal operator that further action will be required on his part. This may be done in the following format:

```
IF SOCIAL-SECURITY-NO IS NOT NUMERIC
    MOVE 'EMPLOYEE ID NUMBER IS IN
    ERROR' TO ERR-MSGO
    MOVE 'H' TO ERR-MSGA
EXEC CICS TRANSID ('C001')
    COMMAREA (WORK-COMM-AREA0 LENGTH(25))
END-EXEC.
```

```
LINKAGE SECTION.            *   * WORKING-STORAGE SECTION.
01 DFHCOMMAREA.             *   * 01 WORK-COMM-AREA.
   02  COM-DATA             *   *    02 RECORD-INDICATOR.
       PICTURE X(20).       *   *       03 TRANSMIT-F
                            *   *          PICTURE X.
                            *   *       03 FILLER PIC X(2).
                            *   *    02 FILLER    PIC X(17).
                            *   * 01 COMLEN1
----------------------------    *       PIC S9(4)
                                *       COMPUTATIONAL
                                *       VALUE +3.
----------------------------    * 01 ERROR-BYTE
PROCEDURE DIVISION.         *   *       PIC X(2).
HANDLE-COMM.                *   * COMLEN2 PIC S9(4)
EXEC CICS HANDLE AID        *   * COMPUTATIONAL, VALUE +1.
PF1(UPDATE)                 *   ----------------------------
      *                     *
      *                         ----------------------------
END-EXEC.
START-PROCESSING.
IF EIBCALEN GREATER THAN ZEROS
MOVE COM-DATA TO RECORD-INDICATOR.
IF RECORD-INDICATOR = 'ONE' MOVE 'TWO' TO
RECORD-INDICATOR, EXEC CICS SEND MAP('MAP1')
MAPSET('SET1') CURSOR ERASE END-EXEC
EXEC CICS RETURN TRANSID('C001')
COMMAREA(WORK-COMM-AREA) LENGTH(COMLEN1) END-EXEC.
IF RECORD-INDICATOR = 'TWO' EXEC CICS RECEIVE MAP
MAP('MAP1') MAPSET('SET1') END-EXEC
PERFORM EDIT1 THRU EDIT1-EXIT
EXEC CICS RETURN TRANSID('C001')
COMMAREA(WORK-COMM-AREA) LENGTH(COMLEN1) END-EXEC.
----------------------------------------------------------

----------------------------------------------------------
UPDATE1.
IF ERROR-BYTE = 'OK' AND DFHAID=DFHPF1
MOVE 'F' TO TRANSMIT-F

        ........rewrite or update record here.........

EXEC CICS XCTL PROGRAM('PGM002')
COMMAREA(WORK-COMM-AREA) LENGTH(COMLEN2)
END-EXEC, ELSE.........insert error routine........
```

Fig. 16. Code that shows how information can be altered in the COMMAREA to trigger different functions, such as sending or receiving maps.

where ERR-MSGO is an area on the output map (designated by the character O) that is allocated to the display of systems messages. An H is interpreted by CICS as a high-intensity attribute byte. Thus moving the character H into the error message would place substantial emphasis on such a message.

Since the current program transaction identifier happens to be C001, an error condition would allow you to reinvoke such a transaction, so that

49

the terminal operator may continue his data verification routine uninterrupted.

If the edit is successfully completed, the bottom half of the UPDATE1 paragraph will materialize; that is the current program will exit into PGM002 to continue in another path.

SUMMARY

A HANDLE CONDITION statement may be coded by the application programmer to provide a branching mechanism in the program logic as a response to a number of systems-related conditions, such as not finding a specific record or detecting a duplicate key error. A specific HANDLE CONDITION remains in effect until it is redefined by the application programmer.

The HANDLE AID, or Handle Attention Identifier, command is used in reference to the keyboard. In the CICS application program hierarchy, the HANDLE AID command will take precedence over the HANDLE CONDITION command.

The communications (COM) area is also available for the programmer analyst. The COMMAREA is used to relay and receive messages that are either internal or external to a given application program.

QUESTIONS

1. What is the function of the HANDLE CONDITION?
2. How many conditions can you specify in a single HANDLE CONDITION statement?
3. Once you have issued a HANDLE CONDITION, how long is it going to stay in effect?
4. Why do you have to refer to the DFHAID block in your application program?
5. Explain the need for using the communications area (COMMAREA)?
6. Why is it necessary to reinvoke an on-line program?
7. Why is it necessary at times to provide a "first time" as oposed to a "second time" routine?

5

Maps and Mapsets

HIGHLIGHTS
- **Overview**
- **Attribute Bytes**
- **Map Generation**
- **Screen Definition Facility (SDF)**

5.1 OVERVIEW

The purpose of this chapter is to review some of the conventions available to the application programmer in creating and working with maps. In this chapter I have focused on an IBM Basic Mapping Support (BMS) interactive package referred to as Screen Definition Facility, or SDF. This package, unlike its macro level BMS equivalent, allows the programmer to design maps in an on-line environment.

What Are Maps?

Maps are preformatted screen displays logically arranged by function or by task. A number of these can belong to a *mapset*. They define the position and the attributes of various fields or data elements. Let us now review some essential terms.

Physical Map. For input operations, the physical map defines the maximum length and starting position of each field to be read. For output operations, the physical map defines starting positions, length, field characteristics, and default data.

Symbolic Map. The symbolic map is the dsect or copy book that is copied into the application program used to reference the data fields in the map and their corresponding length and attribute characters.

Creation. Maps are created by map definition macros. These are:

DFHMDS   Mapset Definition
DFHMDI   Map Definition
DFHMDF   Field Definition

Through SDF, fields can be named so that the application programmer can refer to them by name in his program. The naming of each data ele-

51

ment appearing on the map may be done either by the programmer or generated through SDF. In addition to being able to automatically name fields, SDF allows the programmer to define new maps using existing ones as models.

Whatever methodology you use to create maps, it is imperative that you understand how field names are detected and recognized by the program logic, when and how they are transmitted, and most important, how they can be manipulated and modified in accordance with constantly changing requirements. This is done through the manipulation of *attribute bytes*, for the most part.

5.2 ATTRIBUTE BYTES

To understand data transmission, the concept of *fields* is essential. Fields are zones of consecutive character positions on the screen. The characteristics of a field are defined by the preceding attribute byte, which appears on the screen as a protected blank. Through the manipulation of the attribute byte, it is possible to define a field with initial *properties* and then redefine it as it becomes necessary. The application programmer, via a copy statement, will have access to a number of systems-supplied BMS functions in his program. When compiled, the following statement:

```
01   DFHBMSCA COPY DFHBMSCA
```

will result in the expanded statements shown in Fig. 5-1.

When a field is defined as unprotected, it means that it will accept data entered by the terminal operator. An unprotected field can be modified, but, a protected field (such as a header or a constant) cannot be modified by the user.

Autoskip fields are essentially protected fields that the cursor automatically skips during data entry from the terminal.

The intensity of a field may be described to the system in a number of ways. Dark means that the data in the field is invisible. It is not left off or deleted from the screen, but simply displayed in dark. This is most often used for security purposes: A password can be entered or data that you do not want the users to see can be passed or stored.

Bright means that a field is intensified to alert the operator of a possible error condition, or perhaps to describe certain mandatory data elements that may not be left blank on the screen.

When the attribute byte is set to be numeric, only numeric data (0-9) are permissible. The numeric attribute ensures that the data entry keyboard is set to numeric shift for this field, unless the user presses the alpha shift key. If the keyboard numeric lock feature is installed and the shift is set to numeric, the entry of non-numeric data will not be allowed. Note that

```
01  DFHBMSCA.
    02   DFHBMPEM    PIC X VALUE ' '. (Printer end of message)
    02   DFHBMPNL    PIC X VALUE ' '. (Printer new line char.)
    02   DFHBMASK    PIC X VALUE '0'. (Autoskip)
    02   DFHBMUNP    PIC X VALUE ' '. (Unprotected)
    02   DFHBMUNN    PIC X VALUE '&'. (Unprotected numeric)
    02   DFHBMPRO    PIC X VALUE '-'. (Protected)
    02   DFHBMBRY    PIC X VALUE 'H'. (Bright intensity)
    02   DFHBMDAR    PIC X VALUE '<'. (Nondisplay)
    02   DFHBMFSE    PIC X VALUE 'A'. (Modified data tag mdt on)
    02   DFHBMPRF    PIC X VALUE '/'. (Protected and mdt on)
    02   DFHBMASF    PIC X VALUE '1'. (Autoskip and mdt on)
    02   DFHBMASB    PIC X VALUE '8'. (Autoskip bright intensity)
    02   DFHSA       PIC X VALUE ' '.
    02   DFHCOLOR    PIC X VALUE ' '.
    02   DFHPS       PIC X VALUE ' '.
    02   DFHHLT      PIC X VALUE ' '.
    02   DFH3270     PIC X VALUE ' '.
    02   DFHVAL      PIC X VALUE 'A'.
    02   DFHALL      PIC X VALUE ' '.
    02   DFHERROR    PIC X VALUE ' '. (Error code)
    02   DFHDFT      PIC X VALUE ' '.
    02   DFHDFCOL    PIC X VALUE ' '. (Default color)
    02   DFHBLUE     pic x value '1'. (Blue)
    02   DFHRED      PIC X VALUE '2'. (Red)
    02   DFHPINK     PIC X VALUE '3'. (pink)
    02   DFHGREEN    PIC X VALUE '4'. (green)
    02   DFHTURQ     PIC X VALUE '5'. (Turquoise)
    02   DFHYELLO    PIC X VALUE '6'. (Yellow)
    02   DFHNEUTR    PIC X VALUE '7'. (Neutral)
    02   DFHBASE     PIC X VALUE ' '. (Based pgm. symbol set)
    02   DFHDFHI     PIC X VALUE ' '. (No highlight - default)
    02   DFHBLINK    PIC X VALUE '1'. (Blinking)
    02   DFHREVRS    PIC X VALUE '2'. (Reverse video)
    02   DFHUNDLN    PIC X VALUE '4'. (Underlining)
    02   DFHMFIL     PIC X VALUE ' '. (Mandatory fiLL)
    02   DFHMENT     PIC X VALUE ' '.
    02   DFHMFE      PIC X VALUE ' '.
```

Fig. 5-1. The expanded statements that result from the compilation of the DFHBMSCA COPY DFHBMSCA statement.

the programmer should never assume the presence of a numeric lock. Even if every terminal that is installed has such a feature in the beginning, as the system expands and additional terminals are acquired, it is possible that some of the newer acquisitions may not have those features.

When using the attribute byte of a field in order to position the cursor, the application programmer normally wants to position the cursor at the beginning of a specific field. When validating data, the programmer might want to position his cursor at the beginning of an erroneous field. If there are three of those fields, the last field flagged in the program will contain the cursor following the completion of a transaction. As a result, some programmers have the tendency to reverse the sequence in which the fields are edited.

Setting the *modified data tag* (MDT) is necessary to ensure that the contents of the field is returned following each data transmission. Without this feature, a field that has not been entered during the most current cycle would be lost (the length of the field would be equal to zero) following the next data transmission.

An attribute byte may be set to determine whether data for this field should be left or right justified at run time. It is also possible to pad fields with blanks or zeros.

Depending upon the hardware features of a given terminal, it is possible to display information in various colors. For example, a field that is initially transmitted in green may be modified to red upon failure to meet certain edit criteria. You may also wish to express the severity of a condition through a color coding scheme.

In addition, a field may be displayed in reverse video form, may be underscored, or may blink.

I mentioned earlier that the application programmer might want to rely on a number of attributes conveniently rolled into one. For example, assume that we would like to display a given field in normal intensity, unprotected, with the modified data tag on. Also, the cursor should be positioned as specified, with the field being left justified and padded with blanks. These conditions may be defined and constructed utilizing the IBM attribute bit character definition charts presented in Fig. 5-2, and the corresponding attribute chart showing functional definitions presented in Fig. 5-3.

The attribute definition chart and the attribute character chart showing functional definitions that represent a few abbreviated entries out of an IBM green card work very much in unison.

Let's assume that we would like to "invent" a symbol for the following function:

Unprotected
Numeric
Modified data tag on
High intensity display
Selector pen detectable

If you look on the attribute character bit definition chart (Fig. 5-2), all the above mentioned criteria would be satisfied by the entry at EBCDIC hexadecimal D9 (ASCII hexadecimal 52). Hexadecimal D9 (decimal 217) on the attribute character chart (Fig. 5-3) shows that the functional definition is equal to an R. Thus, translating all this into an ANS COBOL statement, we might say:

```
01   UNP-NUM-MDT-HI-PEN         PIC X value 'R'.
```

Furthermore, we may create a procedure statement as follows:

Move UNP-NUM-MDT-HI-PEN to GRSPYA.

ATTRIBUTE BIT CHARACTER DEFINITION

P R O	A/N	ATTRIBUTE MDT ON	HI INT	SEL PEN DET	NON DIS PRT	BITS 23	BITS 4567	EBC DIC HEX	AS CH HEX
U						00	0000	40	20
U		Y				00	0001	C1	41
U				Y		00	0100	C4	42
U		Y		Y		00	0101	C5	43
U			H	Y		00	1000	C8	48
U		Y	H	Y		00	1001	C9	49
U			-	-	Y	00	1100	4C	3C
U		Y	-	-	Y	00	1101	4D	28
U	N					01	0000	50	26
U	N	Y				01	0001	D1	4A
U	N				Y	01	0100	D4	D4
U	N	Y		Y		01	0101	D5	4E
U	N		H	Y		01	1000	D8	51
U	N	Y	H	Y		01	1001	D9	52
U	N		-	-	Y	01	1100	5C	2A
U	N	Y	-	-	Y	01	1101	5D	29
P						10	0000	60	2D
P		Y				10	0001	61	2F
P				Y		10	0100	E4	55
P		Y		Y		10	0101	E5	56
P			H	Y		10	1000	E8	59
P		Y	H	Y		10	1001	E9	5A
P			-	-	Y	10	1100	6C	25
P		Y	-	-	Y	10	1101	6D	5F
P	S					11	0000	F0	30
P	S	Y				11	0001	F1	31
P	S			Y		11	0100	F4	34
P	S	Y		Y		11	0101	F5	35
P	S		H	Y		11	1000	F8	38
P	S	Y	H	Y		11	1001	F9	39
P	S		-	-	Y	11	1100	7C	40
P	S	Y	-	-	Y	11	1101	7D	27

```
S = skip    U = unprotected    P = protected
Y = yes     H = high           N = numeric
```

Fig. 5-2. The attribute bit character definition chart.

```
           DECIMAL    HEX    CHAR     BINARY
                             EQUIV    EQUIV
           --------------------------------------
             D8       216     Q       1101 1000
             D9       217     R       1101 1001
             ↓        ↓       ↓       ↓    ↓

             F8       248     8       1111 1000
             F9       249     9       1111 1001
             ↓        ↓       ↓       ↓    ↓
```

Fig. 5-3. The attribute character chart showing functional definitions.

```
          POSSIBLE DEFINED ATTRIBUTES, EQUATE CHARACTERS

  !   HIGH INTENSITY, AUTOSKIP, LEFT JUSTIFIED, FILLED BLANKS
  #   NORMAL INTENSITY, AUTOSKIP, LEFT, BLANK
  ¢   NORMAL, UNPROTECTED, LEFT, BLANK
  $   NORMAL, UNPROTECTED, CURSOR, LEFT, BLANK
  *   HIGH, UNPROTECTED, LEFT, BLANK
  +   NORMAL UNPROTECTED, MDT, LEFT, BLANK
  =   NORMAL, UNPROTECTED MDT, CURSOR, LEFT, BLANK
  @   NORMAL, UNPROTECTED, RIGHT, ZERO FILLED
  %   NORMAL, UNPROTECTED, CURSOR, RIGHT, ZERO
  ]   NORMAL, UNPROTECTED, MDT, RIGHT, ZERO
  &   NORMAL, UNPROTECTED, MDT, CURSOR, RIGHT, ZERO
```

Fig. 5-4. Special characters assigned to combined attribute functions.

Here, the variable GRSPYA could represent the attribute byte of the map field GROSS PAY.

In section 5.4, we will be creating our own attribute set to be used in conjunction with developing new maps and mapsets via SDF. Figure 5-4 shows some special characters that have been assigned to combined attribute functions. This table of SDF attribute symbols can be utilized by the application programmer. As an example, the table shows that the], or right bracket, was set up to represent a field that will be displayed on the screen in normal intensity. It will be an unprotected field with the modified data tag turned on. Also, the field will appear initially zero filled and right justified. You may define your own symbols according to your specific needs.

When designing screen layouts (maps), consider the space that cannot be used due to the attribute byte. A classical example would be the entering of a social security number by an operator. Due to the delimiter you must place at the beginning and end of each variable, you cannot have a constant (such as a hyphen) immediately following or preceding a variable. The closest you could get to this would be the following:

123 - 45 - 6789

There are various ways to approach this problem. One is to make the operator key in the hyphens, thus making one eleven-character field on your map. Another solution would be to make three fields, one for each section of the number. Still another methodology would be to create one field, and place the hyphens in characters four and seven. In this case, the operator would either have to skip over the hyphens or type over them. Finally, a field of length nine could be created, and the operator would type in only the number with no hyphens. When we actually discuss the creation of maps, this will become more apparent.

5.3 MAP GENERATION

Whether we use BMS techniques to code up lengthy DFHMDF statements for every data element on the screen or utilize the Screen Definition Facility (SDF) package, we must issue a copy statement in order to have access to a program-generated set of statements. (Refer to the PPT or Program Processing table for additional information.) The format of the copy statement is as follows:

```
01  MAPNAME COPY MAPSET.
```

Let us illustrate this. Consider the table maintenance screen in Fig. 5-5.

TABLE MAINTENANCE SCREEN

MAINTENANCE:

CLASS CODE:

DESCRIPTION:

REVISE DATE:

                MAINTENANCE CODES: A = ADD A RECORD
                                    D = DELETE A RECORD
                                    R = REVISE A RECORD
                                    I = INQUIRY
                                    X = REACTIVATE RECORD

PF3:RETURN TO MAIN MENU
PF6:UPDATE   PF10: SIGN OFF

ERROR OR ALERT MESSAGES DISPLAYED HERE.

Fig. 5-5. The table maintenance screen, including a number of maintenance codes and command key assignments.

It represents a means to update some on-line records. Essentially a record may be added, revised, or deleted. The terminal operator may also be able to inquire about the contents of a given file. A special reactivate function was designed for those still under ISAM (Indexed Sequential Access Method). When a record is deleted from a file via ISAM, the record is only marked for deletion. The actual deletion occurs when computer operations has a chance to reorganize the files, dumping data from the overflow areas back to the prime areas. Since the record is only marked for deletion and not physically deleted as would be the case under VSAM, the application programmer can remove the flag (prior to the reorganization) and thus "reactivate" the record.

Once the map is resident in the PPT (Program Processing Table), and has been coded via BMS, SDF, or other means, the programmer may issue the following statement:

```
01  MAPSETI   COPY MAPSETO.
```

This statement will generate the entries shown in the program in Fig. 5-6. Note that these statements are segregated into two logical areas:

- The input definition represented by the MAPSETI map definition, which is in turn redefined by the other logical area.
- The output section, or MAPSETO area.

Let's take the maintenance code which was initially defined by SDF as a one position data element with the generic field name MAINT. Once the program compiles, the field MAINT will acquire an extra suffix attachment as follows:

L : Defines the length of a given field.
A : The attribute byte of a field originally shown with the suffix F, which is redefined to an A.
I : Designates an input form of the field.
O : Designates the output form.

When L is attached to the root field name, MAINT + L, or MAINTL, the programmer is able to test the length of the field in order to determine whether or not anything was entered into the field. If MAINTL = zeros, then nothing was entered.

Figures 5-7 through 5-11 illustrate how the ability to test the length of a field can be put to use in a program. Figure 5-7 shows that the operator failed to enter the maintenance code. In order to check the status of the maintenance code field, the programmer can issue the set of commands shown in Fig. 5-8. Statement 1 checks the length of the maintenance code

```
01  MAPSETI.
    02  FILLER PIC X(12).
    02  MAINTL COMP PIC S9(4).
    02  MAINTF PIC X.
    02  FILLER REDEFINES MAINTF.
        03  MAINTA PIC X.
    02  MAINTI PIC X.
    02  CLASSL COMP PIC S9(4).
    02  CLASSF PIC X.
    02  FILLER REDEFINES CLASSF.
        03  CLASSA PIC X.
    02  CLASSI PIC X(5).
    02  DESCL COMP PIC S9(4).
    02  DESCF PIC X.
    02  FILLER REDEFINES DESCF.
        03  DESCA PIC X.
    02  DESCI PIC X(20).
    02  REVISEL COMP PIC S9(4).
    02  REVISEF PIC X.
    02  FILLER REDERINES REVISEF.
        03  REVISEA PIC X.
    02  REVISEI PIC X(6).
    02  ERR-LINEL COMP PIC S9(4).
    02  ERR-LINEF PIC X.
    02  FILLER REDEFINES ERR-LINEF.
        03  ERR-LINEA PIC X.
    02  ERR-LINEI PIC X(40).
01  MAPSETO REDEFINES MAPSETI.
    02  FILLER PIC X(12).
    02  FILLER PIC X(3).
    02  MAINTO PIC X.
    02  FILLER PIC X(3).
    02  CLASSO PIC X(5).
    02  FILLER PIC X(3).
    02  DESCO PIC X(20).
    02  FILLER PIC X(3).
    02  REVISEO PIC X(6).
    02  FILLER PIC X(3).
    02  ERR-LINEO PIC X(40).
```

Fig. 5-6. The entries generated by the MAPSETI COPY MAPSETO statement.

(MAINTL). If the length is zero, then nothing was entered into the field. Because the field is a mandatory data-element this omission would result in an error condition. When this occurs, the program logic would branch to the paragraph called MAINTENANCE-ERROR, which is shown in Fig. 5-11.

Statements 2 through 6 introduce a number of compare and branch operations. Actually, as we review Fig. 5-9, we find that every one of the branch procedures relate to an exit control (XCTL) command. That is to say that every maintenance routine has a separate transaction module to branch to.

Statement 7 is invoked when the code entered by the terminal operator is not A, D, R, I, or X. Obviously, we are again faced with another error condition, which must be overcome in the following manner:

Move an error message into the output (or input) form of ERR-LINE (ERR-LINEI or ERR-LINEO). Then turn the text of the error message to red by issuing a move with a variable that will make the field turn red. This is done by moving a special character to ERR-LINEA, which is the attribute byte of ERR-LINE. Finally, before transmitting the map back to the terminal operator in statement 9, position the cursor at the missing field by moving a −1 to the length of the field MAINT, which is MAINTL.

TABLE MAINTENANCE SCREEN

MAINTENANCE:

CLASS CODE: 1225

DESCRIPTION: CUSTODIAN

REVISE DATE: 120286

MAINTENANCE CODES: A = ADD A RECORD
                    D = DELETE A RECORD
                    R = REVISE A RECORD
                    I = INQUIRY
                    X = REACTIVATE RECORD

PF3: RETURN TO MAIN MENU
PF6: UPDATE   PF10: SIGN OFF

ERROR OR ALERT MESSAGES DISPLAYED HERE.

Fig. 5-7. The table maintenance screen, showing that the operator failed to enter a maintenance code.

```
(1)   IF MAINTL = ZEROS GO TO MAINTENANCE-ERROR.
(2)   IF MAINTI = 'A' GO TO ADD-ROUTINE.
(3)   IF MAINTI = 'D' GO TO DELETE-ROUTINE.
(4)   IF MAINTI = 'R' GO TO REVISE-ROUTINE.
(5)   IF MAINTI = 'I' GO TO INQUIRE-ROUTINE.
(6)   IF MAINTI = 'X' GO TO REACTIVATE-ROUTINE.
(7)   MOVE 'ERRONEOUS CODE ENTERED' TO ERR-LINEO.
(8)   MOVE DFHRED TO ERR-LINEA.
(9)   MOVE -1 TO MAINTL.
(10)  EXEC CICS SEND MAP('MAPSETI')
(11)       CURSOR DATAONLY END-EXEC.
(12)  EXEC RETURN TRANSID('TRID')
(13)       COMMAREA(WORK-COMM-AREA) LENGTH(LEN) END-EXEC.
```

Fig. 5-8. Statements to check the contents of the maintenance code field.

```
ADD-ROUTINE.
    EXEC-CICS XCTL PROGRAM('ADDPGM')
    COMMAREA(WORK-COMM-AREA)
    LENGTH(LEN) END-EXEC.
DELETE-ROUTINE.
    EXEC CICS XCTL PROGRAM('DELPGM')
    COMMAREA(WORK-COMM-AREA)
    LENGTH(LEN) END-EXEC.
REVISE-ROUTINE.
    EXEC CICS XCTL PROGRAM('REVPGM')
    COMMAREA(WORK-COMM-AREA)
    LENGTH(LEN) END-EXEC.
INQUIRE-ROUTINE.
    EXEC CICS XCTL PROGRAM('INQPGM')
    COMMAREA(WORK-COMM-AREA)
    LENGTH(LEN) END-EXEC.
REACTIVATE-ROUTINE.
    EXEC CICS XCTL PROGRAM('REAPGM')
    COMMAREA(WORK-COMM-AREA)
    LENGTH(LEN) END-EXEC.
```

Fig. 5-9. Code that will cause the execution of the appropriate programs.

```
LINKAGE SECTION.
01  DFHCOMMAREA            PIC X(6).

In working storage section.......
01  LEN COMP PIC S9(4) VALUE +6.
01  WORK-COMM-AREA.
    02  CA-MAINT-CODE      PIC X.
    02  CA-CLASS           PIC X(5).
```

Fig. 5-10. The linkage and working storage sections.

```
MAINTENANCE-ERROR.
    MOVE 'MANDATORY FIELD MISSING' TO ERR-LINE0.
    MOVE DFHRED TO ERR-LINEA.
    MOVE -1 TO MAINTL.
    EXEC CICS SEND MAP('MAPNAME') MAPSET('MSNAME')
    CURSOR DATAONLY END-EXEC.
    EXEC CICS RETURN TRANSID('TRID')
    COMMAREA(WORK-COMM-AREA) LENGTH(LEN) END-EXEC.
```

Fig. 5-11. The routine invoked when the terminal operator has failed to enter a maintenance code.

In order to successfully position the cursor, it is necessary to issue a send map command (more of which will be discussed in subsequent chapters) with the cursor option as shown in statements 10 and 11. You will also notice that the "dataonly" option is used here. Once the map is sent for the first time, it need not continually be sent over and over again. By using this option, we are only sending the data back, and not the whole map, which is helpful for response time.

Once the map is issued, we must reinvoke the program in order to give the terminal operator a chance to correct the problems. If all editing criteria is met, then one of the statements in Fig. 5-9 will be executed.

5.4 SCREEN DEFINITION FACILITY (SDF)

Screen definition facility is a tool that allows the user to specify maps and mapsets. It also provides the application programmer with a library to maintain them. Field names can be defined by the programmer or through SDF as defaults.

In order to sign on to SDF, you must type SDF when using an IBM 3279 type terminal or equivalent and then press the Enter key. This will trigger the sign-on screen (Fig. 5-12). You must enter your user identification and password and again press the Enter key to proceed.

Next a user master selection screen will be displayed (Fig. 5-13). Note that by using function key PF3, you are able to terminate SDF. From among the five possible selections presented on the screen, function 5, normal functions has been selected. This provides a range of activities from map generation to editing. (Figure 5-14)

Before continuing, let us briefly review some of the functions available on the master selection screen.

1-START UP:	This command is used only once whenever the system is brought up for the first time. Start up is required to enable the system to generate mapsets.
2-SHUT DOWN:	The system is automatically disabled. (The user can no longer sign on to SDF/CICS.)
3-USER LIST 4-SUBMIT LIST:	These commands display the list of all requests under your identification code.
5-NORMAL FUNCTIONS:	This command will direct the user to the next logical sequence in the SDF path, which will display the initial selection map.

As mentioned above, the initial selection screen, (Fig. 5-14) was triggered via function 2 of the prior step. Here SDF gives you 11 possible selections. Let's briefly review what some of the above functions represent.

1-MAP EDITOR:	This function allows us either to edit or specify a new map, or else to redefine an existing one.
2-MAP SET EDITOR:	This function is used either to edit or to specify a new mapset.

```
SCREEN DEFINITION FACILITY / CUSTOMER INFORMATION CONTROL SYSTEM    R4.0
XXXXXX   XXXXXXXXX   XXXXXXXXXX     XX   XXXXXXX  XXXXX   XXXXXXX     XXXXXX
XXXXXXXX XXXXXXXXX   XXXXXXXXXX    XXXX  XXXXXXXXX XXXXX XXXXXXXXX   XXXXXXXX
XXX       XXX  XXX    XXX           XX XX   XXX    XXXXX   XXX        XXX
XXXXXXXX  XXX  XXX    XXXXXXX       XX  XX  XXX    XXXXX   XXX       XXXXXXXX
XXXXXXXX  XXX  XXX    XXXXXXXX     XX    XX XXX    XXXXX   XXX       XXXXXXXXX
     XXX  XXX  XXX    XXX          XX    XX XXX    XX XXX  XXX             XXX
XXXXXXXX  XXXXXXXXX   XXXXXXXX    XXXXXXXXXX XXX    XXXXX  XXXXXXXX   XXXXXXXXX
XXXXXX    XXXXXXXXX   XXXXXXX     XX      XX XXX    XXXXX   XXXXXXX    XXXXXXX
              USER ID    ==>                       PASSWORD  ==>
         OPTION AND PARAMETER ==>
         PRESS ENTER KEY TO START, END KEY (PF03) TO TERMINATE
```

Fig. 5-12. The SDF sign-on screen.

```
0 ------------------------------  MASTER USER SELECTION  ------------------------------
OPTION ==>                    1 - START-UP
                              2 - SHUT-DOWN
                              3 - USER LIST
                              4 - SUBMIT LIST
                              5 - NORMAL FUNCTIONS

         USE END KEY (PF03) TO TERMINATE
```

Fig. 5-13. The SDF master selection screen.

```
------------------------   INITIAL SELECTION   ------------------------
OPTION ==>           1 - MAP EDITOR
                     2 - MAP SET EDITOR
                     3 - LIBRARY MANAGEMENT
                     4 - CICS/VS BMS GENERATOR
                     5 - PAGE EDITOR
                     6 - PRINT AND UNLOAD UTILITIES
                     7 - PROFILE EDITOR
                     8 - USER ENVIRONMENT EDITOR
                     9 - DEMO SESSION EDITOR
                    10 - PARTITION SET EDITOR
                    11 - TUTORIAL
                    12 - NEWS


        USE END KEY (PF03) TO TERMINATE
```

Fig. 5-14. The SDF initial selection screen.

```
1 ------------------------   MAP IDENTIFICATION   ------------------------
ENTER MAP TO BE EDITED                      PASSWORD ==>
      MAP SET ==>
      MAP     ==>
ENTER DEVICE TYPE IF REQUIRED
      DEVICE  ==>
ENTER MAP TO BE USED AS BASIS FOR NEW MAP (SKELETON MAP)
      MAP SET ==>
      MAP     ==>


        USE END KEY (PF03) TO TERMINATE
```

Fig. 5-15. The SDF map identification screen.

3-LIBRARY
MANAGEMENT:
This function handles libraries of maps, mapsets, pages, profiles, etc.

4-CICS/VS BMS
GENERATOR:
This module allows you to generate a BMS map through SDF. Unless a map is generated, you won't be able to make reference to its data components in your application program.

5-PAGE
EDITOR:
This function allows you to edit SDF-CICS pages, a collection of maps.

6-UTILITIES:
Through these utilities, you will be able to look at your map in detail, generate printouts, and so on.

The choice of function 1, Map Editor, triggers the map identification screen (Fig. 5-15). The purpose of this screen is to define maps and mapsets. It is also possible to use an existing skeleton map as the basis for new maps. Once you have entered the required information on the map identification screen, you will see the map editor step selection screen (Fig. 5-16). This screen provides the programmer with eight selections. Briefly, some of them are as follows:

1-ALL FUNCTIONS:
This option will create a sequential path starting with options 2 - 7. (Function key 3 has been allocated to perform each option.)

2-MAP CHARACTERISTICS:
This option defines the map in terms of physical requirements, such as map size and position, and the use of automatic naming and partitions, etc., as illustrated in Fig. 5-17.

3-FIELD DEFINITION:
Every data element you plan on displaying as part of your map will have to be defined on the field definition screen (Fig. 5-18).

Let's review some of the command characters appearing on the field definition screen: C indicates a constant, V, a variable, G, a group, and S, spaces. # Indicates the beginning of a constant that happens to be a protected field. @ Indicates the beginning of a variable field.

Note that you may also directly enter the length of the field on the screen in the following manner

#SSN:@,9

```
1 --------- MAP EDITOR STEP SELECTION ---------- MAPSET          MAPNAME
OPTION ==>               1 - ALL FUNCTIONS
                         2 - MAP CHARACTERISTICS
                         3 - FIELD DEFINITION
                         4 - FIELD ATTRIBUTE DEFINITION
                         5 - FIELD INITIALIZATION
                         6 - APPLICATION STRUCTURE SPECIFICATION
                         7 - APPLICATION STRUCTURE REVIEW
                         8 - TEST

USE END KEY (PF03) TO FILE AND EXIT
```

Fig. 5-16. The SDF map editor step selection screen.

```
1.2 --------  MAP CHARACTERISTICS  ----------  MAPSET          MAPNAME
MAP SIZE:  DEPTH  ==> 024              WIDTH      ==> 080
POSITION:  LINE:  ==> NEXT             COLUMN     ==> SAME
JUSTIFY:   LINE   ==>                  COLUMN     ==> LEFT
STRUCTURE FORMAT  ==> FIELD            I/O AREA PREFIX    ==> YES
MAP ATTRIBUTE     ==>                  OUTBOARD FORMAT    ==>
FREE KEYBOARD     ==> YES              ALARM              ==> NO
                                       RESET MDT          ==>
PRINT WIDTH       ==> EOM              START PRINTER      ==> NO
AUTOMATIC NAMING  ==> NO               NAME PREFIX        ==>
GENERATION SEQ.   ==> 001              EXTENDED ATTR.     ==> NO
LVL NUMBER START  ==> 01               LVL NUMBER INCR.   ==> 01
PARTITION NAME    ==>                  ACTIVE PARTITION   ==> NO
```

Fig. 5-17. The SDF map characteristics screen.

```
1.3 ------------- FIELD DEFINITION --------------- MAPSET NAPNAME 3279-2
==>
LINES   1  20    -------------- C(#) V(@) G(%) S(/) --------------- COLS  1  75
01 #SCREEN: 2                 CONSOLIDATED AMERICAN           ADVANCE TO SCREEN:@ #
02 #
03 #                              DEMOGRAPHIC FILE
04 #
05 #
06 #     EMPLOYEE SSN:@  @  @        #
07 #
08 #
09 #            NAME: @                                            #
10 #            ADDRESS: @
11 #            CITY: @                           #
12 #            ZIP CODE:@            #
13 #
14 #                           @ #ENTER SELECTION
15 #
16 #                               A = ADD
17 #                               R = REVISE
18 #                               D = DELETE
19 #
20 #
```

Fig. 5-18. The SDF field identification screen.

After pressing the Enter key, you will now have the following:

#SSN:@   #

Here are some other methods of entering fields:

@123@45@6789#

The result of the above would be:

123 45 6789

Here's another possibility:

@123#-@45#-@6789#

This would appear to the user as:

123 - 45 - 6789

The next screen in the map-creation sequence is the field attribute definition screen (Fig. 5-19). For our specific purpose, we have developed the attribute bytes listed below. Note that the first option refers to the attribute of the field such as protected, unprotected, or skip; while the second option specifies the intensity of display. The third option defines the color of the displayed field (if your terminal has the ability to display color).

```
#   =   ASKIP, NORMAL (BLUE)
¢   =   ASKIP, BRIGHT (WHITE)
(   =   UNPROT, NORMAL (GREEN)
$   =   UNPROT, NORMAL, CURSOR (GREEN)
        (Cursor refers to the initial position of the cursor)
*   =   UNPROT, BRIGHT (RED)
+   =   UNPROT, NORMAL, MDT CURSOR (GREEN)
@   =   UNPROT NORMAL, RIGHT JUSTIFIED, PAD ZEROS
%   =   UNPROT, NORMAL, RIGHT JUSTIFIED, PAD ZEROS, CUR-
        SOR (GREEN)
]   =   UNPROT, NORMAL, RIGHT JUSTIFIED, PAD ZEROS, MDT
        (GREEN)
?   =   UNPROT, DARK, MDT (INVISIBLE)
```

As you can see, you can easily create your own attribute characters using any one of the above combinations or additional ones as required.

Next we access the naming screen (Fig. 5-20), where we can assign

```
1.4 ---------- FIELD ATTRIBUTE DEFINITION ---------- MAPSET NAPNAME 3279-2
==>
LINES   1  20   ---------- (#$*+=%&] ----------          COLS   1  75
01 #SCREEN: 2          CONSOLIDATED AMERICAN         ADVANCE TO SCREEN:( #
02 #
03 #                       DEMOGRAPHIC FILE
04 #
05 #
06 #   EMPLOYEE SSN:%  ]  ]   #
07 #
08 #
09 #          NAME:    (                                   #
10 #          ADDRESS: (                       #
11 #          CITY:    (             #
12 #          ZIP CODE:]
13 #
14 #                    ( #ENTER SELECTION
15 #
16 #                      A = ADD
17 #                      R = REVISE
18 #                      D = DELETE
19 #
20 #
```

Fig. 5-19. The SDF field attribute definition screen.

```
1.6 ------------ FULL SCREEN NAMING ------------ MAPSET NAPNAME 3279-2
==>

          NAME          IND   NAME          IND   NAME                 IND
           1             2     3
           4             5     6
           7             8     9
LINES  1 16   ------------- NO PREFIX DEFINED ------------- COLS  1 75
01 SCREEN: 2                  CONSOLIDATED AMERICAN         ADVANCE TO SCREEN: ATS
02
03                            DEMOGRAPHIC FILE
04
05
06         EMPLOYEE SSN: SS+ S+ SSN3
07
08
09              NAME:     EMP-NAME
10              ADDRESS:  EMP-ADDRESS
11              CITY:     EMP-CITY
12              ZIP CODE: EMP-ZIP-CODE
13
14                     S ENTER SELECTION
15
16                        A = ADD
```

Fig. 5-20. The SDF full-screen naming screen.

names to corresponding data elements. This screen may be omitted if you wish to rely on the application structure review screen (Fig. 5-21). This screen will be displayed in its entirety, but will not include the field names unless you defined them on the previous screen. In other words, the application structure review screen will display all other information (row, column, length, etc.), allowing you to enter your own naming conventions. Once we're through with the application structure review screen, SDF will generate the following items.

Field names for the map.
Input pictures and definitions.
Output pictures and definitions.
An *unformatted map*, indicating field length.
A COBOL DSECT for the map.
A map status report.
A field analysis defining all fields.

Figure 5-22 shows a flowchart representation of SDF functions as we reviewed them.

Figures 5-23 through 5-39 were generated by SDF to provide the analyst with a comprehensive reporting mechanism on what has been entered by him and what the system prompted as the result. Figure 5-23 shows the options in effect. The first format in this series, presented in Fig. 5-24 is referred to as FIELD NAMES FOR MAP MAPSET, MAPNAME. This panel shows the variable field names selected by the analyst. If a field is initially defined as a 10 position variable field, for example, yet the field name actually utilizes 20 positions, only the first 10 positions of the field will be displayed by SDF.

Figure 5-25, INPUT PICTURES FOR MAP, MAPSET, MAPNAME, shows actual field lengths associated with each variable field. Just like in ANS COBOL, for example, the name of an employee is defined as a thirty position alphanumeric field. Note that fields are truncated when the *picture clause* of a field contains less than three positions. The difference between Fig. 5-25 and Fig. 5-26 (OUTPUT PICTURES FOR MAP MAPSET.MAPNAME) is that the latter displays the output format of the screen layout, whereas the previous is strictly an input definition.

Figure 5-27 (UNFORMATTED MAP MAPSET.MAPNAME) is an overview of where each field will appear on the MAP and the number of positions taken up by it. The at sign (@) in the first high-order position is merely an indicator showing the beginning of each field. Thus, a one byte long field would be presented as @, whereas a three byte long field would show as @...

Figure 5-28 (COBOL DSECT FOR MAP MAPSET.MAPNAME) is an overview of a record format defined by SDF with an additional suffix on

```
1.7  --------  APPLICATION STRUCTURE REVIEW  --------  MAPSET         MAPNAME     3279-2
==>
    LVL              ADS OCC  --- MAP ---
    NO. NAME         LEN URS  LEN ROW COL  STATUS   PICIN   PICOUT  COMMENT
   ---------------------------------------------------------------------------------
  1 01 MAPNAME
  2 02 ATS            2        2    1  78           X(02)   X(02)
  3 02 SSN1           3        3    6  19           X(03)   X(03)
  4 02 SSN2           2        2    6  23           X(02)   X(02)
  5 02 SSN3           4        4    6  26           X(04)   X(04)
  6 02 EMP-NAME      30       30    9  28           X(30)   X(30)
  7 02 EMP-ADDRESS   25       25   10  28           X(25)   X(25)
  8 02 EMP-CITY      20       20   11  28           X(20)   X(20)
  9 02 EMP-ZIP-CODE   9        9   12  28           X(09)   X(09)
 10 02 SELECTION      1        1   14  29           X(01)   X(01)
 11 02 ERR-LINE      30       30   24   2           X(30)   X(30)
```

Fig. 5-21. The SDF application structure review screen.

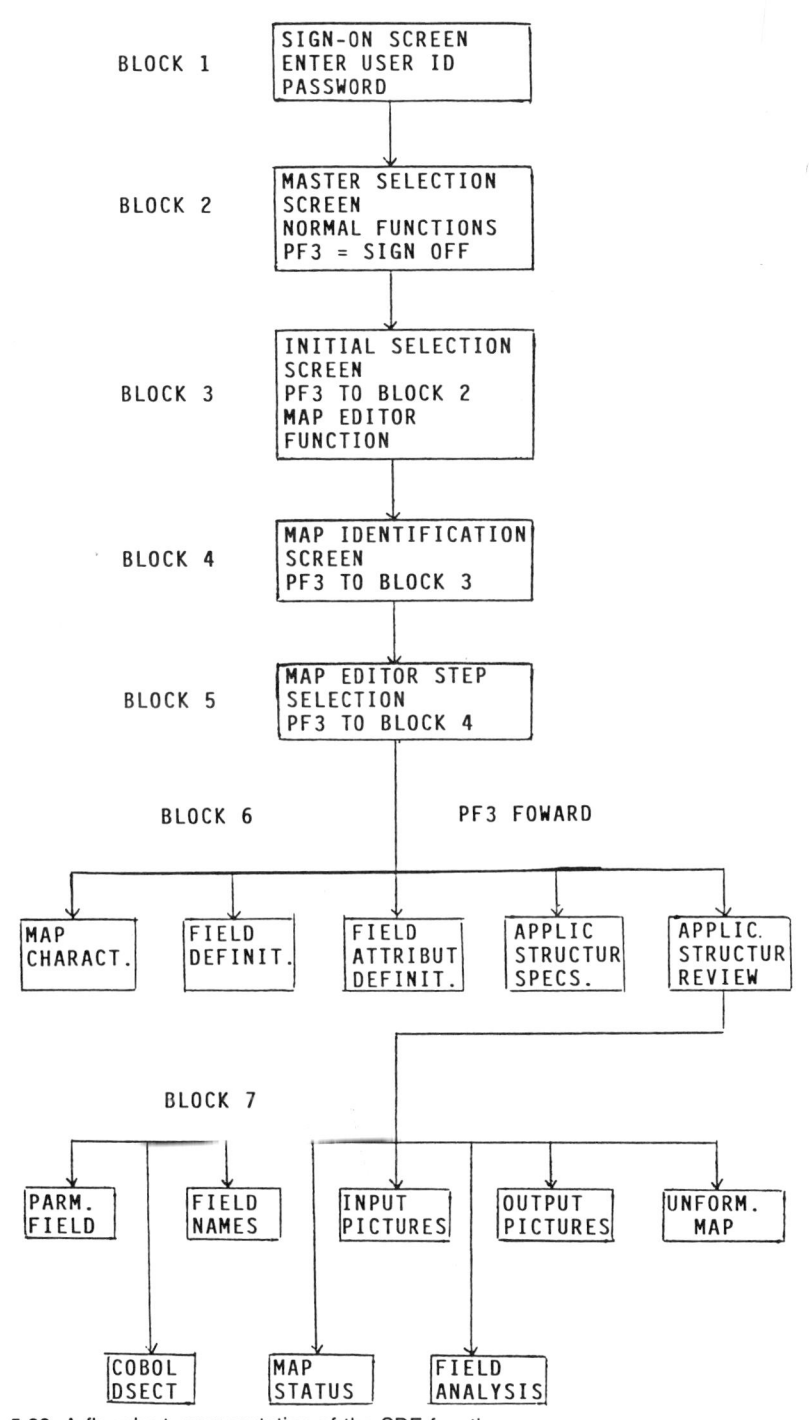

```
BLOCK 1      SIGN-ON SCREEN
             ENTER USER ID
             PASSWORD
                  │
                  ▼
BLOCK 2      MASTER SELECTION
             SCREEN
             NORMAL FUNCTIONS
             PF3 = SIGN OFF
                  │
                  ▼
BLOCK 3      INITIAL SELECTION
             SCREEN
             PF3 TO BLOCK 2
             MAP EDITOR
             FUNCTION
                  │
                  ▼
BLOCK 4      MAP IDENTIFICATION
             SCREEN
             PF3 TO BLOCK 3
                  │
                  ▼
BLOCK 5      MAP EDITOR STEP
             SELECTION
             PF3 TO BLOCK 4

BLOCK 6                          PF3 FOWARD

┌────────┬─────────┬─────────┬─────────┬─────────┐
MAP       FIELD     FIELD     APPLIC    APPLIC.
CHARACT.  DEFINIT.  ATTRIBUT  STRUCTUR  STRUCTUR
                    DEFINIT.  SPECS.    REVIEW

BLOCK 7

┌──────┬──────┬──────┬──────┬──────┬──────┐
PARM.   FIELD   INPUT    OUTPUT    UNFORM.
FIELD   NAMES   PICTURES PICTURES  MAP
  │       │       │        │
  ▼       ▼       ▼        ▼
COBOL           MAP      FIELD
DSECT           STATUS   ANALYSIS
```

Fig. 5-22. A flowchart representation of the SDF functions.

73

```
SDF/CICS OS/VS R4.0   DVD6BTCH - BATCH UTILITY CONTROLLER
============================================================

PARAMETER FIELD -

         *PARM USER=USERNAME/....

OPTIONS IN EFFECT -

         MESSAGES    = ENGLISH
         DEPTH       = NO
         WIDTH       = NO
         LIST        = NO
         ALIGNMENT   = NO
         TERM        = NO
         SYSTUSER    = NO
         OPERSYST    = OS

         REV O=MAPSET.MAPNAME,F=(S,F,I,O,U,A,V,D),D=3279-2
         LOGKEY='861212135919RMAPSET    MAPNAME'
```

Fig. 5-23. The SDF options screen.

each field name. (See our previous discussion on attribute bytes for reference.) Thus the field name ATS receives an L suffix so that the programmer analyst can refer to the length of such a map-defined field in his application program while cross referencing it with SDF.

Figure 5-29 represents a redefinition of Fig. 5-28 in which one of two additional suffixes are attached to the field definition (either an O for OUTPUT or an A for Attribute) available for the various display modes.

The map status report (Fig. 5-30) is an overview of certain statistics with regard to a particular panel.

Figures 5-31 through 5-38 represent what IBM refers to as a *field analysis report*. Here every field is thoroughly defined, each definition showing a field name, a field length, an initial value, attribute characteristics, a group name, a field position, and a structure name. For example, the field ATS, which is a two position field, is displayed in normal intensity and as an unprotected field.

A summary sheet is presented in Fig. 5-39; it shows both input and output fields, with a complete run down. As you can see, SDF is a completely self-documenting tool. It allows you to develop a panel completely on-line, and then generates the follow up procedures in batch mode.

```
SDF/CICS OS/VS R4.0    DVD6BTCH - BATCH UTILITY CONTROLLER
==========================================================================
FIELD NAMES FOR MAP MAPSET.MAPNAME
====================================
         1         2         3         4         5         6         7         8
12345678901234567890123456789012345678901234567890123456789012345678901234567890
+------------------------------------------------------------------------------+
| SCREEN: 2            CONSOLIDATED AMERICAN          ADVANCE TO SCREEN: AT    | 01
|                                                                              | 02
|                            DEMOGRAPHIC FILE                                  | 03
|                                                                              | 04
|                                                                              | 05
| EMPLOYEE SSN:SSNSSSSN3                                                       | 06
|                                                                              | 07
|                                                                              | 08
|               NAME:     EMP-NAME                                             | 09
|               ADDRESS:  EMP-ADDRESS                                          | 10
|               CITY:     EMP-CITY                                             | 11
|               ZIP CODE:EMP-ZIP-CD                                            | 12
|                                                                              | 13
|                       S ENTER SELECTION                                      | 14
|                                                                              | 15
|                         A = ADD                                              | 16
|                         R = REVISE                                           | 17
|                         D = DELETE                                           | 18
|                                                                              | 19
|                                                                              | 20
|                                                                              | 21
|                             PF3: MAIN MENU; PF6: UPDATE; PF10: SIGN OFF      | 22
|                                                                              | 23
| ERR-LINE                                                                     | 24
+------------------------------------------------------------------------------+
12345678901234567890123456789012345678901234567890123456789012345678901234567890
         1         2         3         4         5         6         7         8
```

Fig. 5-24. The SDF field names screen.

75

```
SDF/CICS OS/VS R4.0   DVD6BTCH - BATCH UTILITY CONTROLLER
================================================================
INPUT PICTURES FOR MAP MAPSET.MAPNAME
====================================
             1         2         3         4         5         6         7         8
    1234567890123456789012345678901234567890123456789012345678901234567890123456789012345678901234567890
01  --------------------------------------------------------------------------------
02  SCREEN: 2           CONSOLIDATED AMERICAN        ADVANCE TO SCREEN: X(
03
04                            DEMOGRAPHIC FILE
05
06  EMPLOYEE SSN:X(3 X( X(4)
07
08                    NAME:    X(30)
09                    ADDRESS: X(25)
10                    CITY:    X(20)
11                    ZIP CODE:X(9)
12
13                         X ENTER SELECTION
14
15                           A = ADD
16                           R = REVISE
17                           D = DELETE
18
19
20
21
22
23                                   PF3: MAIN MENU; PF6: UPDATE; PF10: SIGN OFF
24  X(30)
    --------------------------------------------------------------------------------
    1234567890123456789012345678901234567890123456789012345678901234567890123456789012345678901234567890
             1         2         3         4         5         6         7         8
```

Fig. 5-25. The SDF input pictures screen.

76

```
SDF/CICS OS/VS R4.0  DVD6BTCH - BATCH UTILITY CONTROLLER
========================================================

OUTPUT PICTURES FOR MAP MAPSET.MAPNAME
======================================
           1         2         3         4         5         6         7         8
  12345678901234567890123456789012345678901234567890123456789012345678901234567890
01 +------------------------------------------------------------------------------+ 01
02 | SCREEN: 2              CONSOLIDATED AMERICAN          ADVANCE TO SCREEN: X(  | 02
03 |                                                                              | 03
04 |                            DEMOGRAPHIC FILE                                  | 04
05 |                                                                              | 05
06 |    EMPLOYEE SSN:X(3 X( X(4)                                                  | 06
07 |                                                                              | 07
08 |                    NAME:    X(30)                                            | 08
09 |                    ADDRESS: X(25)                                            | 09
10 |                    CITY:    X(20)                                            | 10
11 |                    ZIP CODE:X(9)                                             | 11
12 |                                                                              | 12
13 |                                X ENTER SELECTION                             | 13
14 |                                                                              | 14
15 |                                   A = ADD                                    | 15
16 |                                   R = REVISE                                 | 16
17 |                                   D = DELETE                                 | 17
18 |                                                                              | 18
19 |                                                                              | 19
20 |                                                                              | 20
21 |                                                                              | 21
22 |                                                                              | 22
23 |                  PF3: MAIN MENU; PF6: UPDATE; PF10: SIGN OFF                 | 23
24 | X(30)                                                                        | 24
   +------------------------------------------------------------------------------+
   12345678901234567890123456789012345678901234567890123456789012345678901234567890
           1         2         3         4         5         6         7         8
```

Fig. 5-26. The SDF output pictures screen.

```
SDF/CICS OS/VS R4.0  DVD6BTCH - BATCH UTILITY CONTROLLER
========================================================

UNFORMATTED MAP MAPSET.MAPNAME
==============================
             1         2         3         4         5         6         7         8
    12345678901234567890123456789012345678901234567890123456789012345678901234567890
   +--------------------------------------------------------------------------------+
01 | SCREEN: 2              CONSOLIDATED AMERICAN             ADVANCE TO SCREEN: @. | 01
02 |                                                                                | 02
03 |                              DEMOGRAPHIC FILE                                  | 03
04 |                                                                                | 04
05 |                                                                                | 05
06 |      EMPLOYEE SSN:@.. @. @...                                                  | 06
07 |                                                                                | 07
08 |             NAME:    @........................                                 | 08
09 |             ADDRESS: @........................                                 | 09
10 |             CITY:    @.........                                                | 10
11 |             ZIP CODE:@........                                                 | 11
12 |                                                                                | 12
13 |                         @ ENTER SELECTION                                      | 13
14 |                                                                                | 14
15 |                             A = ADD                                            | 15
16 |                             R = REVISE                                         | 16
17 |                             D = DELETE                                         | 17
18 |                                                                                | 18
19 |                                                                                | 19
20 |                                                                                | 20
21 |                                                                                | 21
22 |                                                                                | 22
23 |                           PF3: MAIN MENU; PF6: UPDATE; PF10: SIGN OFF          | 23
24 | @............................................................................ | 24
   +--------------------------------------------------------------------------------+
    12345678901234567890123456789012345678901234567890123456789012345678901234567890
             1         2         3         4         5         6         7         8
```

Fig. 5-27. The SDF unformatted map screen.

```
SDF/CICS OS/VS R4.0   DVD6BTCH - BATCH UTILITY CONTROLLER
=========================================================

COBOL DSECT FOR MAP MAPSET.MAPNAME
==================================

    1   MAPNAMEI.
        02 FILLER PIC X(12).
        02 ATSL COMP PIC S9(4).
        02 ATSF PIC X.
        02 ATSI PIC X(02).
        02 SSN1L COMP PIC S9(4).
        02 SSN1F PIC X.
        02 SSN1I PIC X(03).
        02 SSN2L COMP PIC S9(4).
        02 SSN2F PIC X.
        02 SSN2I PIC X(02).
        02 SSN3L COMP PIX S9(4).
        02 SSN3F PIC X.
        02 SSN3I PIC X(04).
        02 EMP-NAMEL COMP PIC S9(4).
        02 EMP-NAMEF PIC X.
        02 EMP-NAMEI PIC X(30).
        02 EMP-ADDRESSL COMP PIC S9(4).
        02 EMP-ADDRESSF PIC X.
        02 EMP-ADDRESSI PIC X(25).
        02 EMP-CITYL COMP PIC S9(4).
        02 EMP-CITYF PIC X.
        02 EMP-CITYI PIC X(20).
        02 EMP-ZIP-CODEL COMP PIC S9(4).
        02 EMP-ZIP-CODEF PIC X.
        02 EMP-ZIP-CODEI PIC X(09).
        02 SELECTIONL COMP PIC S9(4).
        02 SELECTIONF PIC X.
        02 SELECTIONI PIC X(01).
        02 ERR-LINEL COMP PIC S9(4).
        02 ERR-LINEF PIC X.
        02 ERR-LINEI PIC X(30).
```
Fig. 5-28. The **SDF COBOL DSECT** screen.

SUMMARY

Maps are preformatted screen displays logically arranged by function or by task. A number of these maps are referred to as *map sets*. The *physical map* defines the maximum length and the starting position of each field to be read, as well as the field length, field characteristics, and default data.

The *symbolic map* is the *copy book* that is copied into the application program used to reference the data field in the map, and the corresponding length and attribute characters.

SDF, or Screen Development Facility, is an IBM software package that enables the programmer analyst to create maps interactively.

Attribute bytes allow the programmer to define a field with initial properties and then redefine it within an application program. The characteristics of a field are defined by the preceding attribute byte, which appears on the screen as a protected blank.

The DFHBMSCA block provides the application programmer with a tool in reference to the attribute byte of each field in the system. For example, the DFHBMPRO (also referred to as -) lends protected status to a field. DFHBMBRY (or H) is used to intensify or highlight a particular field. It is also possible to combine attributes (unprotected, numeric, high intensity, modified data tag on, etc.) using an attribute character chart often referred to as the *Green Card*.

When you are using SDF, the system generates fields on the map with one of the following suffixes as integral part of such fields:

L: Defines the length of a given field
A: Designates the attribute byte of a field
I : Designates the input form of a field
O: Designates the output form of such a field.

```
SDF/CICS OS/VS R4.0   DVD6BTCH - BATCH UTILITY CONTROLLER
===========================================================

COBOL DSECT FOR MAP MAPSET.MAPNAME
==================================

     1    MAPNAMEO REDEFINES MAPNAMEI.
          02 FILLER PIC X(12).
          02 FILLER PIC X(2).
          02 ATSA PIC X.
          02 ATSO PIC X(02).
          02 FILLER PIC X(2).
          02 SSN1A PIC X.
          02 SSN1O PIC X(03).
          02 FILLER PIC X(2).
          02 SSN2A PIC X.
          02 SSN2O PIC X(02).
          02 FILLER PIC X(2).
          02 SSN3A PIC X.
          02 SSN3O PIC X(04).
          02 FILLER PIC X(2).
          02 EMP-NAMEA PIC X.
          02 EMP-NAMEO PIC X(30).
          02 FILLER PIC X(2).
          02 EMP-ADDRESSA PIC X.
          02 EMP-ADDRESSO PIC X(25).
          02 FILLER PIC X(2).
          02 EMP-CITYA PIC X.
          02 EMP-CITYO PIC X(20).
          02 FILLER PIC X(2).
          02 EMP-ZIP-CODEA PIC X.
          02 EMP-ZIP-CODEO PIC X(09).
          02 FILLER PIC X(2).
          02 SELECTIONA PIC X.
          02 SELECTIONO PIC X(01).
          02 FILLER PIC X(2).
          02 ERR-LINEA PIC X.
          02 ERR-LINEO PIC X(30).
```

Fig. 5-29. A redefinition of the SDF COBOL DSECT shown in Fig. 5-28.

```
SDF/CICS OS/VS R4.0   DVD6BTCH - BATCH UTILITY CONTROLLER
=================================================================

MAP STATUS REPORT
=================

OBJECT NAME                  : MAPSET.MAPNAME
OBJECT TYPE                  : MAP
CREATION DATE, TIME          : 86/01/01 14:00:00
MODIFICATION DATE, TIME      : 86/01/02 12:00:00
EDITED BY                    : PROGRAMMER-NAME
GENERATION SEQUENCE NUMBER   : 0001
DEVICE TYPE
     BASE DEVICE             : 3279-2
MAP FORMAT                   : FIELD
MAP POSITION                 : NEXT,SAME
WRITE CTL CHARACTER          : FREE KEYBOARD, NO MDT RESET, NO SOUND ALARM
OUTBOARD FORMATTING          : NO
AUTOMATIC NAMING             : NO
NAME PREFIX                  :
LVL START(INCREMENT)         : 1( 1)
I/O AREA PREFIX              : YES
MAP SIZE (DEPTH, WIDTH)      : 024,080
LINE JUSTIFICATION           :
COLUMN JUSTIFICATION         : LEFT
MAP ATTRIBUTE                :
EXTENDED ATTRIBUTES          : NO
PARTITION NAME               :
ACTIVE PARTITION             : NO
```

Fig. 5-30. The SDF map status report screen.

```
SDF/CICS OS/VS R4.0   DVD6BTCH - BATCH UTILITY CONTROLLER
==================================================================

FIELD ANALYSIS - ALL FIELDS OF MAP MAPSET.MAPNAME
==================================================================

FIELD NAME:                    GROUP NAME      :                      STRUCTURE NAME:
FLD LENGTH: 77                 FIELD POSITION:       1, 1
INIT VALUE: SCREEN: 2                          CONSOLIDATED AMERICAN  ADVANCE TO SCREEN:
ATTRIBUTE : NORMAL, AUTOSKIP

FIELD NAME: ATS                GROUP NAME      :                      STRUCTURE NAME:
FLD LENGTH: 2                  FIELD POSITION:       1, 78
PIC.IN.   : X(02)                              PIC.OUT.: X(02)
ATTRIBUTE : NORMAL, UNPROTECTED, MDT, RIGHT, ZERO

FIELD NAME:                    GROUP NAME      :                      STRUCTURE NAME:
FLD LENGTH: 0                  FIELD POSITION:       1, 80
ATTRIBUTE : NORMAL AUTOSKIP

FIELD NAME:                    GROUP NAME      :                      STRUCTURE NAME:
FLD LENGTH: 0                  FIELD POSITION:       2, 1
ATTRIBUTE : HIGH, AUTOSKIP

FIELD NAME:                    GROUP NAME      :                      STRUCTURE NAME:
FLD LENGTH: 44                 FIELD POSITION:       3, 1
INIT VALUE:                                    DEMOGRAPHIC FILE
ATTRIBUTE : HIGH, AUTOSKIP
```

Fig. 5-31. The SDF field analysis report, part 1.

```
SDF/CICS OS/VS R4.0  DVD6BTCH - BATCH UTILITY CONTROLLER
================================================================

FIELD ANALYSIS - ALL FIELDS OF MAP MAPSET.MAPNAME
================================================================

FIELD NAME:                    GROUP NAME      :                    STRUCTURE NAME:
FLD LENGTH:     0              FIELD POSITION:     4,  1
ATTRIBUTE : NORMAL, AUTOSKIP

FIELD NAME:                    GROUP NAME      :                    STRUCTURE NAME:
FLD LENGTH:     C              FIELD POSITION:     5,  1
ATTRIBUTE : NORMAL, AUTOSKIP

FIELD NAME:                    GROUP NAME      :                    STRUCTURE NAME:
FLD LENGTH:     18       EMPLOYEE SSN           FIELD POSITION:     6,  1
INIT VALUE:
ATTRIBUTE : NORMAL AUTOSKIP

FIELD NAME: SSN1               GROUP NAME      :                    STRUCTURE NAME:
FLD LENGTH:     3              FIELD POSITION:     6, 19
PIC.IN.   : X(03)                                PIC.OUT.: X(03)
ATTRIBUTE : NORMAL, UNPROTECTED, MDT, RIGHT, ZERO, CURSOR

FIELD NAME: SSN2               GROUP NAME      :                    STRUCTURE NAME:
FLD LENGTH:     2              FIELD POSITION:     6, 23
PIC.IN.   : X(02)                                PIC.OUT.: X(02)
ATTRIBUTE : NORMAL, UNPROTECTED, MDT, RIGHT, ZERO
```

Fig. 5-32. The SDF field analysis report, part 2.

83

```
SDF/CICS OS/VS R4.0  DVD6BTCH - BATCH UTILITY CONTROLLER
=========================================================================

FIELD ANALYSIS - ALL FIELDS OF MAP MAPSET.MAPNAME
=================================================

FIELD NAME: SSN3              GROUP NAME :                      STRUCTURE NAME:
FLD LENGTH: 4                 FIELD POSITION:    6, 26
PIC.IN X(04)                          PIC.OUT X(04)
ATTRIBUTE : NORMAL, UNPROTECTED, MDT, RIGHT, ZERO

FIELD NAME:                   GROUP NAME :                      STRUCTURE NAME:
FLD LENGTH:   0               FIELD POSITION:    6, 30
ATTRIBUTE : NORMAL, AUTOSKIP

FIELD NAME:                   GROUP NAME :                      STRUCTURE NAME:
FLD LENGTH:   0               FIELD POSITION:    7,  1
ATTRIBUTE : NORMAL, AUTOSKIP

FIELD NAME:                   GROUP NAME :                      STRUCTURE NAME:
FLD LENGTH:   0               FIELD POSITION:    8,  1
ATTRIBUTE : NORMAL, AUTOSKIP

FIELD NAME:                   GROUP NAME :                      STRUCTURE NAME:
FLD LENGTH: 27                FIELD POSITION:    9,  1
INIT VALUE:            NAME:
ATTRIBUTE : NORMAL, AUTOSKIP
```

Fig. 5-33. The SDF field analysis report, part 3.

```
SDF/CICS OS/VS R4.0   DVD6BTCH - BATCH UTILITY CONTROLLER
==============================================================================

FIELD ANALYSIS - ALL FIELDS OF MAP MAPSET.MAPNAME
==============================================================================

FIELD NAME: EMP-NAME              GROUP NAME :                      STRUCTURE NAME:
FLD LENGTH: 30                    FIELD POSITION:    9, 28
PIC.IN X(30)                               PIC.OUT X(30)
ATTRIBUTE : NORMAL, UNPROTECTED, MDT, LEFT, BLANK

FIELD NAME:                       GROUP NAME :                      STRUCTURE NAME:
FLD LENGTH:   0                   FIELD POSITION:    9, 58
ATTRIBUTE : NORMAL, AUTOSKIP

FIELD NAME:                       GROUP NAME :                      STRUCTURE NAME:
FLD LENGTH: 27                    FIELD POSITION:   10,  1
INIT VALUE:                       ADDRESS:
ATTRIBUTE : NORMAL, AUTOSKIP

FIELD NAME: EMP-ADDRESS           GROUP NAME :                      STRUCTURE NAME:
FLD LENGTH: 25                    FIELD POSITION:   10, 28
PIC.IN   : X(25)                           PIC.OUT.: X(25)
ATTRIBUTE : NORMAL, UNPROTECTED, MDT, LEFT, BLANK

FIELD NAME:                       GROUP NAME :                      STRUCTURE NAME:
FLD LENGTH:   0                   FIELD POSITION:   10, 53
ATTRIBUTE : NORMAL, AUTOSKIP
```

Fig. 5-34. The SDF field analysis report, part 4.

```
SDF/CICS OS/VS R4.0    DVD6BTCH - BATCH UTILITY CONTROLLER
================================================================

FIELD ANALYSIS - ALL FIELDS OF MAP MAPSET.MAPNAME
================================================================

FIELD NAME:                         GROUP NAME :                     STRUCTURE NAME:
FLD LENGTH: 27                      FIELD POSITION:    11,    1
INIT VALUE:                   CITY:
ATTRIBUTE : NORMAL, AUTOSKIP

FIELD NAME: EMP-CITY                GROUP NAME :                     STRUCTURE NAME:
FLD LENGTH: 20                      FIELD POSITION:    11,   28
PIC.IN   : X(20)                                       PIC.OUT.: X(20)
ATTRIBUTE : NORMAL, UNPROTECTED, MDT, LEFT, BLANK

FIELD NAME:                         GROUP NAME :                     STRUCTURE NAME:
FLD LENGTH:  0                      FIELD POSITION:    11,   58
ATTRIBUTE : NORMAL, AUTOSKIP

FIELD NAME:                         GROUP NAME :                     STRUCTURE NAME:
FLD LENGTH: 27                      FIELD POSITION:    12,    1
INIT VALUE:                ZIP CODE:
ATTRIBUTE : NORMAL, AUTOSKIP

FIELD NAME: EMP-ZIP-CODE            GROUP NAME :                     STRUCTURE NAME:
FLD LENGTH:  9                      FIELD POSITION:    12,   28
PIC.IN.  : X(09)                                       PIC.OUT: X(09)
ATTRIBUTE : NORMAL, UNPROTECTED, MDT, RIGHT, ZERO
```

Fig. 5-35. The SDF field analysis report, part 5.

```
SDF/CICS OS/VS R4.0   DVD6BTCH - BATCH UTILITY CONTROLLER
=================================================================

FIELD ANALYSIS - ALL FIELDS OF MAP MAPSET.MAPNAME
=================================================================

FIELD NAME:                    GROUP NAME    :                    STRUCTURE NAME:
FLD LENGTH:    0               FIELD POSITION:   12,  37
ATTRIBUTE : NORMAL, AUTOSKIP

FIELD NAME:                    GROUP NAME    :                    STRUCTURE NAME:
FLD LENGTH:    0               FIELD POSITION:   13,   1
ATTRIBUTE : NORMAL, AUTOSKIP

FIELD NAME:                    GROUP NAME    :                    STRUCTURE NAME:
FLD LENGTH:    0               FIELD POSITION:   14,   1
ATTRIBUTE : NORMAL, AUTOSKIP

FIELD NAME: SELECTION          GROUP NAME    :                    STRUCTURE NAME:
FLD LENGTH:    1               FIELD POSITION:   14,  29
PIC.IN.   : X(C1)                              PIC.OUT: X(01)
ATTRIBUTE : NORMAL, UNPROTECTED, MDT, LEFT, BLANK

FIELD NAME:                    GROUP NAME    :                    STRUCTURE NAME:
FLD LENGTH:    0               FIELD POSITION:   14,  30
INIT VALUE:ENTER SELECTION
ATTRIBUTE : NORMAL, AUTOSKIP
```

Fig. 5-36. The SDF field analysis report, part 6.

```
SDF/CICS OS/VS R4.0    DVD6BTCH - BATCH UTILITY CONTROLLER
==================================================================================
FIELD ANALYSIS - ALL FIELDS OF MAP MAPSET.MAPNAME
==================================================

FIELD NAME:                       GROUP NAME    :                    STRUCTURE NAME:
FLD LENGTH:    0                  FIELD POSITION:   15,  1
ATTRIBUTE : NORMAL, AUTOSKIP

FIELD NAME:                       GROUP NAME    :                    STRUCTURE NAME:
FLD LENGTH:   37                  FIELD POSITION:   16,  1
INIT VALUE:                                     A = ADD
ATTRIBUTE : NORMAL, AUTOSKIP

FIELD NAME:                       GROUP NAME    :                    STRUCTURE NAME:
FLD LENGTH:   39                  FIELD POSITION:   17,  1
INIT VALUE:                                     R = REVISE
ATTRIBUTE : NORMAL, AUTOSKIP

FIELD NAME:                       GROUP NAME    :                    STRUCTURE NAME:
FLD LENGTH:   39                  FIELD POSITION:   18,  1
INIT VALUE:                                     D = DELETE
ATTRIBUTE : NORMAL, AUTOSKIP

FIELD NAME:                       GROUP NAME    :                    STRUCTURE NAME:
FLD LENGTH:    0                  FIELD POSITION:   19,  1
ATTRIBUTE : NORMAL, AUTOSKIP
```

Fig. 5-37. The SDF field analysis report, part 7.

```
SDF/CICS CS/VS R4.0   DVD6BTCH - BATCH UTILITY CONTROLLER
==========================================================================

FIELD ANALYSIS - ALL FIELDS OF MAP MAPSET.MAPNAME
=================================================

FIELD NAME:                        GROUP NAME    :                    STRUCTURE NAME:
FLD LENGTH:  0                     FIELD POSITION: 20,  1
ATTRIBUTE : NORMAL, AUTOSKIP

FIELD NAME:                        GROUP NAME    :                    STRUCTURE NAME:
FLD LENGTH:  0                     FIELD POSITION: 21,  1
ATTRIBUTE : NORMAL, AUTOSKIP

FIELD NAME:                        GROUP NAME    :                    STRUCTURE NAME:
FLD LENGTH:  0                     FIELD POSITION: 22,  1
ATTRIBUTE : NORMAL, AUTOSKIP

FIELD NAME:                        GROUP NAME    :                    STRUCTURE NAME:
FLD LENGTH:  0                     FIELD POSITION: 23,  1
ATTRIBUTE : NORMAL, AUTOSKIP

FIELD NAME: ERR-LINE               GROUP NAME    :                    STRUCTURE NAME:
FLD LENGTH: 30                     FIELD POSITION: 24,  1
PIC.IN.   : X(30)                                  PIC.OUT: X(30)
ATTRIBUTE : HIGH, UNPROTECTED, LEFT, BLANK

FIELD NAME:                        GROUP NAME    :                    STRUCTURE NAME:
FLD LENGTH: 50                     FIELD POSITION: 24, 31
INIT VALUE:PF3: MAIN MENU; PF6: UPDATE; PF10: SIGN OFF
ATTRIBUTE : HIGH AUTOSKIP
```

Fig. 5-38. The SDF field analysis report, part 8.

```
SDF/CICS O / S R4.0   DVD6BTCH - BATCH UTILITY CONTROLLER
==========================================================================
FIELD ANALYSIS - NAMED FIELDS OF MAPSET.MAPNAME
==========================================================================

FIELD NAME       GROUP NAME      STRUCTURE NAME    LNGTH   INPUT PICTURE   OUTPUT PICTURE
-----------------------------------------------------------------------------------------
ATS                                                   2        X(02)           X(02)
SSN1                                                  3        X(03)           X(03)
SSN2                                                  2        X(02)           X(02)
SSN3                                                  4        X(04)           X(04)
EMP-NAME                                             30        X(30)           X(30)
EMP-ADDRESS                                          25        X(25)           X(25)
EMP-CITY                                             20        X(20)           X(20)
EMP-ZIP-CODE                                          9        X(09)           X(09)
SELECTION                                             1        X(01)           X(01)
ERR-LINE                                             30        X(30)           X(30)
```

Fig. 5-39. The SDF field analysis summary sheet.

QUESTIONS

1. What is meant by the terms *physical map* and *symbolic map*?
2. What purpose does the attribute byte serve?
3. What function does the DFHBMSCA block perform in CICS?
4. Briefly define the following terms:

   Protected fields
   Unprotected fields
   Intensified (highlighted) fields
   Blinking fields
   MDT (modified data tag)

5. Explain the following BMS statement:

```
01   PMAPSETI.
     02 FILLER PIC X(12).
     02 NAMEL PIC COMP S9(4)..
     02 NAMEF PIC X.
     02 FILLER REDEFINES NAMEF.
        03 NAMEA PIC X.
     02 NAMEI PIC X(30).
```

6

The Terminal Control Commands

HIGHLIGHTS
- **The Send Map Command**
- **The Converse Command**
- **(Conversational Programming)**
- **Miscellaneous Terminal Control Commands**
- **The Receive Map Command**

6.1 THE SEND MAP COMMAND

Sending a map is the terminal control's equivalent of performing a write statement. Essentially, it is used to write data to a terminal from an application program. Once the programmer has developed and preformatted a map and made the proper entries in the Program Processing Table (PPT), he can issue the SEND MAP command to display all that data on the screen.

A comprehensive table presented in Fig. 6-1 summarizes the options that can be used in conjunction with the SEND MAP command. It is not likely that anyone would use all the options during a given transaction; however, let us review briefly some of the most frequently used commands associated with the SEND MAP instruction.

MAP. MAP is used to specify the name of the MAP being displayed on the screen. It should not exceed seven positions.

MAPSET. MAPSET is used to specify the name of the MAPSET to which a set of maps belong. The names are arranged in some logical order by the application programmer or by the systems analyst. MAPSET is a resident of the CICS Program Library and an entry of it must be made in the Program Processing Table or PPT. If the MAPSET option is not specified, the name given in the MAP option is assumed to be that of the MAPSET.

PAGING. PAGING specifies that data will not be sent immediately to the terminal. Rather it will be placed in temporary storage to be displayed by the operator on request.

FROM. The FROM option names an area in the program that contains the data to be sent to the terminal.

LENGTH. The LENGTH option specifies the actual length of the data to be written (SENT) to the terminal.

TERMINAL. TERMINAL specifies that input data is to be read from

```
EXEC CICS SEND MAP(name)
  [MAPSET(name)]
  [PAGING  /  SET(pointer-ref)  /   TERMINAL [WAIT]]
  [FROM(data-area)]
  [LENGTH(data-area)]
  [ACCUM]
  [DATAONLY  / MAPONLY]
  [REQID(name)]
  [ALARM]
  [CURSOR [(data-value)]]
  [ERASE   /    ERASEUP]
  [FREEKB]
  [FRSET]
  [HONEOM   /   L40   /   L64   /   L80]
  [NLEOM]
  [PRINT]
  [FMHPARM]            logical units only
  [LAST]               logical units only
  [LDC(name)]          logical units only
END-EXEC.
```

Fig. 6-1. An overview of the SEND MAP command with an array of options available for the applications programmer.

the terminal that originated the transaction or that data will be sent to the terminal following paging.

WAIT. When the WAIT option is specified, CICS will not return control to the application program until the WRITE operation has been completed. When this option is not used, control is returned as soon as the SEND command has been accepted. The WAIT option should not be used, unless the application requires it.

ACCUM. The ACCUM option specifies that it is one of a number of commands that are used to build a logical message, which is completed by a SEND PAGE command.

DATAONLY. DATAONLY specifies that only the application program data is to be sent to the terminal, rather than the entire MAP, whenever a transmission is triggered.

MAPONLY. MAPONLY specifies that only default data from the MAP is to be written. This being the case, the FROM option must not be specified.

REQID. REQID specifies a two character prefix in reference to a temporary storage (more of this in later chapters).

ALARM. ALARM specifies the activation of the IBM 3270 alarm feature.

CURSOR. CURSOR is used to specify the position of the cursor on the screen following the completion of each SEND MAP command.

ERASE. ERASE specifies that the screen is to be erased and the cursor returned to the upper left-hand corner of the screen before the output is displayed.

ERASEUP. ERASEUP specifies that all unprotected fields will be erased before the subsequent output displays.

FREEKB. FREEKB specifies that the keyboard should be unlocked after the data is written.

CTLCHAR. The CTLCHAR option is used to specify that the control character associated with the message is to be written to the IBM 3270 terminal. The DATA VALUE specified in this option must be a one byte field (hexadecimal) containing the desired attribute configuration. Each bit in this field (also known as the WRITE CONTROL CHARACTER or WCC) represents an attribute characteristic such as START POINTER and RESTORE THE KEYBOARD (Fig. 6-2).

HONEOM. HONEOM specifies that the IBM 3270 is to honor all new characters and the first end of message character that appears in the displayable fields in the data stream.

L40. L40 specifies the line length for the 3270 printer: a carriage return and line feed are forced after 40 characters have been printed on the line.

L64. L64 specifies the line length for the 3270 printer: a carriage return and a line feed are forced after 64 characters have been printed on the line.

L80. L80 specifies the line length for the 3270 printer: a carriage return and a line feed are forced after 80 characters have been printed on the line.

When transmitting via the SEND MAP command, the application programmer can transmit three types of data:

- Constants (such as headings, footings, etc.)
- Variable data (such as user data)
- Device control data (such as instructions to clear the screen or sound the alarm before displaying the data).

Let's look at a relatively simple example. Suppose you want to SEND

```
BITS  2-3        0  0  -  HONEOM
                 0  1  -  L40
                 1  0  -  L64
                 1  1  -  L80

        4        1  =     START PRINTER AT END OF WRITE
        5        1  =     SOUND ALARM
        6        1  =     RESTORE KEYBOARD
        7        1  =     RESET MODIFIED DATA TAG.
```

Fig. 6-2. The Write Control Character, or WCC, in structural detail.

a MAP to the terminal operator with the following specifications:

The name of the MAP is: PMM090A
The name of the MAPSET is: PMS090A

You want to erase all unprotected fields before sending your map, be able to position your cursor following the SEND command, and transmit only data and not the entire map. You would give the command

```
EXEC CICS SEND MAP('PMM090A') MAPSET('PMS090A')
ERASEUP CURSOR DATAONLY END-EXEC.
```

Here is an example of how the ERASEUP command works. Figure 6-3 shows the way the screen looks prior to the ERASEUP command, and Fig. 6-4 shows what the screen would look like following the SEND MAP ERASEUP command.

```
        .......PROTECTED......    ......UNPROTECTED
        NAME, LAST & FIRST        JOHN HENDERSON
        ADDRESS                   241 PARK AVE
        CITY & STATE              ELMHURST, IL.,
        ZIP CODE                  60126
        TELEPHONE                 (312) 833-1234
```
Fig. 6-3. A screen display before the use of the ERASEUP command.

```
        .......PROTECTED......    ......UNPROTECTED
        NAME, LAST & FIRST
        ADDRESS
        CITY & STATE
        ZIP CODE
        TELEPHONE
```
Fig. 6-4. The same screen display after the use of the ERASEUP command.

6.2 THE CONVERSE COMMAND

The CONVERSE command allows you to perform conversational programming. It allows the programmer to communicate back and forth with the terminal. The overall effect of this is like issuing a SEND MAP COMMAND, following it up with a WAIT TERMINAL instruction, and then completing the cycle with a RECEIVE command. All that is done without ever issuing the RETURN TRANSID statement. Figure 6-5 is an overview of the CONVERSE command:

DEST. The DEST option is only essential for certain devices. It specifies the destination of a message.

MAXLENGTH. MAXLENGTH specifies the maximum amount of

```
EXEC CICS CONVERSE
    FROM(data-value)
    FROMLENGTH(data-value)
    [INTO(data-area)   /   SET(pointer-ref)]
    TOLENGTH(data-area)
    [DEST(name)]
END-EXEC.
                          Condition code: LENGERR
```
Fig. 6-5. The structure of the CONVERSE command.

data that CICS is to recover in response to a RECEIVE or CONVERSE command.

NOTRUNCATE. NOTRUNCATE specifies that when the data available exceeds the length requested in the RECEIVE or CONVERSE command, the remaining data is not to be discarded, but retained for retrieval by subsequent RECEIVE commands.

Consider the lines shown in Fig. 6-6. They do the following. (1) send a message to the terminal operator asking him whether he'd like to update a particular file, (2) receive the answer YES or NO in the same cycle, and (3) trigger the next transaction as the result, without issuing a single return option.

The data area in the FROM option provides the name of the area where the message to be written resides. In conjunction with the TOLENGTH option, it specifies the name of the area where CICS will place the actual length of the data received from the terminal.

The data value in the FROMLENGTH option can be either a literal or the name of the field containing the message length.

```
WORKING-STORAGE SECTION.
01  TERMINAL-OP-MSG      PIC X(50) value is
                         'WOULD YOU LIKE TO UPDATE FILEX? YES OR NO?'.
01  TERMINAL-OP-reply    PIC x(3).
01  REPLY-LENGTH         PIC S9(4) COMP.
                         *
                         *
                         *
PROCEDURE DIVISION.
                         *
                         *
    EXEC CICS CONVERSE
    FROM (TERMINAL-OP-MSG)
    FROMLENGTH(32)
    INTO(TERMINAL-OP-REPLY)
    TOLENGTH(REPLY-LENGTH)
    ERASE
    END-EXEC.
```
Fig. 6-6. The DATA and the PROCEDURE DIVISIONS of conversational coding.

97

The INTO option refers to move mode (as opposed to locate mode), meaning that when the INTO option is specified, CICS will translate it into a move statement.

The SET option refers to the locate mode. Keep in mind that the SET and the INTO options are mutually exclusive.

The ERASE option clears the screen prior to writing.

6.3 MISCELLANEOUS TERMINAL CONTROL COMMANDS

The commands presented in this section are those that an application programmer may or may not utilize. In order to give you a rather comprehensive summary of most CICS command functions, however, I felt that the following commands should be discussed in a cursory manner.

- The SEND PAGE command is used to complete and transmit a logical message built by one or more SEND MAP command(s) using the PAGING option or the SEND TEXT command.
- The PURGE COMMAND is used to discontinue the building of such logical messages. The portion of the message already built in the main storage or in temp storage will be deleted.
- The ROUTE command is used to initiate the building of a logical message to be transmitted to one or more terminal(s). This should be followed by a SEND TEXT or a SEND MAP command. The last message sent in the sequence must be a SEND PAGE.
- The ISSUE command, such as ISSUE, RESET, and ISSUE DISCONNECT relate to specific types of terminals or lines. Generally, an application programmer will not need to use these commands unless specifically requested by a systems programmer.
- To use the following command, an on-line printer must be available.

EXEC CICS ISSUE PRINT

- The printer must not be used by another task, and it must be eligible. What we mean is that it must have been specified by the systems programmer in the Terminal Control Table (TCT).
- The programmer uses the SEND TEXT command to format an output without actually having to map it. It is possible to build messages (utilizing the ACCUM option) by issuing several TEXT commands, which then must be completed via a SEND PAGE command.

6.4 THE RECEIVE MAP COMMAND

The RECEIVE MAP command shown in Fig. 6-7 reads the data from the terminal into an application program. This command will enable the programmer to review and utilize data entered by the terminal operator.

```
EXEC CICS RECEIVE MAP(name)
     [MAPSET(name)]
     [INTO(data-area)]
     [FROM(data-area) LENGTH(data-area)]
     [SET(pointer-ref)]
     [TERMINAL]
     [ASIS]
END-EXEC.


        Condition   LENGERR
```
Fig. 6-7. The RECEIVE MAP command structure.

The INTO option refers to move mode, meaning that access is obtained by moving the data into a given area. Use this option the same way you'd read a file into a predefined area in your batch program, as shown in Fig. 6-8.

```
READ FILEA AT END GO TO.............
MOVE FILEA-RECORD TO WORKING-STORAGE-FILEA.

(where WORKING-STORAGE-FILEA is defined as...)

01   WORKING-STORAGE-FILEA       PIC X(200).

(and FILEA-RECORD as.....)
01   FILEA-RECORD                PIC X(200).
```

Fig. 6-8. The more frequently used move mode, a concept also used in batch programming.

The SET option, on the other hand, refers to locate mode. This means that addressability is established only after an area outside the program is located and its address placed in the pointer reference.

Using what we have learned thus far about SENDING and RECEIVING maps, let us briefly review an additional technique we might want to utilize in order to convey messages back and forth through self-invoked programs.

It is possible to define a field or fields on the map to be used for communications in place of the COMMAREA option. Let us assume that at the time the MAP001I was generated (as part of the mapset MST001I), we created a one-position numeric field named CHECK and initialized it in non-display mode. After the fifth time we receive the map, we would like to branch to the program that'll generate an error message. (Assuming that, if the operator is still encountering error conditions, we might want to alert him of the fact, so that he would try to handle the problem differently.) Figure 6-9 shows the lines used.

Statement 1 checks the length of the communications area to determine, whether or not anything was passed to the current program from the prior one or from the self-invoked cycle. If nothing was entered, an error routine is triggered, as shown in statement 2.

99

```
 1  *      IF EIBCALEN GREATER THEN ZERO, MOVE COMM-DATA
    *      TO WORK-COMM-AREA...
 2  *      ELSE GO TO ERROR-ROUTINE.
 3  *SEND-OR-RECEIVE.
 4  *      IF COM-FIELD = 'RECV' GO TO RECEIVE-MAP.
 5  *      MOVE 'RECV' TO COM-FIELD.
 6  *      EXEC CICS SEND MAP('MAP001I') MAPSET('MST001I')
 7  *      CURSOR END-EXEC.
 8  *      EXEC CICS TRANSID('C009')
 9  *      COMMAREA(WORK-COM-AREA)
10  *      LENGTH(COMLEN1) END-EXEC.
11  *RECEIVE-MAP.
12  *      EXEC CICS RECEIVE MAP('MAP001I') MAPSET
13  *      ('MST001I') END-EXEC.
14  *      ADD 1 TO CHECKL.
15  *      IF CHECKL = 6 MOVE ZEROS TO CHECKL
16  *      EXEC CICS XCTL PROGRAM('MAINPGM')
17  *      END-EXEC.
18  *      MOVE SPACES TO COM-FIELD.
19  *      ...........perform edit routine here..........
20  *      GO TO SEND-OR-RECEIVE.
------------------------------------------------------------

    * LINKAGE SECTION           *    * 01 WORK-COMM-AREA.
    *   01   DFHCOMMAREA.       *    *    02 COM-FIELD
    *        02 COM-DATA        *    *       PIC S((4) COMP
    *        PIC X(4).          *    *       VALUE +4.

    * 01 MAP001I COPY MST001I
    * 01 MAP001I.
    *    02 CHECKL           PIC S9(4) COMPUTATIONAL.
    *    02 CHECKF           PIC X.
    *    02 FILLER REDEFINES CHECKF
    *       03 CHECKA        PIC X.
    *    02 CHECKI           PIC X.
```

Fig. 6-9. The use of a nondisplay map field to pass on data.

If COM-FIELD contains the code RECV, we are going to branch to the RECEIVE-MAP paragraph (statement 4). Otherwise, we are to set up a RECEIVE ROUTINE for the next transaction cycle (statement 5).

Statements 6 and 7 will SEND a MAP to the terminal operator, while positioning the cursor as specified in the application program.

Statements 8, 9, and 10 will invoke the next transaction cycle and continue to edit.

During the RECEIVE MAP cycle, starting with statement 11, the map is received from the terminal operator to be read and analyzed by the program (statements 12 and 13).

Statement 14 defines a map field that was generated at the time both MAP and MAPSET were created. CHECKL appears on the screen in nondisplay mode. It is essentially a numeric field; it uses the numeric attribute version on the map. Here we're going to use it as an internal counter, adding 1 to it following each RECEIVE command.

Statement 15 checks the counter CHECKL for the sixth transaction sequence. That is, the programmer now wants to determine whether the task has been already invoked at least five times prior to the current cycle. If the answer is YES, then he'll clear the counter by moving zeros into the field and branch to the program MAINPGM (a warning screen) (statements 16 and 17).

Once editing is done, he'll issue a branch to the SEND-OR-RECEIVE paragraph (statement 20) where the code is already set up for sending a map and reinvoking the current transaction.

Afterward, if CHECKL is still within the constraint of Less-Than-Six-Cycles, he'll perform whatever edit functions are in order (statement 19).

Finally, he'll issue a SEND MAP command through a routine coded in the SEND-OR-RECEIVE paragraph (statement 20).

SUMMARY

SENDING a map is terminal control's equivalent of performing a WRITE statement. It is used to WRITE data to a terminal from an application program.

The CONVERSE command is used by CICS when *conversational*, as opposed to pseudo-conversational, programming is required. The effect of this is the same as the effect of issuing a SEND MAP command, following it up with a WAIT TERMINAL instruction, and then completing the cycle with a RECEIVE COMMAND.

Pseudo-conversational programming sequences require RECEIVE MAP and SEND MAP instructions back-to-back, followed by the RETURN option.

The SEND PAGE COMMAND is used to complete and transmit a logical message built by one or a number of SEND MAP commands, using the paging message or the send text option.

The PURGE command is used to discontinue such logical messages.

The ROUTE command is available to initiate the building of a logical message to be transmitted to one or a number of terminals.

The ISSUE command, such as ISSUE, RESET, and ISSUE DISCONNECT relate to specific types of terminals or lines.

The RECEIVE MAP command reads the data from the terminal into the application program. This command will enable the programmer to review and utilize data entered by the terminal operator.

QUESTIONS

1. What function(s) does the SEND MAP command perform?
2. What is meant by pseudo-conversational programming? Describe a

pseudo-conversational cycle.
3. What is the function of the SEND TEXT command?
4. A RECEIVE MAP command is equivalent to a READ or WRITE command. What's being read or written?

Briefly explain the following commands:

SEND PAGE
PURGE
ROUTE
ISSUE.

7

File Control Commands

HIGHLIGHTS

- Overview
- The READ Command
- The WRITE Command
- The REWRITE Command
- The DELETE Command
- The File BROWSE Commands

7.1 OVERVIEW

A number of file control commands are available under CICS. These include the READ, WRITE, DELETE, and BROWSE commands. Conceptually speaking, the READ statement under CICS command greatly resembles its batch counterpart. A file is read into a predefined area in the WORKING-STORAGE section for subsequent processing. Under CICS command, however, the file to be read must be at first defined in the File Control Table (FCT).

When you are updating a file, it is necessary to perform both READ and WRITE functions within the same transaction cycle. You cannot read a file and update it after reinvoking the application program or transaction for the second time. This sounds fairly obvious in batch processing; however, in an on-line environment, where the same program may be reinvoked or reprocessed even a dozen times in a matter of minutes, this isn't entirely self-evident. Think of it this way. Each time an on-line transaction is reinvoked using the RETURN and the TRANSID options, it can be equated to rerunning the same batch program. You may not READ a batch file, make subsequent modifications in it, and fail to record (WRITE) the results of it until after the job is terminated.

When a new record is added to a file, it will be necessary to issue a WRITE statement. If, however, a record is already in existence a REWRITE command is in order.

A record may be disabled and taken off the file permanently through the DELETE command. Under VSAM and KSDS (Virtual Storage Access Method using KEY SEQUENCED RECORDS), DELETE will physically remove the record from a direct access file, as specified. Under the ISAM technique (INDEXED SEQUENTIAL ACCESS METHOD), a record is not to be removed physically right away, but only flagged for deletion and then

103

dropped at the time the overflow and the prime areas are reorganized.
You can release a record that you have READ for update if you decided not to update after all.

7.2 THE READ COMMAND

The READ command reads the file from a dataset contained on a direct access device. Datasets under CICS are normally structured through the use of one of the following access methods.

VSAM or Virtual Storage Access Method
ISAM or Indexed Sequential Access Method
DAM or Direct Access Method

Actually VSAM may be divided into the following categories:

KSDS or Key Sequenced Disk Storage
ESDS or Entry Sequenced Disk Storage
RRDS or Relative Record Disk Storage

All three access methods support the processing of fixed- and variable-length blocked and unblocked records.

Figure 7-1 shows the READ command and its standard format.

Once a record is read, and the respective record retrieved or created,

```
EXEC CICS READ
     DATASET(name)
     [INTO(data-area) / SET (pointer-ref)]
     [LENGTH(data-area)]
     RIDFLD(data-area)
     [KEYLENGTH(data-value) [GENERIC]]     VSAM only
     [SYSID(name)]
     [SEGSET(name) / SEGSETALL]
     [RBA / RRN / DEBKEY / DEBREC]
     [GTEQ / EQUAL]          VSAM only
     [UPDATE]


     Conditions: DSIDERR, DUPKEY, ILLOGIC, INVREQ
                 IOERR, ISCINVREQ, LENGERR, NOTFND,
                 NOTOPEN, SEGIDERR, SYSIDERR.



     RBA and RRN for VSAM only.
     DEBKEY and DEBREC for blocked DAM only.
```

Fig. 7-1. Overview of the READ command showing possible condition codes. Condition codes are indicative of specific errors.

104

CICS will place a copy of that record INTO a data area specified by the application program.

The DATASET name option will essentially cross reference the file name as used by the program and the way it's defined in the File Control Table (FCT). If there is any discrepancy or if no such entry can be located in the FCT, CICS will generate an exception condition to be logged under DSIDERR.

Whenever the length option is specified, CICS command will place the actual length of the record to be retrieved into the data area. The length field must be a half-word binary field (PIC S9(4) COMP). The DATASET is an alphanumeric field up to eight characters.

The RIDFLD option (Record Identification Field) is used to specify the structural make-up of the key. (For VSAM, if RBA is coded, the key must be the relative byte address. If RRN is specified, it's simply referring to the relative record number.)

The KEYLENGTH option is used whenever a key is specified in the RIDFLD option. When the LENGTH value doesn't agree with the length specified in the File Control Table, an INVREQ (invalid request) exception condition occurs.

The search argument can be a partial, or generic, key. When the generic option is used, the KEYLENGTH option is mandatory, and it must specify the length of the partial key. Note that the generic option is only valid for VSAM Datasets. The generic key is found at the beginning of the full key.

Figure 7-2 illustrates the idea of generic key. In the first instance, we're trying to locate a name (ALEXANDER), utilizing only four positions of the name. In the second example we have increased the inquiry base to six (ALEXAN).

When the UPDATE option is used, it specifies that an UPDATE (or DELETE) operation is about to follow. When the UPDATE option is not specified, a READ only operation is assumed.

The GTEQ and EQUAL options are invoked to locate one or a number of specific records. When the GTEQ option is specified, for example, the

```
        FULL KEY                FULL KEY

        . . . . . . . .         . . . . . . . . .

        ALEXANDER               ALEXANDER

        PARTIAL KEY             PARTIAL KEY

        . . . .                 . . . . . .

        ALEX                    ALEXAN
```

Fig. 7-2. An illustration of the concept of a generic key. In the first instance, the operator is trying to locate the name Alexander using the four letters ALEX. In the second instance, the six letters ALEXAN are used.

READ is to return the first record whose key is equal to or greater than the key provided. This option is normally used with the full or the generic key.

Figure 7-3 shows a comprehensive list of file control exceptions that may occur in conjunction with a READ statement. Note that unless exception conditions are specified during the execution of the READ command, the default action for all conditions is abnormal termination (ABEND) of the task.

Let us briefly review the READ function. Assume that on the menu screen we use the field UPDTSELECT (or UPDTSELECTI, referring to the input form of the map field) to define a user-selection criterion. UPDTSELECTI can be an R for revision, an A for adding a new record to the file, or a D for deleting an existing record. Figure 7-4 shows our HANDLE CONDITION.

Suppose we are reading a file with the intent to add a new record to

DSIDERR	DATASET ID DOESN'T MATCH THE ENTRY IN THE FILE CONTROL TABLE.
DUPKEY	TWO RECORDS EXIST WITH THE SAME KEY WHEN RETRIEVAL THROUGH AN ALTERNATE INDEX ALLOWS FOR DUPLICATES.
DUPREC	AN ATTEMPT WAS MADE TO ADD A RECORD WITH AN IDENTICAL KEY.
ENDFILE	END-OF-FILE HAS BEEN REACHED ON A BROWSE OR READPREV COMMAND.
ILLOGIC	AN ERROR THAT DOESN'T FALL INTO ANY OTHER RESPONSE CATEGORIES OCCURRED (VSAM ONLY.)
INVREQ	REQUEST IS NOT COMPATIBLE WITH THE INFORMATION IN THE FILE CONTROL TABLE.
IOERR	AN INPUT/OUTPUT ERROR THAT COULD NOT BE HANDLED OTHERWISE OCCURRED.
LENGERR	INCORRECT LENGTH SPECIFIED FOR FIXED-LENGTH RECORDS, OR THE LENGTH OF AN INPUT RECORD SPECIFIED IS LESS THAN THE RECORD SIZE IN THE FILE CONTROL TABLE.
NOSPACE	THERE IS NO SPACE LEFT ON THE FILE FOR WRITING OR REWRITING OPERATIONS.
NOTFND	THERE IS NO RECORD ON THE FILE WITH THE KEY SPECIFIED IN THE RIDFLD. ON A RETRIEVE COMMAND IT MEANS THAT THE REQUESTED DATA COULD NOT BE FOUND IN TEMPORARY STORAGE.
NOTOPEN	THE FILE YOU TRIED TO ACCESS WAS CLOSED AT THE TIME.
ISCINVREQ	OCCURS WHEN THE REMOTE SYSTEM INDICATES A FAILURE THAT DOES NOT CORRESPOND TO A KNOWN CONDITION.
SEGIDERR	OCCURS WHEN THE NAME SPECIFIED IN THE SEGSET OPTION IS NOT DEFINED IN THE FCT.
SYSIDERR	OCCURS WHEN THE SYSID OPTION SPECIFIES EITHER A NAME THAT IS NOT DEFINED IN THE INTESYSTEMS TABLE OR A SYSTEM TO WHICH THE LINK IS CLOSED.

Fig. 7-3. Condition codes for processing errors.

```
HANDLE-CONDITION-ROUTINE.
    EXEC CICS HANDLE CONDITION
    NOTFND(CHECK-RECORD)
    IOERR(SIGN-OFF)
    MAPFAIL(RETURN-TRANSID)
    END-EXEC.
```

Fig. 7-4. The initial HANDLE CONDITION for the problem.

it, but as the READ command is issued, our procedure will have to be fool proof. What if the record we're trying to add to the file already exists? Likewise, what if the record we're about to revise has never been added to the file? Or perhaps it has been deleted a long time ago?

We start our procedure (Fig. 7-5) by reading the dataset PMSTABC lines 1 through 4. Essentially, we read it into an area presented in Fig. 7-6.

The key to the file (RECORD-KEY) is 17 positions long and has been predefined. The length of the record (WSTORAGE-AREA) is shown in Fig. 7-6.

If the record is not in existence, line 5 (Fig. 7-5) will never be reached since the HANDLE CONDITION in Fig. 7-4 will take charge, causing a branch to the CHECK-RECORD paragraph, which is defined under the option NOTFND. So, if by some odd chance we had an A (ADD) record which continues to test the logic of line 5 without taking a detour as specified under the NOTFND label, we actually have a record that's already in exis-

```
   *  READ1.
1  *     EXEC CICS READ DATASET('PMSTABC')
2  *        INTO(WSTORAGE-AREA)
3  *        RIDFLD(RECORD-KEY)
4  *        LENGTH(LEN) UPDATE END-EXEC.
5  *     IF UPDTSELECTI = 'A'
6  *        MOVE ' RECORD ALREADY EXISTS' TO
   *        ERR-LINE0
7  *        MOVE PROT-WHITE-BRIGHT TO ERR-LINEA,
8  *        MOVE -1 TO UPDTSELECTL
9  *        EXEC CICS SEND MAP('PMM090A') MAPSET
10 *        ('PMS090A'), CURSOR END-EXEC.
11 *        EXEC CICS RETURN TRANSID('C009')
12 *        COMMAREA(WORK-CUMM-AREA)
   *        LENGTH(COMLEN1)
13 *        END-EXEC.
14 *  CHECK-RECORD.
15 *     IF UPDTSELECTI = ('R' OR 'D') MOVE
16 *        'RECORD ALREADY EXISTS' TO ERR-LINE0
17 *        MOVE UNPROT-RED-MDT TO ERR-LINEA
18 *        MOVE -1 TO UPDTSELECTL
19 *        GO TO ......................
20 *  CONTINUE-PROCESSING.
21 *     IF UPDTSELECTI = ('R' or 'D') NEXT
   *        SENTENCE
22 *     ELSE GO TO ERR-IN-READ.
```

Fig. 7-5. Procedures required to update a file.

```
            WORKING-STORAGE SECTION.

            01  WSTORAGE-AREA.
                02  WS-CODE         PIC X.
                02  RECORD-KEY      PIC X(17).
                02  REST-OF-DATA    PIC X(52).
```

Fig. 7-6. Entries in the WORKING STORAGE section for the file update shown in Fig. 7-5.

tence bearing the wrong update code.

So now we are ready to transmit an error message (lines 6 through 10) and reinvoke the current program for continued resolution of the problem. If, however, we do reach the CHECK-RECORD paragraph and the record type in question is either an R or a D (revision or deletion), again, we have no business of being there, and we must display a corresponding error message. Note that the only logical path to the CHECK-RECORD label is via the NOTFND option specified in the HANDLE CONDITION routine.

7.3   THE WRITE COMMAND

Just as it is in batch systems, the WRITE command under CICS is essentially designated to create, or WRITE, a new record on a direct-access device, following a READ instruction. The WRITE statement doesn't necessarily have to follow a READ command as long as it is performed before the termination of the current task.

The WRITE statement is shown in Fig. 7-7. FROM specifies the data area from which the record is to be updated. The LENGTH option refers to the length of the record as defined; it must be a half-word binary field:

```
01   LEN   S9(4) COMPUTATIONAL VALUE +70.
```

```
            EXEC CICS WRITE
            DATASET(name)
            FROM(data-area)
            [LENGTH(data-value)]         mandatory with SYSID
            RIDFLD(data-area)
            [KEYLENGTH(data-value)]      mandatory with SYSID
            [SYSID(name)]
            [RBA/RRN]                    VSAM only
            [MASSINSERT]                 VSAM only
            [SEGESTALL]

            Conditions     DSIDERR, DUPREC, ILLOGIC, INVREQ,
                           IOERR, ISCINVREQ, LENGERR, NOSPACE,
                           NOTOPEN, SYSIDERR
```

Fig. 7-7. Standard format for the WRITE statement used to add a new record to a file.

```
READ1.
    EXEC CICS READ DATASET('PMSTABC')
    INTO(WSTORAGE-AREA)
    RIDFLD(RECORD-KEY)
    LENGTH(70) UPDATE
    END-EXEC.
          .
          .
WRITE-ADD.
    EXEC CICS WRITE FROM(WSTORAGE-AREA)
    DATASET ('PMSTABC')  RIDFLD
    (RECORD-KEY)
    LENGTH(70) END-EXEC.
```

Fig. 7-8. The READ and WRITE instructions within the same program (transaction) cycle.

RIDFLD refers to the identification of the record to be added. The length of the RIDFLD or record key is further defined in the KEYLENGTH option, which specifies the length of the record key on the file. MASSINSERT exists only for VSAM datasets; it specifies that the WRITE command is part of the mass insert operation.

When using the WRITE command, most of the exception conditions are similar, if not completely identical, to those presented in Fig. 7-3. In addition, observe the NOSPACE option. It specifies that there is no more space left on a direct access device for adding or updating a new record. The default action for all of the file control exception conditions is abnormal termination of the task.

When you are writing or adding a record to the file, it is important to realize the following:

1. The file must have been read with the UPDATE option during the execution of the current task.
2. A WRITE statement must be issued before the termination of the task or else the record will not be created.

Figure 7-8 shows both steps within the same cycle. Should there be an XCTL (Exit Control statement) or a RETURN statement between the logic separating the READ1 and the WRITE-ADD paragraphs, the result of the WRITE statement (for reasons explained earlier) will be negative.

7.4 THE REWRITE COMMAND

The function of the REWRITE command is to update an already existing record, thus rewriting it. A new record obviously cannot be rewritten since it doesn't exist. Standard format for the REWRITE is shown in Fig. 7-9.

Options for the REWRITE command have been summarized under the WRITE command. It is also important to understand that like the WRITE

```
EXEC CICS REWRITE
  DATASET(name)
  FROM(data-area)
  [LENGTH(data value)]        mandatory with SYSID
  [SYSID(name)]
  [SEGSETALL]
END-EXEC.

Conditions: DSIDERR, DUPREC, ILLOGIC, INVREQ, IOERR,
            ISCINVREQ, LENGERR, NOSPACE, NOTOPEN,
            SYSIDERR.
```

Fig. 7-9. The REWRITE command structure.

```
EXEC CICS REWRITE
  FROM(WSTORAGE)
  DATASET('PMSTABC')
END-EXEC
```

Fig. 7-10. A simple example of a REWRITE statement based on previously developed code.

command, the REWRITE command requires that the existing record must have been read earlier with an update option.

Figure 7-10 shows a simple REWRITE statement based on previously discussed coding problems. For exception conditions, please refer to Fig. 7-3.

7.5 THE DELETE COMMAND

The DELETE command is valid for VSAM key-sequenced datasets only. It is used to delete a single record or a group of records. If a generic key option is provided, it is possible to delete a group of records with a single statement. Review the command format presented in Fig. 7-11 available only for VSAM files.

Both the RIDFLD and the KEYLENGTH options are required with the generic DELETE. Essentially, the generic option is used when all records

```
EXEC CICS DELETE
  DATASET(name)
  [RIDFLD(data area)]            mandatory with generic
  [KEYLENGTH(data-value)]        generic or SYSID
  [GENERIC[NUMREC(data area)]]
  [SYSID(name)]
  [RBA/RRN]
END-EXEC.

Conditions: DSIDERR, ILLOGIC, INVREQ, IOERR,
            ISCINVREQ, NOTFND, NOTOPEN, SYSIDERR
```

Fig. 7-11. Standard format for the DELETE command, which is available only for VSAM files.

with the partial key (the starting characters of a full key) are to be deleted. When the generic option is used with the numeric one, an area is provided by the system where CICS can place the number of records that were deleted.

When you choose to delete a single record, it is assumed that you located the individual record at the time the file was read. Afterward, CICS keeps track of all reference requirements. Thus, when the DELETE command is used (Fig. 7-12) the system "remembers" the record marked for deletion as long as both the READ and the DELETE commands are within the same task.

Figure 7-13 shows that we can delete the records through the generic option using the first three positions of the social security number string. The RIDFLD option (the Record Identification Field) contains the full or the partial key of the records to be deleted. This option should not be specified when the records to be deleted have just been read for update. This is because the READ has already identified the records.

KEYLENGTH is mandatory when a partial key is being specified. When it is used with the full key, the value is compared with the entry made in the File Control Table (FCT). If the values differ, the INVREQ exception condition will occur.

Generic delete is a powerful tool, and the application programmer must have a thorough understanding of the potential problems this command is likely to create if used improperly.

Figure 7-14 shows the data division set up for this generic delete.

```
EXEC CICS DELETE
DATASET('PMSTABC')
END-EXEC.
```

Fig. 7-12. A statement that will delete a record from the dataset PMSTABC.

Group delete.

Fig. 7 13. Generic deletion based on three bytes of the record key.

```
EXEC CICS DELETE
DATASET('PMSTABC')
RIDFLD(PARTIAL-KEY)
KEYLENGTH (3)
GENERIC
NUMERIC(NO-OF-RECS-DEL)
END-EXEC.
```

```
WORKING-STORAGE SECTION.

01  WSTORAGE-AREA.
    02  WS-CODE          PIC X.
    02  RECORD-KEY.
        03  PARTIAL-KEY  PIC X(13)
        03  FILLER       PIC X(14).
    02  REST-OF-DATA     PIC X(52).
```

Fig. 7-14. The DATA DIVISION set up for the generic delete.

111

7.6 THE FILE BROWSE COMMANDS

The browse operation in CICS command is equivalent to the sequential accessing of records in a dataset. To accomplish this, CICS command utilizes five related statements:

STARTBR
READNEXT
READPREV
RESETBR
ENDBR

Forward sequential retrieval is available for all three access methods (ISAM, DAM, VSAM); however, backward sequential retrieval is only available for VSAM. Specific or generic keys may also be used to start the browse operation.

7.6.1 STARTBR or Start Browse

The Start Browse command, or STARTBR, is intended for starting and positioning the pointer. Although the data is not yet available, it is from this point in the dataset that the records will be made available for sequential reading. Figure 7-15 shows a standard format for a STARTBR command.

Note that the definition of the KEYLENGTH is mandatory with GENERIC or SYSID unless RBA or RRN is coded. The exception condition ILLOGIC is only available under VSAM.

The GENERIC option establishes that the specified key is a partial key. GTEQ (greater than or equal to) means that the browsing operation will start at the first record having a key equal to the one specified, or failing that, at the first record having a greater key.

The EQUAL option, which is only available for VSAM datasets, will be satisfied only by a record having the same key (complete or generic) as

```
EXEC CICS STARTBR
DATASET(name)
RIDFLD(data-area)
[KEYLENGTH(data value)[GENERIC]]
[REQID(data value)]
[SYSID(name)]
[RBA / RRN / DEBKEY / DEBREC]
[GTEQ / EQUAL]
```

Conditions: DSIDERR, ILLOGIC, INVREQ,
IOERR, ISCINVREQ, NOTFND, NOTOPEN,
SYSIDERR.

Fig. 7-15. Standard format for the Start Browse command.

```
01  SSNO.
    02   SSNO1           PIC    9(3).
    02   SSNO2           PIC    9(2).
    02   SSNO3           PIC    9(4).
```

Fig. 7-16. The Social Security number field defined in three parts so that only one part of it can be used in generic searches.

```
EXEC CICS STARTBR
     DATASET('PERSNLMT')
     RIDFLD(SSNO)
     GENERIC
     KEYLENGTH(3)
END-EXEC.
```

Fig. 7-17. Code that sets up the browse based on the first three digits of the Social Security number.

that specified in the RIDFLD option. REQID is used when more than one browsing operation is to be performed concurrently. The data value contains a unique identifying number for each browse operation. When this is not specified, the default value is zero and only one browsing may be performed at any time against the dataset. RIDFLD points to an area with the key (partial or full) where scanning is to begin. Note that if the key is a generic one, the KEYLENGTH option must also be specified.

Let's say we want to initiate a BROWSE based on the employee's social security number. In Fig. 7-16 we have subdivided our nine position social security number string into three separate fields under SSNO, the way we would normally hyphenate it. Assume that we only want to utilize the first three digits of the social security number field to initiate a generic search. Figure 7-17 shows what the code would look like. Note that the RIDFLD will carry the full nine positions of the key, while the KEYLENGTH option is only defined as a three character long data element (SSNO1).

7.6.2 The READNEXT Command

After the STARTBR command, the application programmer will issue a READNEXT statement to sequentially retrieve records from a dataset. (Note that prior to the READNEXT command, a STARTBR command must have been issued or else an INVREQ exception condition will occur.)

Standard format for the READNEXT command is shown in Fig. 7-18.

Using the previous example with the social security number string, note the relationship between the STARTBR and READNEXT commands shown in Fig. 7-19. Statement 2 utilizes a dataset PERSNLMT, which has a table entry equivalent in the File Control Table. RIDFLD, in statement 3, contains the entire social security number string defined in Fig. 7-16. Statement 4 specifies that we are attempting to search a number of records

```
EXEC CICS READNEXT
     DATASET(name)
     [INTO(data area) / SET(pointer-ref)]
     [LENGTH(data area)]
     RIDFLD(data area)
     [KEYLENGTH(data value)]
     [REQID(data value)]
     [SYSID(name)]
     [SEGSET(name) / SEGSETALL]
     [RBN / RRN]
     END-EXEC.

     Conditions: DSIDERR, DUPKEY, ENDFILE, ILLOGIC,
     INVREQ, IOERR, ISCINREQ, LENGERR, NOTFND,
     NOTOPEN, SEGIDERR, SYSIDERR
```

Fig. 7-18. Standard format for the READNEXT command.

```
 1  *  EXEC CICS STARTBR
 2  *            DATASET('PERSNLMT')
 3  *            RIDFLD(SSNO)
 4  *            GENERIC
 5  *            KEYLENGTH(3)
 6  *            END-EXEC.
    *
    *
    *
 7  *       EXEC CICS READNEXT
 8  *            INTO('WS-RECORD')
 9  *            LENGTH(REC-SIZE)
10  *            DATASET('PERSNLMT')
11  *            RIDFLD(SSNO)
12  *            KEYLENG(9)   END-EXEC.
```

Fig. 7-19. The relationship between the STARTBR and READNEXT commands.

using the generic (or partial) key option. Statement 5 specifies that the key-length will only be partially defined up to three rather than the full nine positions, which is the SSNO1 field. Once the STARTBR command is issued or the pointer is set by the first qualified criterion, we're ready to proceed with the READNEXT command (statement 7). The file now is ready to accommodate the respective record. Figure 7-20 shows the File Control Table with the information required to do browsing.

7.6.3 The READPREV Command

The READPREV command, valid with VSAM datasets only, is used to retrieve records sequentially, but in a reverse order. Before the first READPREV command is issued, a STARTBR command must have been coded (just as if we were to perform a READNEXT operation). Otherwise an INVREQ exception condition will occur. Figure 7-21 illustrates the differences between the READNEXT and READPREV operations.

```
WORKING-STORAGE SECTION.
01 WS-RECORD      PIC X(200).
---------------------------

PERSNLMT DFHFCT TYPE=DATASET,DATASET=PERSNLMT,              C
ACCMETH=VSAM,MODE=VSAM,STRNO=1,                             C
SERVREQ=(GET,SHARE,UPDATE,NEWREC,BROWSE,DELETE),            C
RECFORM=(VARIABLE,UNBLOCKED),FILSTAT=(ENABLE,OPENED),       C
LOG=NO,          NO AUTO LOGGING                            C
   JID=NO,       NO AUTO JOURNALLING                        C
   JREQ=(RU,WN,WU)   READUP,WRUPD,WRNEW
```

Fig. 7-20. The File Control Table with the information required for browsing.

```
 SOCSEC NO   EMPLOYEE NAME  | SOCSEC NO   EMPLOYEE NAME
 123-45-6789 SMITH, TOM     | 222-80-1900 PENDELTON, J
 124-44-3280 HENDERSON,P.   | 222-70-2183 PRESLEY, ALEX
 130-31-2170 JACKSON, J     | 211-80-1234 DUVALL, DENNY
 201-10-0197 ALEXANDER S    | 201-10-0197 ALEXANDER, S
 211-80-1234 DUVALL, DENNY  | 130-31-2170 JACKSON, JAY
 222-70-2183 PRESLEY, ALEX  | 124-44-3280 HENDERSON, P
 222-80-1900 PENDELTON, J   | 123-45-6789 SMITH, TOM
 235-10-1240 MILTON, BILL   | 122-95-8034 JERGEN,TERRY
 244-43-0876 ANDREOZZI, G   | 120-01-7011 BRINKMANN, P
 250-00-9705 JOHNSTON, PAT  | 101-70-8102 HAUWILLER, T

       The READNEXT              The READPREV
       Command                   Command
```

IF THE READNEXT INSTRUCTION IS TO START WITH THE SOCIAL SECURITY NUMBER 123-45-6789
(ASSUMING THE FILE IS SET UP IN THAT KEY SEQUENCE) WE MAY DO THE FOLLOWING:

MOVE 123-45-6789 TO THE RECORD-KEY
ISSUE A STARTBR
CONTINUE ISSUING A READNEXT COMMAND

IF THE READPREV INSTRUCTION IS TO START WITH THE SOCIAL SECURITY NUMBER 222-80-1900,
WE MAY DO THE FOLLOWING:

MOVE 222-80-1900 TO THE RECORD-KEY
ISSUE A STARTBR
CONTINUE ISSUING THE READPREV COMMAND

Fig. 7-21. The differences between the READNEXT and the READPREV commands. READPREV is available only under VSAM.

```
EXEC CICS READPREV
DATASET(name)
[INTO(data area) / SET(pointer-ref)]
[LENGTH(data area)]
RIDFLD(data area)
[KEYLENGTH(data value)]
[REQID(data value)]
[SYSID(name)]
[SEGSET(name) / SEGSETALL]
[RBA / RRN]
END-EXEC.


    Conditions:  DSIDERR, DUPKEY, ENDFILE, ILLOGIC,
    INVREQ, IOERR, ISCINVREQ, LENGERR, NOTFND, NOTOPEN,
    SEGIDERR, SYSIDERR
```

Fig. 7-22. Standard format for the READPREV command.

Standard format for the READPREV command is shown in Fig. 7-22. The INTO option simply refers to move mode. SET, on the other hand, operates in locate mode utilizing the pointer reference. LENGTH specifies the maximum record length expected by the application program. It also provides CICS with an area in which it can place the actual length of the record retrieved. The DATASET option provides the name of the file being read. The data area specified by the RIDFLD must be synonymous with the STARTBR (or the last RESETBR) operation. Upon the completion of the READPREV command, CICS will place the full key value of the record retrieved in the data area of the RIDFLD. The RBA and the RRN options are used for VSAM files only, utilizing a relative address (RBA) or a relative record number (RRN) as the key. Finally, the REQID identifies the browsing operation when more than one browse is being processed concurrently against the same file. The data value in this option has to match the value specified in the STARTBR or RESETBR command.

7.6.4 The ENDBR Command

The ENDBR command is used to end a browsing operation. When not used, browsing will remain active until the end of the task (application program). Figure 7-23 shows the standard format for the ENDBR command, and Fig. 7-24 shows an example of the ENDBR command.

```
            EXEC CICS ENDBR
            DATASET(name)
            [SYSID(name)]


            Conditions: DSIDERR, ILLOGIC, IOERR,
            ISCINVREQ, NOTOPEN, SYSIDERR
```

Fig. 7-23. Standard format for the ENDBR command.

```
              EXEC CICS ENDBR
              DATASET('PERSNLMT")
              REQID (2)
              END-EXEC.
```

Fig. 7-24. An example of the ENDBR command.

7.6.5 The RESETBR Command

The RESETBR command is used when a browsing operation is to continue from a different point. In fact, it is the same as issuing an End Browse, followed by a STARTBR statement. This command cannot be utilized unless a STARTBR command has been issued previously in the program. In short, the Reset Browse command is:

RESETBR = ENDBR + STARTBR

Figure 7-25 shows the standard format for the RESETBR command.

SUMMARY

The READ command reads the file from a dataset contained on a direct access device. The Dataset Name Option refers to the file name as used in the File Control Table (FCT). The RIDFLD or Record Identifier option is used to specify the key of the record for further reference.

When an UPDATE option is used, it specifies that an UPDATE or DELETE operation is about to follow. However, when no such option is specified, a READ ONLY operation is assumed.

The GTEQ and the EQUAL options are invoked to locate one or a number of specific records.

The WRITE command is designed to create a new record on a direct access device following a READ command. In order to successfully create a record, both the READ and the WRITE instructions must be issued within the same task, and the READ command must contain the UPDATE option.

```
         EXEC CICS RESETBR
         DATASET(name)
         RIDFLD(data area)
         [KEYLENGTH(data value) [GENERIC]]
         [REQID(data value)]
         [SYSID(name)]
         [GTEQ / EQUAL]
         [RBA / RRN]
         END-EXEC.



         Conditions:   DSIDERR, ILLOGIC, INVREQ,
            IOERR, ISCINVREQ, NOTFND, NOTOPEN, SYSIDERR.
```

Fig. 7-25. Standard format for the Reset Browse command.

The function of the REWRITE command is to update an already existing record, thus rewriting it.

The DELETE command is only valid for VSAM key sequenced datasets.

If a GENERIC key option is provided, it is possible to delete a group of records within the same statement.

The BROWSE operation in CICS command is equivalent to the sequential accessing of each record. The following statements are associated with the browse command:

STARTBR   Issued to initialize sequential reading
READNEXT   Issued to sequentially retrieve records
READPREV   Issued to retrieve records in reverse order (Available for VSAM only)
ENDBR   Issued to end the browsing operation
RESETBR   Issued as a compound ENDBR + STARTBR command

QUESTIONS

1. Is the update option in the READ command necessary when you are to rewrite an existing record on the file?
2. When do you use the GTEQ and EQUAL options in the READ command?
3. What is the DUPKEY exception condition the result of?
4. True or false: the DELETE command is valid for all datasets, whether VSAM, ISAM, or DAM.
5. True or false: the WRITE command is used to update an existing record.
6. Which one of the following is not a file browse command?

STARTBR
READNEXT
READMORE
RESETBR
READPREV

7. What function do the browse commands perform?
8. Specifically, what does the READNEXT command do?
9. True or false: the READPREV command is only valid for ISAM (Indexed Sequential Access Method) type datasets.
10. What does the length option specify in the READPREV command?
11. A RESETBR command in fact is the combination of what two other browse commands?

8
Case Study I

This case study, (Case Study I) represents a review of a number of topics we discussed earlier so that you acquire a better understanding of some of the associated codes. This chapter provides a comprehensive review of the paging or browsing mechanism as well as concrete examples of some of the topics we discussed up to this point.

Figure 8-1 presents a screen containing job related information periodically reviewed by the personnel staff in order to comply with Civil Service regulations. The key to this file is CLASS CODE, which is arranged in ascending order adhering to current job descriptions. REVISION refers to an action date when personnel reviews jobs with the intent of revising or validating them.

PRO-LINE, or Promotional Line, describes job potentials with regards to the next promotable step. If the operator decides to start the browse from the very first page, he'll have to depress PF Key 1. (In order to keep the application program fairly simple, we only considered forward processing using the READNEXT Command.)

CLASS CODE	DESCRIPTION	REVISION	PRO-LINE
1111	COMPUTER OPERATOR I	11-12-85	111-5674
1112	COMPUTER OPERATOR II	11-12-85	111-6774
1120	COMPUTER OPERATOR III	11-12-85	111-7774
1300	PROGRAMMER ANALYST I	10-22-84	233-6781
1301	PROGRAMMER ANALYST II	10-22-84	133-6783
1302	SENIOR PROGRAMMER	10-22-84	133-6783
2000	PROJECT LEADER	11-01-85	200-1221
2001	SYSTEMS ANALYST I	11-01-85	200-1224
2002	SYSTEMS ANALYST II	11-01-85	200-1225
3001	ACCOUNTANT JR	11-15-85	000-1935
3990	ACCOUNTANT I	09-01-85	001-1990
3999	ACCOUNTANT II	09-01-85	001-2000
4000	AUDITOR	09-01-85	002-2001
4001	AUDITOR MANAGER	09-01-85	003-2001
5000	PURCHASING AGENT	10-10-85	009-1234

.............SYSTEMS MESSAGES HERE.............

PF1 START OVER PF3: RETURN TO MENU PF10: SIGN OFF

Fig. 8-1. A screen layout that is reviewed and updated periodically by the personnel officer.

PF Key 3 will cause a branch to the main menu. PF Key 10 will sign off the terminal operator, once his work is completed. Notice that a maximum of 15 jobs may be displayed on the screen at a time. By pressing the Enter key, the terminal operator will be able to display the next 15 entries.

Because of the relatively small size of the file, we may think of it as an on-line table, which is updated from time to time. It wasn't necessary for us to set up pointers for repositioning the inquiry. This, however, will be done in our second case study, which deals with temporary storage facilities. Figure 8-2 shows a flowchart reviewing the logic of the BROWSE operation. Block 1 determines whether or not this is the first time the application program has gained control through an indicator in the COMMAREA, whose content is being moved to CA-FIRST-PASS. If the cycle is not the first one, the program is to branch to block 2 after the key of the next record is set up and the map is received.

Block 3 is where the STARTBR, or Start Browse, operation is to begin, regardless whether it is a first time routine or whether it is one of the subsequent paths. Note that the STARTBR operation starts with the KEYLENGTH of zero. It is essential to initialize the key with low values. (If you were to begin with the last entry on the file and read backward, which is essentially what the READPREV command does, you must initialize the KEYLENGTH with high values of hexadecimal FF.)

Once the READNEXT command is invoked (block 4), the application program stays in a self-induced loop until either one of two conditions are met:

1. The 15-record display cycle ends, or
2. The end of the file is reached prior to the completion of the 15 record display.

If neither one of the above conditions prevail, CICS command will start moving data elements defined on the map to the output area, which is the display terminal. Afterward, the logic will check to make sure that the 15 record limit has not been exceeded. If it hasn't, the program will branch back to acquire the next record through a READNEXT command in block 4.

If it hasn't done so already, the program will store the key representing the first entry of the next 15 display records in the COMMAREA, transmit a map to the terminal operator with the previous entries, and stop the browse procedures (ENDBR) while reinvoking the transaction for the next cycle in block 6.

If there are no more records to read, the program generates a message saying "END OF DISPLAY" on the bottom of the screen (SYSTEMS MESSAGES).

Another ENDBR is shown in block 7 without reference since ENDBR's may be triggered in a number of different ways, the logic of which we didn't

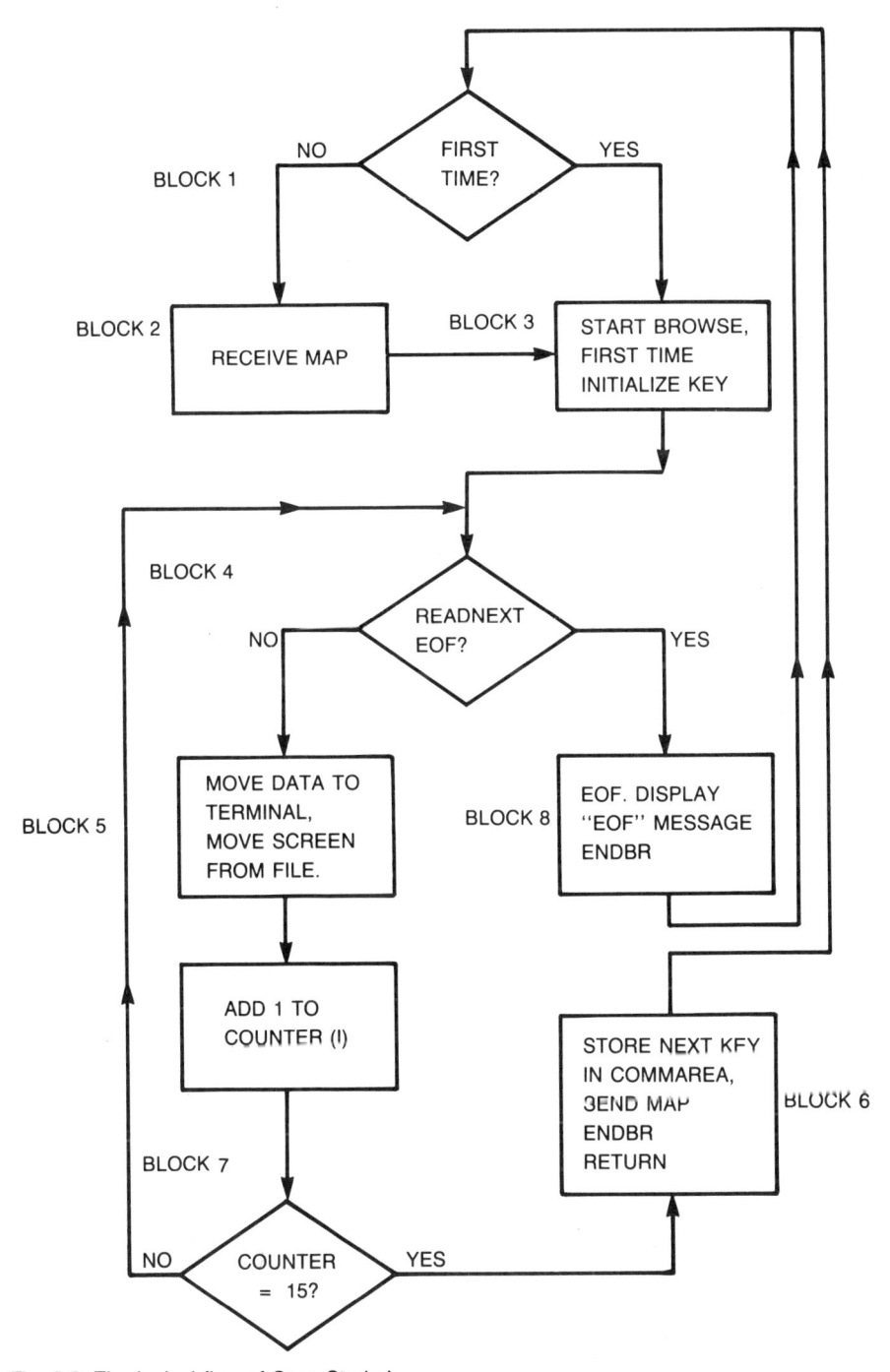

Fig. 8-2. The logical flow of Case Study I.

```
    PROCEDURE DIVISION.
        EXEC CICS HANDLE AID
        ANYKEY (RESET-ATTR)
        PF3 (RTRN-TO-MAIN-MENU)
        PF1 (START-OVER)
        PF 10 (LOFOFF) END-EXEC.
        EXEC CICS HANDLE CONDITION MAPFAIL(RESET-ATTR)
        ENDFILE(EOJ)
        ERROR(PROG-ERR) END-EXEC.
        IF EIBCALEN GREATER THAN ZERO NEXT SENTENCE
        ELSE GO TO RTRN-TO-MAIN-MENU.
```

Fig. 8-3. The PROCEDURE DIVISION of the on-line program used in Case Study I.

incorporate into the current flow.

Let us now review the logic of the above through the PROCEDURE DIVISION, which is shown in Fig. 8-3.

The initial stages of an on-line program are set up via the HANDLE AID and the HANDLE CONDITION statements. Should the terminal operator press any undefined key on the keyboard, accidentally or unknowingly, the logic of the application program will direct the path through the ANYKEY (RESET-ATTR) routine. As the result, the BROWSE routine should continue uninterrupted.

Function Key 3 will trigger an unconditional branch back to the MAIN MENU program (PGP0010A) in order to give the terminal operator a chance to select a different task, if so desired.

Function Key 1 will initiate the entire browse operation from the beginning of the file.

Function Key 10 will allow the terminal operator to log off the system without having to return to the main menu. The HANDLE CONDITION module specifies an end of job condition (EOJ) with a corresponding message, as well as a generalized error condition under PROG-ERR. The latter is to display the message "PROCESSING TERMINATED."

Finally the contents of the communications area is checked. (EIBCALEN GREATER THAN ZERO). If nothing was passed to the current application program (EIBCALEN = ZERO), a branch to the MAIN-MENU program will occur.

In Fig. 8-4 a counter, I, is set up to clear the screen. This is done through subscripting to show you a specific way to clear the screen. (You might want to do it differently.)

As mentioned before, Fig. 8-1 shows an example of our output screen. The system generates the layout shown in Fig. 8-5 through the Screen Definition Support module. We use

01 MYPPM110   REDEFINES PCM110AI

where PCM110AI designated the original map definition.

```
RESET-SUB.
    IF I = 15 MOVE ZEROS TO I
    GO TO RESET-EXIT.
    ADD 1 TO I.
    MOVE SPACES TO CLASSI(I), DESCI(I), REVI(I),
    PROI(I).
    GO TO RESET-SUB.
RESET-EXIT.
    EXIT.
```

Fig. 8-4. The counter part of the program.

```
02  RED-TABLE OCCURS 15 TIMES.
    03  CLASSL    PIC S9(4) COMP.
    03  CLASSA    PIC X.
    03  CLASSI    PIC X(5).
    03  DESCL     PIC S9(4) COMP.
    03  DESCA     PIC X.
    03  DESCI     PIC X(25).
    03  REVL      PIC S9(4) COMP.
    03  REVA      PIC X.
    03  REVI      PIC X(8).
    03  PROL      PIC S9(4).
    03  PROA      PIC X.
    03  PROI      PIC X(8).
```

Fig. 8-5. The screen layout generated by the SDS module.

Following is an entry representing the COUNTER

```
01  I   PIC 99 VALUE IS ZEROS.
```

The PARA-1 label in Fig. 8-6 stores the contents of the Communications area into the CA-PCM110 field, which is also defined as an eleven position field:

```
01  CA-PCM110.
    05  CA-FIRST-PASS       PIC X.
    05  CA-PWRD.
        10  PWRD1           PIC XX.
        10  PWRD2           PIC XX.
        10  PWRD3           PIC X.
    05  CA-CLASS            PIC X(5)
```

Afterward, the password is moved into position and the initial key is set up from the COM-AREA. Finally, a check is issued to determine whether or not it is the first time around for the current transaction. As you can see in Fig. 8-7, there are separate routines for handling each.

Start browsing is initiated with the keylength being zero in order to begin scanning from the top. Dataset (TBL-DD) was entered in the File Control Table (FCT) earlier. The NEXT-BROWSE paragraph refers to starting

```
    PARA-1.
        MOVE PASS-INFO TO CA-PCM110.
    CHECK-PWRD.
        MOVE PWRD1 TO HOLD-PWRD.
        MOVE 'PCSTABC ' TO TBL-DD.
    BUILD-TB-KEY.
        MOVE CA-CLASS TO 850-KEY.
        IF CA-FIRST-PASS = 'N'
        MOVE CA-CLASS TO 850-KEY
        GO TO RECEIVE-MAP, ELSE
        MOVE 'Y' TO CA-FIRST-PASS.
```

Fig. 8-6. The PARA-1 part of the code.

```
START-BROWSE.
    EXEC CICS HANDLE CONDITION NOTFND(NO-TABLE) END-EXEC.
    EXEC CICS STARTBR
    DATASET(TBL-DD) KEYLENGTH(0)
    GENERIC RIDFLD(850-KEY),
    END-EXEC.
    GO TO READ-NEXT.
RECEIVE-MAP.
    EXEC CICS RECEIVE MAP('PCM110A')
    MAPSET('PCS110A') INTO(PCM110AI)
    END-EXEC.
RESET-ATTR.
    MOVE SPACES TO END-MESS.
NEXT-BROWSE.
    EXEC CICS HANDLE CONDITION
    NOTFND(NO-TABLE) END-EXEC.
    EXEC CICS STARTBR DATASET (TBL-DD)
    KEYLENGTH(5) RIDFLD(850-KEY) END-EXEC.
```

Fig. 8-7. The START-BROWSE and NEXT-BROWSE code.

the browse with an established key, with a keylength of five, meaning that the BROWSE is being continuously performed rather than initiated from the beginning.

The READ-NEXT and the RECORD-TO-SCREEN paragraphs in Fig. 8-8 create a temporary loop pending the retrieval of the next 15 sequential records on the file or the occurrence of an end-of-file condition.

The record to be accessed has been laid out in the DATA DIVISION in the following manner:

```
01  850-TABLE-KEY.
    05  FILLER              PIC X.
    05  850-KEY             PIC X(5).
    05  850-DESCRIPTION     PIC X(25).
    05  850-REVISION        PIC 9(6).
    05  850-PRO-LINE        PIC X(8).
    05  FILLER              PIC X(30).
```

The RECORD-TO-SCREEN module moves the contents of the file to the terminal via subscripting. The revision date, due to the format requir-

```
READ-NEXT.
        EXEC CICS READNEXT INTO(850-TABLE-FILE)
        DATASET(TBL-DD) RIDFLD(850-KEY)
        LENGTH(TB-LEN)
        END-EXEC.
RECORD-TO-SCREEN.
        IF I = 15 GO TO SET-NEXT-CLASS.
        ADD 1            TO I.
        MOVE 850-KEY         TO CLASSI(I).
        MOVE 850-DESCRIPTION TO DESCI(I).
        MOVE 850-REVISION    TO STOR-RV-DATE.
        MOVE  ST-RV-MO       TO SC-RV-MO.
        MOVE  ST-RV-DA       TO SC-RV-DA.
        MOVE  ST-RV-YR.      TO SC-RV-YR.
        MOVE 850-PRO-LINE    TO PROI(I).
        GO TO READ-NEXT.
```

Fig. 8-8. The READ-NEXT and READ-TO-SCREEN paragraphs.

ing hyphenation (XX-XX-XX), is moved to storage first and then transmitted to the terminal. This is how it is set up in the WORKING-STORAGE section:

```
01  WORK-SEC.
    05  STO-RV-DATE.
        10  ST-RV-MO      PIC 99.
        10  ST-RV-DA      PIC 99.
        10  ST-RV-YR      PIC 99.
    05  SC-RV-DATE.
        10  SC-RV-MO      PIC 99.
        10  SC-HY1        PIC X value '-'.
        10  SC-REV-DA     PIC 99.
        10  SC-HY2        PIC X VALUE '-'.
        10  SC-REV-YR     PIC 99.
```

As shown in Fig. 8-9, before returning to CICS through reinvoking the transaction ('SC08'), we are going to terminate the BROWSE routine. Once the transaction is terminated, the BROWSE is terminated; however, it is good practice to end our procedure with an ENDBR statement.

Figure 8-10 shows the rest of the program. You will recognize the paragraph or label names since they were referred to in one of the HANDLE AID or HANDLE CONDITION commands.

```
    SET-NEXT-CLASS.
        MOVE 850-KET TO CA-CLASS.
        GO TO RTRN-TO-CICS.
    EOJ.
        MOVE END-OF-JOB TO END-MESS.
        EXEC CICS ENDBR.
        IF CA-FIRST-PASS = 'Y'
        MOVE 'N' TO CA-FIRST-PASS
        EXEC CICS SEND MAP('PCM110A')
        MAPSET('PCS110A')
        ERASE, END-EXEC
        ELSE
        EXEC CICS SEND MAP('PCM110A') MAPSET('PCS110A')
        FROM (PCM110AO)
        CURSOR DATAONLY END-EXEC.
        EXEC CICS RETURN TRANSID('SC08') COMMAREA
        (CA-PCM110), LENGTH (CA-LEN), END-EXEC.
```

Fig. 8-9. Preparing to return to CICS.

```
    START-OVER.
        GO TO START-BROWSE.
    NO-TABLE.
        EXIT.
    RTRN-TO-MAIN-MENU.
            MOVE SPACES TO CA-FIRST-PASS.
            EXEC CICS XCTL PROGRAM('PGP0010')
            COMMAREA(CA-PCM110) LENGTH(CA-LEN)
            END-EXEC.
    PROG-ERR.
            EXEC CICS SEND FROM (ERR-PROG)
            LENGTH(36) ERASE END-EXEC.
            GOBACK.
    LOGOFF.
            EXEC CICS SEND MAP('PCM000A') MAPSET('PCS000A')
            ERASE MAPONLY END-EXEC.
            EXEC CICS RETURN END-EXEC.
            GOBACK.
```

Fig. 8-10. The paragraphs referenced in the HANDLE AID and HANDLE CONDITION commands.

9

Temporary Storage

HIGHLIGHTS
- Overview
- Temporary Storage Queues
- The Writeq TS Command
- The Readq TS Command
- The Deleteq TS Command

9.1 OVERVIEW

I have spoken earlier of the communications area (COMMAREA) as a means to convey a message, or a number of messages, between two transactions, or a single transaction invoked a number of times. I have also discussed the technique whereby a map can be utilized to retain vital information. Using this technique, however, we are restricted to the use of specific maps. That is to say, if those maps are not sent or received by the transaction, the data we require will not be at our disposal. When using temporary storage facilities, it is possible to retain messages without continuously dumping and receiving them via the communications area. Temporary storage can retain information for the application program until it is purged or deleted by a valid DELETEQ command, or until it is flushed by the system at the end of the day either when CICS is brought down or via specific installation standards.

9.2 TEMPORARY STORAGE QUEUES

CICS command gives the programmer the ability to store his data in temporary storage queues either in main storage or in auxiliary storage on a direct access device. By *main storage* we're referring to the computer's main memory, which can only "remember" things while the system is up. However, when data is stored in auxiliary storage, it is retained past the termination of CICS and can be recovered any time thereafter.

Because of these peculiarities, the application programmer should have a thorough understanding of the specific need to use main as opposed to auxiliary storage facilities. Main storage should be used only if the data is required to be retained for a short period of time, perhaps to pass data from task to task or other similar instances. Once the temporary queues are

127

created by the programmer, they will remain intact until they are deleted. What is nice about these queues is the fact that they can be accessed any number of times, even after the termination of the program that created them.

There are four basic commands associated with Temporary Storage Control. These are:

1. Adding or writing data to a temporary storage queue (WRITEQ TS)
2. Updating or rewriting data to a temporary storage queue (WRITEQ TS REWRITE)
3. Reading data from a temporary storage queue (READQ TS)
4. Deleting a temporary storage queue (DELETEQ TS)

In order to differentiate temporary storage from transient data, which will be discussed in Chapter 11, temporary storage control requires that each of the four commands be followed by a space and then the acronym *TS*, meaning temporary storage. However, if you were to omit this acronym, the command automatically defaults to temporary storage rather than transient data.

Let's briefly look at another example. Assume that an application program processes and prints data on a preprinted form via an on-line printer. This data can be stored in temporary storage, validated, and then transmitted in the order required by the report.

Temporary storage queues are identified by symbolic names assigned by the programmer. Since there may be a number of programmers "inventing" queue names, occasionally the problem of duplicate names arises. In order to avoid conflicts with duplicate names, we recommend to establish naming conventions. For example, you may utilize either the operator, the terminal, or the transaction identifier in conjunction with a prefix or a suffix in addition to the symbolic name supplied by the programmer. As an example, Fig. 9-1 shows the specification of a queue using a symbolic name. Note that we are using the terminal identifier in this example to establish naming conventions.

9.3 THE WRITEQ TS COMMAND

Standard format for the WRITEQ TS command is shown in Fig. 9-2.

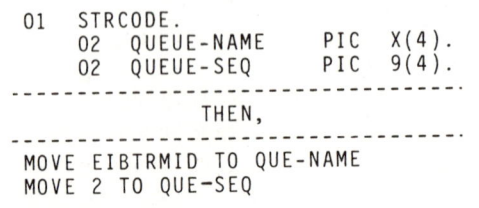

```
01  STRCODE.
    02  QUEUE-NAME    PIC  X(4).
    02  QUEUE-SEQ     PIC  9(4).
-----------------------------------
              THEN,
-----------------------------------
    MOVE EIBTRMID TO QUE-NAME
    MOVE 2 TO QUE-SEQ
```

Fig. 9-1. Possible queue standardizations.

```
EXEC CICS WRITEQ TS
QUEUE(name)
FROM(data area)
[LENGTH(data value)]
[ITEM(data area) [REWRIRE]]
[SYSID(name)]
[MAIN / AUXILIARY]
END-EXEC.

Conditions: INVREQ, IOERR, ISCINVREQ, ITEMERR, NOSPACE,
            QIDERR, SYSIDERR.
```

Fig. 9-2. The temporary storage command WRITEQ.

The WRITEQ TS command is used to store temporary data in a temporary storage queue in main or auxiliary storage. The option MAIN or AUXILIARY will determine just where the data is to be stored. The QUEUE is identified in the queue option. As we mentioned earlier, the name of the queue doesn't appear in any CICS table. Thus it gives the programmer some added flexibility working with this type of storage facilities.

It is possible to store more than a single record or even a single data element in the queue. The ITEM option is essentially designed to identify and monitor certain record types in the queue.

By *writing* a record INTO temporary storage, we mean adding or creating a new set of data. The system will keep a close tab on the number of records placed into the queue. Actually CICS will automatically assign item numbers to the contents of the queue, unless the REWRITE option is specified. If this is the case, the system must know just where in the queue the record to be modified is located. This can only be done via the ITEM NUMBER or an item numbering scheme. If we were to modify the third record in a queue, for example, we must specify among other things that it is the third item we're about to retrieve.

The FROM and the LENGTH options are used to specify to the queue the record to be written and its length.

Let's review the above criteria through some examples. Assume we want to update a queue having the symbolic name STORAGE. Also, assume that Storage contains three sets of records (or items). Primarily, we are interested in updating only the second set. The information required for the update is shown in an area referred to as STATE-IDNET field or:

```
01   STATE-IDNET          PIC X(10).
```

Figure 9-3 shows a set of statements that will update a record in main storage, and Fig. 9-4 illustrates how the queue looks before and after the update. If the WRITEQ TS statement in Fig. 9-3 had been issued without the MAIN option, the default value would have been the auxiliary storage.

Let's review some of the condition codes associated with the WRITEQ Command:

```
              MOVE 'ILLINOIS' TO
              STATE-IDNET.
              EXEC CICS WRITEQ TS
              QUEUE(STORAGE)
              FROM(STATE-IDNET)
              LENGTH(10)
              ITEM(2) REWRITE
              MAIN
              END-EXEC.
```

Fig. 9-3. An update to the second item of the STORAGE queue.

```
          BEFORE                    AFTER
     --------------------    --------------------
     *   CALIFORNIA    *     *   CALIFORNIA    *    ITEM 1
     --------------------    --------------------

     --------------------    --------------------
     *   NEW YORK      *     *   ILLINOIS      *    ITEM 2
     --------------------    --------------------

     --------------------    --------------------
     *   ARIZONA       *     *   ARIZONA       *    ITEM 3
     --------------------    --------------------
```

Fig. 9-4. The STORAGE queue before and after the update of item number 2.

INVREQ occurs when the WRITEQ TS command cannot locate any valid data (the length is zero).

IOERR occurs when there is an unrecoverable input/output error. This is usually not originated by the programmer.

ITEMERR occurs when the item number specified in the WRITEQ TS command utilizes the REWRITE option.

NOSPACE occurs as the result of not having enough space in temporary storage.

QIDERR occurs when the queue specified by a READQ TS command or by a WRITEQ TS command utilizing the REWRITE option cannot be found either in main or in auxiliary storage.

9.4 THE READQ TS COMMAND

Temporary storage is often used as a "scratch pad" facility by the programmer. Rather than storing multi-level data in temporary storage, the programmer may decide to use a give queue in place of the COMMAREA or to store a flag or an indicator. Whatever the case may be, when the information is to be accessed, a READQ TS command should be issued with the ITEM NUMBER (1), or else an ITEMERR condition will occur. Figure 9-5 shows the standard format for the READQ TS command.

The READQ TS command is used to retrieve data from a temporary storage queue either in MAIN or in AUXILIARY storage. Two additional options should be mentioned here:

```
         EXEC CICS READQ TS
         QUEUE(name)
         [INTO(data area) / SET(pointer-ref)]
         [LENGTH(data area)]
         [NUMITEMS(data area)]
         [ITEM(data value) / NEXT]
         [SYSID(name)]   END-EXEC.


         Conditions:   INVREQ, IOERR, ISCINVREQ,
                       ITEMERR, LENGERR, QIDERR,
                       SYSIDERR.
```

Fig. 9-5. Standard format for the READQ TS command.

1. The NEXT option specifies that following the last logical record, the next sequential record is also to be retrieved and
2. NUMITEMS which is essentially a counter set up by CICS to indicate the number of items in the queue.

Following is our previous example using the READQ command.

Figures 9-6 and 9-7 show the retrieval of an item. We are reading the queue STORAGE into a field defined as:

```
01   LOKBOX    PIC X(10).
```

Because it is the third item in the queue STORAGE, the word ARIZONA will now be contained in LOKBOX for further processing.

```
         -------------------
         *  CALIFORNIA   *  ITEM 1
         -------------------
         *  ILLINOIS     *  ITEM 2
         -------------------
         *  ARIZONA      *  ITEM 3
         -------------------
```

Fig. 9-6. The retrieval of the third item, ARIZONA.

```
         EXEC CICS READQ TS
         QUEUE(STORAGE)
         INTO(LOKBOX)
         LENGTH(10)
         ITEM(3)
         REWRITE
         MAIN
         END-EXEC.
```

Fig. 9-7. The coding for the retrieval of the third item, ARIZONA.

9.5 THE DELETEQ TS COMMAND

The DELETEQ TS command is used to delete temporary data associated with the contents of the entire queue. That is to say, the DELETEQ TS command works on the queue, rather than on the item level. Figure 9-8 shows the standard format for the DELETEQ command.

The most common exception condition associated with the DELETEQ TS command is QIDERR, which we briefly discussed in reference to the WRITEW TS command earlier in this chapter. For example, if we were to delete the queue STORAGE, all we need to say is:

```
EXEC CICS DELETEQ TS
QUEUE(STORAGE)
END-EXEC.
```

Note that an extensive case study, Case Study 2, will be presented in Chapter 10. There we have incorporated all relevant temporary storage commands.

```
          EXEC CICS DELETEQ TS
          QUEUE(name)
          [SYSID(name)]  END-EXEC.

          Conditions: ISCINVREQ, QIDERR, SYSIDERR.
```
Fig. 9-8. Standard format for the DELETEQ command.

SUMMARY

Temporary storage facilities are made up of main and auxiliary storage facilities. Temporary storage control requires that each of the commands be followed by a space and then the acronym TS, meaning temporary storage. If TS is omitted, CICS will automatically default to temporary storage rather than to Transient Data Control.

Main storage is used when data is to be stored for only a brief period of time. Auxiliary storage is used for a longer interval. There are four basic commands associated with temporary storage control:

WRITEQ TS means that you are adding data to a temporary storage queue.
THE REWRITE OPTION is used in conjunction with the WRITE TS command to update an existing temporary storage queue.
READQ TS means that you are reading data from a temporary queue.
DELETEQ TS is used to delete an entire temporary storage queue.

Temporary storage queues are identified by symbolic names assigned by the programmer analyst. The use of standard naming conventions are recommended.

When writing records into temporary storage, the system will monitor the number of records placed into the queue. CICS will automatically assign ITEM numbers to the contents of the queue unless the REWRITE option is specified.

The FROM and the LENGTH options are used to specify to the queue the record to be written and its length. The most common error conditions associated with temporary storage are:

INVREQ   occurs when the WRITE command cannot locate any valid data
IOERR   an INPUT/OUTPUT error normally not programmer generated
ITEMERR   occurs when the wrong item number is specified when referring to the queue
NOSPACE   occurs when there is insufficient space for writing to or creating a queue
QIDERR   occurs when the queue cannot be located either in main or in auxiliary storage

QUESTIONS

1. Explain the difference between temporary storage and the communications area in terms of usage.
2. True or false: Temporary storage queues must be defined in the File Control Table (FCT).
3. In using the WRITEQ TS command, why and when do you need to specify the item number?
4. When does the INVREQ exception condition occur?
5. True or false: The DELETEQ TS command is not required to delete a queue since CICS at the end of the transaction will delete it automatically.
6. Under what circumstances does the QIDERR exception condition take place?

10
Case Study 2

HIGHLIGHTS
- **Overview**
- **Program analysis**
- **Summary**

10.1 OVERVIEW

The purpose of this case study is to review temporary storage functions including the paging mechanism that will allow us to *page* forward and backward on the screen. Consider the screen in Fig. 10-1. It shows a directory of all the major study areas a particular university system offers to its student population. The display screen includes a department number, abbreviated as DEPART, and a corresponding DESCRIPTION field. The university code, UNVS, refers to the particular college (H, R, S, etc.).

The screen presented in Fig. 10-1 allows the user to review how a particular course relates to a major department at each college. For example, under the CHEMISTRY DEPARTMENT 2000 at Rawlings Junior College,

```
       COST ANALYSIS REPORT
                                    ENTER SCREEN SELECT
              STUDENT COURSE LISTING


       UNVS       DEPART      DESCRIPTION

        H         2000        DATA PROCESSING
        H         2001        INTRO. TO DATA PROCESSING
        H         2002        INTRODUCTION TO ANS COBOL
        H         2004        DATA BASE CONCEPTS
        H         2005        ON LINE SYSTEMS DESIGN
        H         2006        INTRODUCTION TO PL/I
        H         2007        ADVANCED PL/I
        R         2000        CHEMISTRY, INTRODUCTORY
        R         2001        INORGANIC CHEMISTRY
        R         2002        ORGANIC CHEMISTRY
        R         2003        PHYSICAL CHEMISTRY
        R         2004        ADVANCED ORGANIC CHEMISTRY
        S         2000        BUSINESS ADMINISTRATION

          ERROR OR SYSTEMS MESSAGES....
       PF1: START OVER PF2: BACK PAGE PF3:MAIN MENU
       CLEAR:MAIN MENU
```

Fig. 10-1. A screen showing a number of courses available at each of three community colleges.

designated by the university code H, we may offer Inorganic Chemistry 20-01, or simply 2001, Organic Chemistry 2002, Physical Chemistry 2003, Advanced Organic Chemistry 2004, and so on. The first two positions of the department determine the actual department or the area of major concentration, while the third and the fourth digits relate to a single course within a department. 00 in the last two positions refers to a specific department. Note that each college has substantially different terminology.

Through the use of command keys, as briefly indicated toward the bottom of the screen in Fig. 10-1, we are able to perform a number of functions and maintain sufficient flexibility. Command key 1 is allocated to page forward from the beginning of the file. Command key 2 is designed to page backward from any given point. Command key 3 and the Clear key essentially perform the same functions; that is they both pass control back to the main menu.

A flowchart representation of the program logic is given in Fig. 10-2.

Review the source listing of Case Study II shown in Fig. 10-3. The communications area in the LINKAGE SECTION is defined as a 29 position data element to be moved into the CA-PGRMNB12 field, if and only if the EIBCALEN is greater than zero. This is to make sure that valid data has been passed to the current transaction.

CA-PGRMNB12 is a composite of a number of elements. The first position determines whether it is the first pass of the transaction or one of subsequent cycles with the indicators already set up. The next two positions determine the internal code of a given university. In this program transactions are constantly transmitted to and from a number of universities. All that is defined using 88 level field definitions.

The next three positions, FILLER PIC X9 (03), represent a user-entered password followed by PWRD3, PIC X(01), which designates the mode of access (inquiry versus update).

CA-CURR-SCREEN monitors the page-numbering scheme of the current screen while CA-MAX-SCREEN keeps track of the total number of screens processed. For example, suppose you start reading forward through to the first 10 display pages on the screen. Then you decide to page backward as far as page five. Having glanced at the item on that page, you are now ready once again to proceed forward page by page. In this process, of course, you already have stored pertinent data up to page 10 and you don't have to store additional new data in the queue until you're about to exceed the CA-MAX-SCREEN, which happens to be page 10. Information regarding the next key or display record on the screen is also part of the communications area.

The DFHBMSCA COPY DFHBMSCA represents the DFHBMSCA block that will copy map related information, such as field protection, field intensification (highlighting), and color attributes, into the application program. The MYMAPI COPY MAPSETA triggers the copying of the map

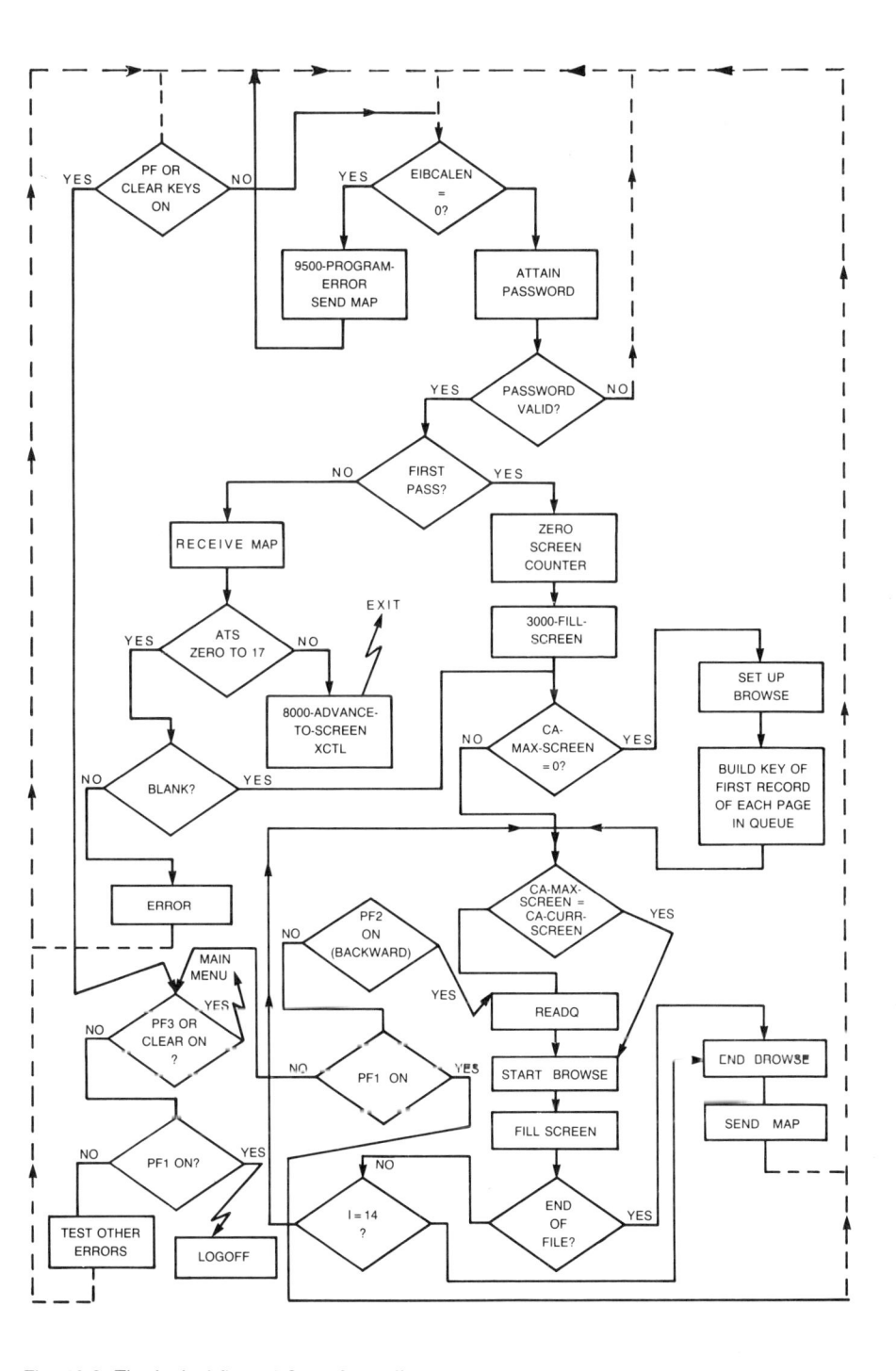

Fig. 10-2. The logical flow of Case Study II.

```
        IDENTIFICATION DIVISION.
        PROGRAM-ID. PGRMNB12.
        DATE-COMPILED.
                        PGRMNB12

                   THIS CICS PROGRAM DISPLAYS THE
                       COURSE DESCRIPTION SCREEN
        ENVIRONMENT DIVISION.
        DATA DIVISION.
        WORKING-STORAGE SECTION.
        01    FILLER.
              05   ATR-GREEN          PIC X(01)  VALUE 'A'.
              05   ATR-RED            PIC X(01)  VALUE 'I'.
              05   XCTL-PROG          PIC X(08).
              05   PGM-ERR-MSG        PIC X(39)  VALUE
                   'PROGRAM ERROR - TASK TERMINATED         '.
              05   WS-TS-KEY.
                   10   FILLER        PIC X(04).
                   10   TS-KEY-TERM   PIC X(04).
              05   WS-GOOD-RECORD-FLAG PIC X(01) VALUE 'N'.
              88   GOOD-RECORD-READ              VALUE 'Y'.
        01    FILLER.
              05   REC-LENGTH         PIC S9(04) VALUE +70.
              05   CA-LENGTH          PIC S9(04) VALUE +29.
              05   TS-LENGTH          PIC S9(04) VALUE +25.
              05   TS-ITEM-NO         PIC S9(04) VALUE ZERO.
              05   I                  PIC S9(04) VALUE ZERO.
        01    CA-PGRMNB12.
              05   CA-FIRST-PASS-FLAG PIC X(01).
              88   CA-FIRST-PASS                 VALUE 'Y'.
              05   CA-PWRD.
                   10   PWRD1         PIC X(02).
                   88   CA-PWRD-H                VALUE 'A1'.
                   88   CA-PWRD-R                VALUE 'B2'.
                   88   CA-PWRD-S                VALUE 'C3'.
                   88   CA-PWRD-OURS             VALUE 'D4'.
```

Fig. 10-3. The program for Case Study II. Continued to page 143.

```
               10   FILLER REDEFINES PWRD1.
                    15   PWRD1-A                PIC X(01).
                    15   FILLER                 PIC X(01).
               10   FILLER                      PIC X(03).
               10   PWRD3                       PIC X(01).
          05   CA-CURR-SCREEN                   PIC S9(03)  COMP-3.
          05   CA-MAX-SCREEN                    PIC S9(03)  COMP-3.
          05   CA-NEXT-KEY                      PIC X(17).
          05   CA-EOF-FLAG                      PIC X(01).
               88   END-OF-FILE                 VALUE 'Y'.
     01   TS-RECORD.
          05   TS-REC-KEY                       PIC X(08).
          05   TS-REC-NEXT-KEY                  PIC X(17).
     ++INCLUDE TABLE
     01   TABLE.
          05   REC-KEY.
               10   REC-UNVS                    PIC X(01).
               10   REC-CRS                     PIC X(16).
          05   REC-DESC                         PIC X(20).
          05   FILLER                           PIC X(43).
     01   DFHBMSCA COPY DFHBMSCA.
     01   MYMAPI   COPY MAPSETA.
     01   LASTMAPI COPY LASTSETA.
     LINKAGE SECTION.
     01   DFHCOMMAREA.
          05   PASS-INFO                        PIC X(29).
     PROCEDURE DIVISION.
          EXEC CICS HANDLE AID
               ANYKEY (2000-ACCEPT-INPUT)
               CLEAR  (9000-PF3-MAIN-MENU)
               PF1    (6000-PF1-START-OVER)
               PF2    (6500-PF2-BACK-PAGE)
               PF3    (9000-PF3-MAIN-MENU)
               PF10   (9900-PF10-LOGOFF)
          END-EXEC.
          EXEC CICS HANDLE CONDITION
               MAPFAIL(2000-ACCEPT-INPUT)
               ILLOGIC(9500-PROGRAM-ERROR)
               ERROR  (9500-PROGRAM-ERROR)
               ENDFILE(7500-END-OF-FILE)
               NOTFND (7500-END-OF-FILE)
          END-EXEC.
          IF EIBCALEN IS GREATER THAN ZERO
               MOVE PASS-INFO TO CA-PGRMNB12.
          IF CA-FIRST-PASS
               MOVE ZERO TO CA-CURR-SCREEN
                            CA-MAX-SCREEN
               GO TO 3000-FILL-SCREEN
          ELSE
               EXEC CICS RECEIVE MAP('MYMAP')
               MAPSET('MAPSETA') INTO (MYMAPI)
               END-EXEC
          ELSE GO TO 9500-PROGRAM-ERROR.
     2000-ACCEPT-INPUT.
          IF ATSL IS GREATER THAN ZERO
          IF ATSI IS NUMERIC
          AND ATSI IS GREATER THAN '00'
          AND ATSI IS LESS THAN '17'
          GO TO 800-ADVANCE-TO-SCREEN
               ELSE
```

```
        IF ATSI IS EQUAL TO SPACES
        GO TO 3000-FILL-SCREEN
            ELSE
        MOVE ATR-RED TO ATSA
        MOVE 'ERRONEOUS SCREEN REQUESTED'
        TO ERR-LINE0
        MOVE -1 TO ATSL
        GO TO 8500-RETURN-TO-CICS
            ELSE
        GO TO 3000-FILL-SCREEN.
    3000-FILL-SCREEN.
        MOVE ATR-GREEN TO ATSA.
        MOVE 'PRESS ENTER FOR NEXT PAGE' TO ERR-LINE0.
        IF CA-MAX-SCREEN IS EQUAL TO ZERO
            MOVE SPACES TO REC-KEY
            MOVE PWRD1-A TO REC-UNVS
            PERFORM 7200-WRITEQ THRU 7200-EXIT
        ELSE
        IF CA-CURR-SCREEN IS EQUAL TO CA-MAX-SCREEN
            MOVE CA-NEXT-KEY TO REC-KEY
        ELSE
            MOVE CA-CURR-SCREEN TO TS-ITEM-NO
            MOVE EIBTRMID TO TS-KEY-TERM
            PERFORM 7300-READQ THRU 7300-EXIT
            MOVE TS-REC-NEXT-KEY TO TS-KEY-TERM.
        MOVE 'N' TO CA-EOF-FLAG.
        EXEC CICS STARTBR
                DATASET ('DDNAME')
                KEYLENGTH (17)
                RIDFLD(REC-KEY)
        END-EXEC.
        PERFORM 7400-READNEXT THRU 7400-EXIT.
        PERFORM 4000-FORMAT-SCREEN THRU 4000-EXIT
                VARYING I FROM 1 BY 1
                UNTIL I IS GREATER THAN 14.
        IF END-OF-FILE
            MOVE 'END OF DATA' TO ERR-LINE0
        ELSE
        IF CA-CURR-SCREEN IS LESS THAN CA-MAX-SCREEN
            ADD 1 TO CA-CURR-SCREEN
        ELSE
            PERFORM 7200-WRITEQ THRU 7200-EXIT.
        GO TO 8500-RETURN-TO-CICS.
    4000-FORMAT-SCREEN.
        MOVE REC-UNVS    TO UNIVO    (I).
        MOVE REC-CRS     TO CRSO     (I).
        MOVE REC-DESC    TO DESCO    (I).
        PERFORM 7400-READNEXT THRU 7400-EXIT.
    4000-EXIT.
        EXIT.
    4200-CLEAR-SCREEN.
        MOVE SPACES TO UNIVO(I)
                    CRSO(I)
                    DESCO(I).
    4200-EXIT.
        EXIT.
    6000-PF1-START-OVER.
        MOVE 1 TO CA-CURR-SCREEN.
        GO TO 2000-ACCEPT-INPUT.
```

```
6000-EXIT.
    EXIT.
6500-PF2-BACK-PAGE.
    IF CA-CURR-SCREEN IS GREATER THAN 2
        SUBTRACT 2 FROM CA-CURR-SCREEN
    ELSE
    MOVE 1 TO CA-CURR-SCREEN.
    GO TO 2000-ACCEPT-INPUT.
6500-EXIT.
    EXIT.
7100-DELETEQ.
    EXEC CICS HANDLE CONDITION
        QIDERR (7100-EXIT)
    END-EXEC.
    MOVE EIBTRMID TO TS-KEY-TERM.
    EXEC CICS DELETEQ TS QUEUE (WS-TS-KEY) END-EXEC.
7100-EXIT.
    EXIT.
7200-WRITEQ.
    ADD 1 TO CA-CURR-SCREEN CA-MAX-SCREEN.
    MOVE EIBTRMID TO TS-KEY-TERM.
    MOVE WS-TS-KEY TO TS-REC-KEY.
    MOVE REC-KEY TO TS-REC-NEXT-KEY CA-NEXT-KEY.
    MOVE CA-CURR-SCREEN TO TS-ITEM-NO.
    EXEC CICS WRITEQ TS
        QUEUE (WS-TS-KEY)
        FROM (TS-RECORD)
        LENGTH (TS-LENGTH)
        ITEM (TS-ITEM-NO)
         MAIN
    END-EXEC.
7300-READQ.
    EXEC CICS READQ TS
        QUEUE (WS-TS-KEY)
        INTO (TS-RECORD)
        LENGTH (TS-LENGTH)
        ITEM (TS-ITEM-NO)
    END-EXEC.
7300-EXIT.
    EXIT.
7400-READNEXT.
    MOVE 'N' TO WS-GOOD-RECORD-FLAG.
    PERFORM 7500-READ THRU 7500-EXIT UNTIL END-OF-FILE
    OR GOOD-RECORD-READ.
7400-EXIT.
    EXIT.
7500-READ.
    EXEC CICS READNEXT INTO (TABLE)
        DATASET ('DDNAME')
        RIDFLD (REC-KEY)
        LENGTH (REC-LENGTH)
    END-EXEC.
    IF REC-UNVS IS EQUAL TO PWRD1-A
        MOVE 'Y' TO WS-GOOD-RECORD-FLAG
    ELSE
        EXEC CICS ENDBR DATASET (DDNAME) END-EXEC
        MOVE 'Y' TO CA-EOF-FLAG.
    GO TO 7500-EXIT.
7500-END-OF-FILE.
    MOVE 'Y' TO CA-EOF-FLAG.
```

```
            MOVE 'Y' TO CA-EOF-FLAG.
        GO TO 7500-EXIT.
    7500-END-OF-FILE.
        MOVE 'Y' TO CA-EOF-FLAG.
    7500-EXIT.
        EXIT.
    800-ADVANCE-TO-SCREEN.
        IF ATSI IS EQUAL TO '01'
            MOVE 'PGRMNB01' TO XCTL-PROG
        ELSE
        IF ATSI IS EQUAL TO '02'
            MOVE 'PGRMNB02' TO XCTL-PROG
        ELSE
        IF ATSI IS EQUAL TO '03'
            MOVE 'PGRMNB03' TO XCTL-PROG
        ELSE
        IF ATSI IS EQUAL TO '04'
            MOVE 'PGRMNB04' TO XCTL-PROG
        ELSE
        IF ATSI IS EQUAL TO '05'
            MOVE 'PGRMNB05' TO XCTL-PROG
        ELSE
        IF ATSI IS EQUAL TO '06'
            MOVE 'PGRMNB06' TO XCTL-PROG
        ELSE
        IF ATSI IS EQUAL TO '07'
            MOVE 'PGRMNB07' TO XCTL-PROG
        ELSE
        IF ATSI IS EQUAL TO '08'
            MOVE 'PGRMNB08' TO XCTL-PROG
        ELSE
        IF ATSI IS EQUAL TO '09'
            MOVE 'PGRMNB09' TO XCTL-PROG
        ELSE
        IF ATSI IS EQUAL TO '10'
            MOVE 'PGRMNB10' TO XCTL-PROG
        ELSE
        IF ATSI IS EQUAL TO '11'
            MOVE 'PGRMNB11' TO XCTL-PROG
        ELSE
        IF ATSI IS EQUAL TO '12'
            MOVE 'PGRMNB12' TO XCTL-PROG
        ELSE
        IF ATSI IS EQUAL TO '13'
            MOVE 'PGRMNB13' TO XCTL-PROG
        ELSE
        IF ATSI IS EQUAL TO '14'
            MOVE 'PGRMNB14' TO XCTL-PROG
        ELSE
        IF ATSI IS EQUAL TO '15'
            MOVE 'PGRMNB15' TO XCTL-PROG
        ELSE
        IF ATSI IS EQUAL TO '16'
            MOVE 'PGRMNB16' TO XCTL-PROG
        ELSE
        IF ATSI IS EQUAL TO '00'
            MOVE 'PGRMNB00' TO XCTL-PROG.
        PERFORM 7100-DELETEQ THRU 7100-EXIT.
```

```
    MOVE 'Y' TO CA-FIRST-PASS-FLAG.
    MOVE +7 TO CA-LENGTH.
    EXEC CICS XCTL PROGRAM (XCTL-PROG)
        COMMAREA (CA-PGRMNB12)
        LENGTH (CA-LENGTH)
    END-EXEC.
8000-EXIT. EXIT.
8500-RETURN-TO-CICS.
    IF CA-FIRST-PASS MOVE 'N' TO CA-FIRST-PASS-FLAG
        EXEC CICS SEND MAP (MYMAP) MAPSET (MAPSETA) ERASE END-EXEC
    ELSE
        EXEC CICS SEND MAP (MYMAP) MAPSET (MAPSETA) DATAONLY END-EXEC.
    EXEC CICS RETURN TRANSID ('TRID') COMMAREA (CA-PGRMNB12)
                LENGTH (CA-LENGTH) END-EXEC.
8500-EXIT. EXIT.
9000-PF3-MAIN-MENU.
    PERFORM 7100-DELETEQ THRU 7100-EXIT.
    MOVE +7 TO CA-LENGTH.
    MOVE 'Y' TO CA-FIRST-PASS-FLAG.
    EXEC CICS XCTL PROGRAM ('PGRMNB01') COMMAREA (CA-PGRMNB12)
                LENGTH (CA-LENGTH) END-EXEC.
9000-EXIT. EXIT.
9500-PROGRAM-ERROR.
    PERFORM 7100-DELETEQ THRU 7100-EXIT.
    EXEC CICS SEND FROM (PGM-ERR-MSG) LENGTH (39) ERASE END-EXEC.
    EXEC CICS RETURN END-EXEG.
9900-PF10-LOGOFF.
    PERFORM 7100-DELETEQ THRU 7100-EXIT.
    EXEC CICS SEND MAP (LASTMAP) MAPSET (LASTSETA) ERASE
```

```
            MAPONLY
        END-EXEC.
        EXEC CICS RETURN
        END-EXEC.
        GOBACK.
    9900-EXIT.
        EXIT.
```

into working storage.

The HANDLE AID shows the assignment of the command keys. PF1 and 2 are now allocated to the paging mechanism, while command Key 3 and the CLEAR key are assigned to the main menu path. Although they are performing the same function, the Clear key and Command key 3 were selected for different logical reasons. Command key 10 will allow the terminal operator to sign off the system any time he wishes to do so. ANYKEY, as you can see, is dedicated to all other undefined keys on the board.

First of all, we must check the validity of the ATS byte in order to see if branching to one of the 16 possible screen displays in the system is viable. Note that the ATS byte is located near the upper right hand corner of the screen.

The HANDLE CONDITION is set up to resolve certain exception conditions, such as end-of-file routine for the browse, a NOTFND exception, if the record being searched is not found, and a generalized error routine for other errors.

ILLOGIC is essentially a catch all class for errors detected by VSAM that don't fall into one of the other categories VSAM recognizes. By far, the most common cause is trying to read from or write into a brand new (empty) VSAM key sequenced dataset (KSDS). In order to use KSDS or CICS, you must batch load at least one record into it, since VSAM will not build the index component until the first record arrives.

Following these standard conventions, the communications area (DFHCOMMAREA) is checked to verify the status of the data being passed through it. If no data has been transmitted through the communications area, the previous queue will be deleted, and an error message "PROGRAM ERROR TASK PGRMNB12 TERMINATED" will be displayed on the screen.

If, on the other hand, the communications area does have valid data to pass on, the first-pass-versus-subsequent-pass condition will be checked. Should the first-pass condition prevail, the counters that keep track of the relative position of the screens are initialized to zero in order to set up the browse.

If an entry is made under *ENTER SCREEN SELECT* referred to by the field named ATS, or *advance to screen,* and located in the upper right-hand corner of the screen, it is checked for validity. Only a space will allow you to continue. Here you may enter a range of numbers from 00 to 16, causing the program to branch from the current task into one of 17 alternate program paths. (See the 8000-ADVANCE-TO-SCREEN paragraph.)

If ATS equals a space, it means that nothing was entered by the user. Thus the current program remains in effect. If, however, anything other than the specified numbers were entered, an error message will be generated by the logic of the application program. This will include the proper repositioning of the cursor using the −1 option for the length field.

The 3000-FILL-SCREEN paragraph addresses three conditions:

1. If CA-MAX-SCREEN = 0, the browse hasn't started yet and no page was sent to the terminal for display.
2. If the two counters, one that keeps track of the current page and the other that monitors that was already written into the queue, are equal the browse will proceed with the next (forward) record to be placed in the queue.
3. If the current counter is less than the maximum counter, then the temporary storage or queue is to be read in order to display the first record of the current page.

Once the First Pass cycle is in progress, we want to set up the next flag area. Afterward, a browse is initiated.

The + + INCLUDE TABLE statement brings a record layout into the expanded WORKING-STORAGE area form, for example, PANVALET or the LIBRARIAN, for subsequent use as follows:

```
01   TABLE.
     05  REC-KEY.
         10   REC-UNVS           PIC X(01).
         10   REC-CRS            PIC X(16).
     05  REC-DESC                PIC X(20).
     05  FILLER                  PIC X(43).
```

After the STARTBR operation, READNEXT is issued with the counter I set up to monitor the display of 14 lines maximum on the screen. The EXEC CICS ENDBR designates the end of the browse operation. The entry for the I counter is set up in the WORKING-STORAGE in the following manner.

```
05   I   PIC   S9(04) VALUE ZERO.
```

Under paragraph 4000-FORMAT-SCREEN, the output map is formatted. Note that the word REC-CRS refers to the department code for internal reasons, since the field is associated with assignments by the Board of Higher Education.

```
01  MYMAPI COPY MAPSET.
01  MYMAPI.
    02  FILLER PIC X(12).
    02  ATSL COMPUTATIONAL  PIC S9(4).
    02  ATSF                PIC X.
    02  ATSI                PIC X(2).
    02  DESC-52I OCCURS 14 TIMES.
        03  UNIVL COMPUTATIONAL PIC S9(4).
        03  UNIVF               PIC X.
        03  UNIVI               PIC X.
        03  CRSL COMPUTATIONAL  PIC S9(4).
        03  CRSF                PIC X.
        03  CRSI                PIC X(4).
        03  DESCL COMPUTATIONAL PIC S9(4).
        03  DESCF               PIC X.
        03  DESCI               PIC X(20).
    02  ERR-LINEL COMPUTATIONAL PIC S9(4).
    02  ERR-LINEF               PIC X.
    02  ERR-LINEI               PIC X(30).
01  MYMAPO REDEFINES MAPSET.
```

Fig. 10-4. The map produced with the help of SDF.

Also note that during our first case study, we have created a screen where we have defined every field. (This is essentially the way basic mapping support, or BMS, works.) However, with SDF, we defined only the first detail line using the matrix option to arrive at the map shown in Fig. 10-4.

Paragraph 6000-PF1-START-OVER sets the counter back to make the first page available for the terminal operator.

By pressing Command Key 1, we'll initialize the current screen position counter by moving 1 to CA-CURR-SCREEN. This will start paging from the first screen on.

By pressing Command Key 2, we'll be setting up the page backward (READPREV) operation. In order to accomplish monitoring the pages in the temporary storage queue, we will allocate or store the key of the first record of each page in WS-TS-KEY, to be referred to by the ITEM number. Thus, if we were to build a 60 page screen display, we would subsequently build 60 corresponding items in the queue.

Assume you're on the fifth page, with the current screen, or CA-CURR-SCREEN pointing to the first record of the sixth page. By pressing Command Key 2, we'll subtract 2 from CA-CURR-SCREEN, which stands at 6. The result, 4, will be moved to temporary storage, disengaging the proper item number for the screen, which now becomes 4. Thus, 4 is our current page to be displayed.

Note that when we are on the first page, a different set of logic must apply. Here we check to make sure that the current screen is greater than 2. Otherwise, we want the first screen to reappear.

Anytime, we're to exit out of the present transaction other than through reinvoking the current task, we must delete all existing queues.

This program is built utilizing the two conventional sections: the main logic and the subroutines, which form the rest of PGRMNB12. Note that the item number is optional with a WRITEQ command. However, when the WRITEQ option is used in conjunction with the REWRITE option, or when the READQ is invoked, we must always specify the item number.

EIBTRMID refers to the particular terminal, thus lending a unique name to the queue.

The rest of the code shows a number of perform statements and the use of the Exit Control (XCTL) command. Other labels from the HANDLE CONDITION and HANDLE AID are defined here.

SUMMARY

The program in this chapter utilizes a number of techniques you may want to use in your own application programs. For example we have presented a paging mechanism that will come in handy.

In this chapter we have also reviewed topics such as working with temporary storage facilities. We have reviewed additional topics already discussed in prior chapters, such as the browse mechanism, the further use of the communications area, and other important CICS options. Finally, we have included comprehensive notes and a procedural flowchart (Fig. 10-1). In order to highlight the main logic and the subroutines triggered by the perform statements.

11

Transient Data Control

HIGHLIGHTS
- Overview
- Automatic Task Initiation (ATI)
- The Destination Control Table
- The Writeq TD Command
- The Readq TD Command
- The Deleteq TD Command

11.1 OVERVIEW

You can use transient data as batch input to non-CICS programs. Unlike temporary storage facilities, which we reviewed in Chapter 9, transient data queues must be defined in the Destination Control Table, or DCT.

When the programmer performs a WRITE routine, he places the record at the very tail end of the queue. Then, when he issues a READ command, the first record on the queue will be retrieved, printed, or otherwise displayed, and then automatically deleted by CICS afterward. This is a rather simple process, and transient data control, unlike the temporary storage mechanism, has no way of finding or maintaining a particular record or item in the queue. Thus when compared with temporary storage procedures, transient data control offers relatively few options.

As shown in Fig. 11-1, data utilizes both *intrapartition* and *extrapartition* queues associated with the CICS partition, where the destination of the data may be a file or a terminal.

Assume your business runs daily prelists of accounts receivables. Your terminal operator, through one of your application programs, enters and writes all that data to an intrapartition transient queue. Then, at night, the information is printed out. (Note that by using transient queues, printing doesn't require extensive formatting since CICS does all that work for you.)

Extrapartition queues, as we mentioned earlier, may be used on subsequent batch input to Non-CICS programs. In other words, you may enter all your data on-line, write it to a tape via an extrapartition destination, and then process the tape through a regular batch program.

Let us now briefly introduce a couple of definitions or topics. A task that is processed under CICS is normally initiated at a terminal, with the task having complete control over the initiating terminal. This mode of operation is often referred to as *synchronous transaction processing*.

Support for *asynchronous transaction processing* can also be generated

149

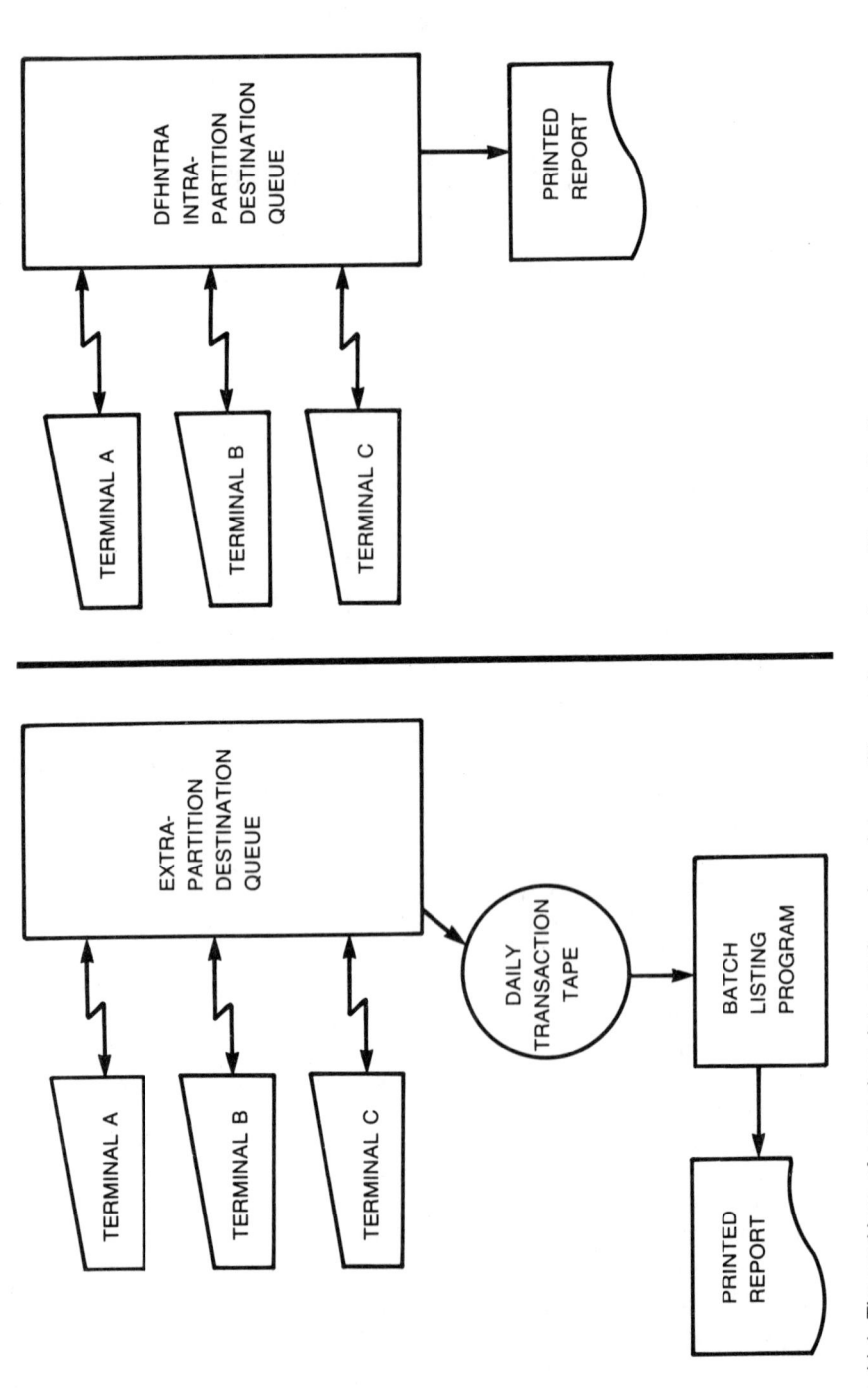

Fig. 11-1. The workings of a transient data set through an intrapartition and an extrapartition destination queue.

into the CICS system. This is done in order to make batch processing a possibility within CICS. Here a task is initiated at the terminal, but the data is to be read to an asynchronous transaction processing unit, or ATP.

11.2 AUTOMATIC TASK INITIATION (ATI)

Automatic task initiation is one of a number of features of intrapartition destinations. Essentially, it is an easy way to initiate, or trigger, a task automatically. The trigger level is usually set in by the systems programmer via a set of entries made in the Destination Control Table (DCT). When the number of entries (created by WRITEQ TS commands) in the queue reaches the specified trigger level, the given task is automatically initiated. In order to retrieve data from the file and subsequently delete it, the application programmer will issue repetitive READQ TD commands. Once the file or queue is depleted in this fashion, a new cycle will be initiated when the trigger level is reached one more time.

11.3 THE DESTINATION CONTROL TABLE

In this section we are going to give you some cursory exposure to what we call *intrapartition destination*. In most computer installations, the responsibility and the maintenance of the Destination Control Table remains with the software department, especially with medium to large sized installations. However, since smaller shops provide less in the way of specialization and as a rule, expect a great deal more versatility of their technicians, we think some presentation on this topic is in order.

Standard format for the Intrapartition Destination Control Table is presented in Fig. 11-2. Note that underlined options designate default procedures.

Let's briefly review the meaning of these statements:

- TYPE indicates an intrapartition destination.
- DESTID – NAME means that the symbolic name is the same as that used in the transient data to specify the destination (four characters maximum allowed).

```
          DFHDCT      TYPE=INTRA
                      ,DESTID=NAME
                      (,DESTFAC=TERMINAL / FILE)
                      (,DESTRCV=NO / PH / LG)
                      (,REUSE=YES / NO)
                      (,RSL=0 / NUMERIC / PUBLIC)
                      (,TRANSID=NAME)
                      (,TRIGLEV=1 / NUMBER)
```

Fig. 11-2. Destination Control Table showing a number of options.

151

- DESTFAC will specify the type of destination the queue represents; it will indicate whether we are directing our output to a terminal or to a file.
- DESTRCV will be specified by you in the event CICS abnormally terminates, (abend); it indicates whether you'd like to recover your destination queue. If the answer is yes, you'll have at least two options at your disposal. If DESTRCV = NO, the destination is not recoverable. If DESTRCV = PH or LG, the destination is either physically or logically recoverable.
- REUSE = YES means that the intrapartition storage tracks for this destination are to be released after they have been read and returned for other uses. REUSE = NO means that the intrapartition storage tracks for this destination are not to be released until a transient-data-purge request is issued.
- RSL = 0/NUMBER/PUBLIC: the number, in a range from 1 to 24, refers to the security level, and PUBLIC means that any transaction is allowed to access the source.
- TRANSID = NAME must be coded to identify the transaction that is to be automatically initiated when the trigger level is reached.
- TRIGLEV = 1NUMBER is coded with the number of records to be accumulated for a destination before these records are automatically processed. Your maximum number of records may be as high as 32,767. Using the example in Fig. 11-2, the Destination Control Table will look like this:

```
DFHDCT    TYPE=INTRA
          DESTID=PAY1
          TRIGLEV=5
          DESTFAC=TERMINAL
```

Note that in this example we set the TRIGGER LEVEL at 5, meaning that we are to start writing to the terminal five records at a time. Indirect destinations allow a single transient queue to be referred to by an identifier.

11.4 THE WRITEQ TD COMMAND

As shown in Fig. 11-3, when the WRITE TD command is used, QUEUE supplies the unique four-character name for the queue. It must be defined first in the Destination Control Table. FROM designates the storage area from which the queue is to be written. LENGTH refers to the length of the record to be written to the queue. If the queue is of fixed length, then the length need not be specified. Intrapartition queues are always variable length record, and therefore, the length is always required. SYSID or System ID is for the Virtual Telecommunications Access Method or (VTAM).

Assume you want to print some information off your payroll master and you are to format that information into separate lines of print images. The

11.4 The Writeq TD Command

```
EXEC CICS WRITEQ TD
  QUEUE(name)
  FROM(data area)
  [LENGTH(data value)]
  [SYSID(name)] END-EXEC.

Conditions:  IOERR ISCINVREQ, LENGERR,
             NOSPACE, NOTOPEN, QIDERR,
             SYSIDERR
```

Fig. 11-3. Standard format for a transient write, including all relevant exception conditions.

first print image (Employee Profile) has the total length of 90 characters. The second print image (Salary-History) contains only 44 characters. Figure 11-4 shows how this is set up in the DATA DIVISION.

When the Payroll Master is read through and EXEC CICS READQ TD command, the records shown in Fig. 11-4 are built into the logic of the application program and include certain print control characters (0 specifying the top of the page, for example, and 1 specifying a single line spacing) in the first position of each record. In fact, you may visualize the entire operation as shown in Fig. 11-5.

Now that both print lines are stored in the program, we want to write them to a transient data queue. For the purpose of using a single line for printing, we refer to a general paragraph name PRINT-IMAGE. RLENGTH defines a number of different length records, as shown in Fig. 11-6. (Note that we define the printer as 133 position long to accommodate a one byte carriage control field.)

```
01  EMPLOYEE-PROFILE.
    02  PRINT-CNTRL1           PIC X VALUE '0'.
    02  EMPLOYEE-NAME          PIC X(30).
    02  EMPLOYEE-STREET-ADD    PIC X(30).
    02  EMPLOYEE-CITY          PIC X(12).
    02  EMPLOYEE-STATE         PIC X(2).
    02  EMPLOYEE-ZIP-CODE      PIC 9(5).
    02  EMPLOYEE-AREA-CODE     PIC 9(3).
    02  EMPLOYEE-TELEPHONE     PIC X(7).
01  SALARY-HISTORY.
    02  PRINT-CNTRL2           PIC X VALUE '1'.
    02  EMPLOYEE-CLASS-CODE    PIC X(5).
    02  EMPLOYEE-DEPARTMENT    PIC X(10).
    02  EMPLOYEE-SALARY-IND    PIC X.
    02  EMPLOYEE-SALARY        PIC S9(5)V99.
    02  EMPLOYEE-RATE          PIC S9(2)V999.
    02  EMPLOYEE-PRIOR-CLASS
                               PIC X(5).
    02  EMPLOYEE-PRIOR-DEPT    PIC X(10).
```

Fig. 11-4. DATA DIVISION statements for sequential processing.

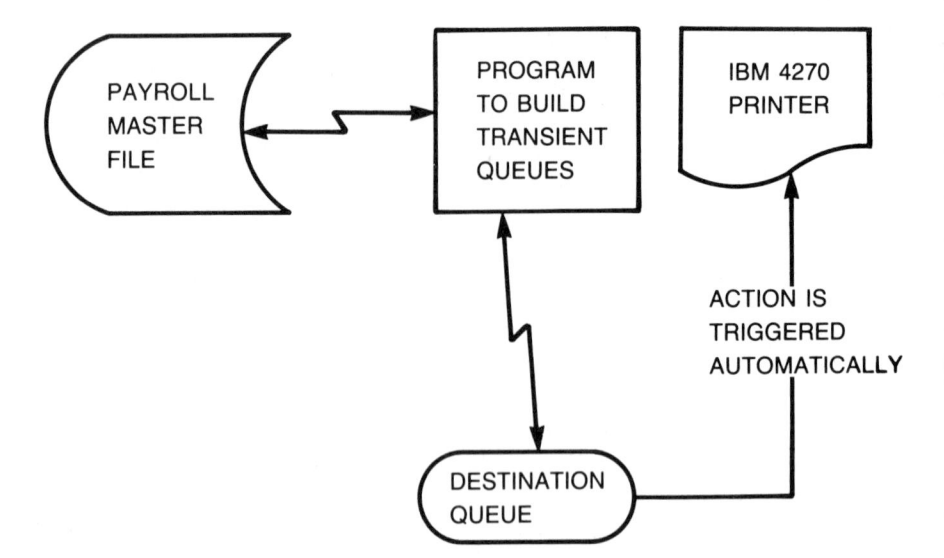

Fig. 11-5. A batch printing mechanism using transient data.

In Fig. 11-7, we show how the report lines are transmitted to do batch reporting via CICS. In statement 1 we move the EMPLOYEE-PROFILE Image to a generalized print line specified in the WORKING-STAGE area, where we define the total length of the record as 90 positions. PRINT-LENGTH is defined in statement 11 as a binary half word (numeric) data element.

Once the first line is set up for transfer to the transient queue, we'll issue a perform statement that will execute lines 13 through 20, writing

```
READ-PAYROLL-MASTER.
        MOVE 134 to RLENGTH.
        EXEC CICS READ DATASET('MASTFLE')
        INTO(BI-RECORD-HOLD)
        RIDFLD(SOCSECNO)
        LENGTH(RLENGTH)
        END-EXEC.
        GO TO SET-UP-QUEUES.

************************************************

01   BI-RECORD-HOLD.
        02   EMPLOYEE-PROFILE      PIC X(90).
        02   SALARY-HISTORY        PIC X(44).
```

The record length of 134 represents the total length of the EMPLOYEE-PROFILE + SALARY-HISTORY.

Fig. 11-6. The DATA and PROCEDURE DIVISION statements for setting up the transient batch printing mechanism.

```
00        SET-UP-QUEUES.
01            MOVE EMPLOYEE-PROFILE TO PRINT-IMAGE.
02            MOVE 90 TO PRINT-LENGTH.
03            PERFORM WRITE-DESTINATION-QUEUE THRU
04            WRITE-DESTINATION-QUEUE-EXIT.
05            MOVE SPACES TO PRINT-IMAGE.
06            MOVE SALARY-HISTORY TO PRINT-IMAGE.
07            MOVE 44 TO PRINT-LENGTH.
08            PERFORM WRITE-DESTINATION-QUEUE THRU
09            WRITE-DESTINATION-QUEUE-EXIT.
10            GO TO READ-PAYROLL-MASTER.
          *****************************************

          (FROM THE DATA DIVISION)
11        01  PRINT-LENGTH    PIC S9(4) COMPUTATIONAL.
12        02  QUENAME         PIC X(4).

          *****************************************

13        WRITE-DESTINATION-QUEUE.
14            EXEC CICS WRITEQ TD
15            QUEUE(QUENAME)
16            FROM(PRINT-IMAGE)
17            LENGTH(PRINT-LENGTH)
18            END-EXEC.
19        WRITE-DESTINATION-QUEUE-EXIT.
20            EXIT.
```

Fig. 11-7. The procedural flow for batch printing.

data into the queue (QUENAME) from the PRINT-IMAGE having the record length of 90 bytes.

In statement 5, we clear the PRINT-IMAGE line for the next operation, beginning in statement 6, and move the SALARY-HISTORY record to print position. Once the line is printed, we return to read another record off the Payroll Master, shown in statement 10. When the queue reaches a predefined trigger level, data from the destination queue will start printing until all that is depleted.

Two additional commands should be mentioned here briefly. These are the ENQ and the DEQ commands. Both ENQ and DEQ are designed to protect a resource from concurrent use by more than one task. Therefore, once you start writing to the queue, make sure you issue a DEQ statement so that no one else will have access to the queue while you're still using it. Once you're done with the process, issue a DEQ command to have the system release valuable resource. Figures 11-8 through 11-11 show the use of the ENQ and DEQ commands.

11.5 THE READQ TD COMMAND

Standard format for the READQ TD command is shown in Fig. 11-12. Note that as you're reading the queue, and you reach the end of it, a QZERO condition will occur. This condition should always be tested in the applica-

```
EXEC CICS ENQ
[RESOURCE(data name)]
[LENGTH(data value)]
END-EXEC
```

Fig. 11-8. The ENQ command format.

Conditions:
    ENQBUSY

Fig. 11-9. The DEQ command format.

```
EXEC CICS DEQ
[RESOURCE(data name)]
[LENGTH(data value)]
END-EXEC
```

```
EXEC CICS
ENQ RESOURCE(QUENAME)
END-EXEC
```

Fig. 11-10. Using the ENQ command as reviewed in the previous problem (refer to Figs. 11-4, 11-6, and 11-7).

Fig. 11-11. Using the DEQ command as reviewed in the previous problem (refer to Figs. 11-4, 11-6, and 11-7).

```
EXEC CICS
DEQ RESOURCE(QUENAME)
END-EXEC
```

```
EXEC CICS READQ TD
QUEUE(name)
[INTO(data area) / SET(pointer-ref)]
[LENGTH(data area)]
[SYSID(name)]
```

Conditions: IOERR, ISCINVREQ, LENGERR,
               NOTOPEN, QBUSY, QIDERR, QZERO,
               SYSIDERR.

Fig. 11-12. Transient-data read options with exception condition codes.

tion program at the time your HANDLE CONDITIONS are defined and set up.

QUEUE represents the symbolic name of the queue to be read. The INTO option specifies the data area that CICS will place the record into. If you specify the INTO option, then you must also define the LENGTH option. LENGTH specifies the data area that contains the maximum length of the record used by the program. If the record exceeds the value defined, it will be truncated and the LENGERR condition will occur.

Assume the following:

```
01   PRINT-LENGTH      S9(4) VALUE COMPUTATIONAL VALUE + 90.
```

We have added a value clause to the previously used PRINT-LENGTH field. QUENAME now contains three different types of records.

1 EMPLOYEE-PROFILE   90 Characters
2 SALARY-HISTORY   44 Characters
3 DEDUCTION-SEGMENT   105 Characters

We're going through a reiterative process reading the transient data queue into the PRINT-IMAGE field with a maximum length of 90:

```
EXEC CICS READQ   TD
QUEUE('PAY1')
INTO(PRINT-IMAGE)
LENGTH(PRINT-LENGTH)
END-EXEC.
```

When the DEDUCTION-SEGMENT is read, the record will be truncated and the LENGERR condition will occur, since PRINT-LENGTH is now set at the 90 character max limit.

11.6 THE DELETE COMMAND

The format for the DELETEQ TD command is simple:

```
EXEC CICS DELETEQ TD
QUEUENAME(name)
[SYSID(name)]

Conditions: ISCINVREQ, QIDERR, SYSIDERR
```

The DELETEQ TD command will delete the entire transient data queue for you. In the Destination Control Table (DCT), a REUSE option is available. If REUSE = YES, then the DELETEQ is not necessary, and we will be simply depleting the queue via the READQ TD statement. If REUSE = NO and it is desired to use the queue a number of times, it will be necessary to code the DELETEQ command.

Using our previous example, we may say:

```
EXEC CICS DELETEQ TD
    QUEUE('PAY1')
    END-EXEC.
```

SUMMARY

Transient data is used as batch input to non-CICS programs and must be defined through the Destination Control Table. Transient Data utilizes both intrapartition and extrapartition destination queues associated with the CICS partition, where the destination of the data may be a file or a terminal.

Automatic Task Initiation (ATI) is one of a number of features of intrapartition destination; it is used to trigger or initiate a transaction automatically.

The READQ TD command will read the contents of a queue. Note that as you are reading the queue, you are actually depleting the contents of such. At the end, a QZERO condition will occur; this condition should be referred to in your HANDLE CONDITION statement.

The WRITEQ TD command will add a record or a data element to the transient queue, as you specify it.

The DELETEQ TD command will delete the entire transient data queue for you. If REUSE = YES in your Destination Control Table, then the DELETEQ TD command is redundant.

The READQ, the WRITEQ, and the DELETEQ commands must be followed by the TD, or Transient Data, acronym: otherwise TS, or Temporary Storage, will be assumed.

The ENQ and DEQ commands are used to protect a resource from concurrent use by more than one task.

Trigger level or TRIGLEV is specified to define to the system the number of records to be accumulated for a destination before those records are automatically processed.

The extrapartition transient queue allows CICS to access batch files via the on-line system's sequential (rather than VSAM or other) access methods.

Intrapartition transient queues on the other hand are utilized to collect data entered interactively, but processed later on through a batch program.

QUESTIONS

1. What is the general purpose of transient data?
2. Describe what is meant by extrapartition destination.
3. Explatin what is meant by intrapartition destination.
4. True or false: When specifying a READQ command without TD (an acronym for transient data), the read automatically defaults to temporary storage, or TS.
5. What does the REUSE option represent in the destination control table?
6. What is the function of the TRIGLEV option?
7. Describe the mechanism available to maintain and update transient data record.
8. Explain the function of the ENQ and DEQ commands.

12

Interval Control

HIGHLIGHTS
- Overview
- ASKTIME Command
- DELAY Command
- POST Command
- WAIT Command
- START Command
- RETRIEVE Command
- CANCEL Command

12.1 OVERVIEW

The interval control functions provided by CICS are designed to allow a task to be scheduled and executed some time in the future. Such functions are called time-controlled functions, and in this chapter we will briefly review a number of basic commands associated with those functions.

When you need the current date or time of day, you simply query the system via the ASKTIME command. When you want to delay the processing of a particular task, because of other events still pending, you can issue a DELAY command. You need to rely on the POST command to attain some notification from the system as to whether or not the time allocated to the task has expired.

The START command is used to start a task at a specific time. When you need data sent by the START command, simply issue a RETRIEVE statement. Finally, when you decide to cancel a previously issued DELAY, POST, or START commands, you will issue a CANCEL command. Note that there are some definite rules for cancelling previously issued tasks. For example, a DELAY command can only be cancelled prior to its expiration. A START command can be cancelled only prior to the expiration of the original command.

The time during which a task will execute is called *expiration time*. Expiration time may be expressed by assuming the 24-hour clock identical to the military time concept. Thus, 10:30 A.M. is expressed as 103000, and 4:00 P.M. is equivalent to 16000000. Midnight is 000000. This may also be referred to as the *absolute time of the day*.

12.2 THE ASKTIME COMMAND

This command is used only when you need to update the EIBDATE and the EIBTIME fields in the EIB block. Initially, the above two fields contain the date and the time when the task was started. If during the processing of your transaction you will need to retrieve and update data, you will be able to do so through the EIBDATE and the EIBTIME modules.

The format for the EIBDATE is PIC S9(7) COMP-3. The date is in packed decimal format: OOYYDDD+, whereby YY represents the last two digits of the calendar year, and DDD the julian date. EIBTIME is in the same packed decimal format, specified by OHHMMSS+, with HH representing the hour, MM the minutes, and SS the seconds. Note that the interval control request needs a unique identifier if it is ever to be cancelled. This can be specified in your application program via the request identifier, or else CICS will provide one for you and place it in the EIBREQID, part of the exec interface block we covered earlier.

12.3 THE DELAY COMMAND

You may issue a DELAY command to request CICS to suspend the processing of the requested (issuing) task until a specified time of the day. Note that this command cancels any POST request for this task. Assume you would like to suspend the processing of a task for two minutes. The following would need to be coded:

```
EXEC CICS DELAY
     INTERVAL(200)
     REQUID(TASK1)
END-EXEC.
```

Now, assume you want to delay a task until 11:00 A.M.

```
EXEC CICS DELAY
     TIME(110000)
     REQUID(TASK1)
END-EXEC.
```

The standard format for the DELAY command is shown in Fig. 12-1.

12.4 THE POST COMMAND

You may request to be notified by CICS that the time that was assigned to your task has expired. Note that a given task may only have one outstanding POST at the time. What the POST command does is to make a timer available to your task initially set to binary zero, and this will remain available during the task that is issuing the POST command.

If you were to issue a DELAY command, a START command, or even a new POST command during your current task, they will supercede your last POST command.

```
EXEC CICS DELAY
     (INTERVAL(HHMMSS) TIME(HHMMSS))
     (REQID(NAME))
END-EXEC.

Where HH specifies the hours
      MM specifies the minutes
      SS specifies the seconds.
```

Fig. 12-1. Standard format for the DELAY command.

Let's say that you request a timer for a task that you want posted after 25 seconds.

```
EXEC CICS POST
     INTERVAL(25)
     REQUID(TASK1)
     SET(CNTR)
END-EXEC.
```

SET will specify a pointer that will actually point you to the address where the timer is located (a four-position field). If you do not specify a REQID in your statement, CICS will assign one automatically and return it to your application program in the EIBREQID field (review the EIB block).

```
EXEC CICS POST
     TIME(SPECS)
     SET(ADRS)
END-EXEC.
```

The standard format for the POST command is given below:

```
EXEC CICS POST (INTERVAL(HHMMSS) / INTERVAL(0) / TIME(HHMMSS))
     SET(POINTER-REF)
     (REQID(NAME))
     END-EXEC.
```

12.6 THE WAIT COMMAND

The WAIT command is issued to synchronize a task with the completion of an event initiated by the same task or by another. The WAIT EVENT command provides a convenient way of giving up control to some other task until the event being waited on is completed.

```
EXEC CICS WAIT EVENT
     ECADDR(POINTER-VALUE)
END-EXEC.
```

Note that the pointer value contains the address of an event control area that is specified by the ECADDR option.

12.6 THE START COMMAND

CICS will let you start a transaction (task) through another task. We usually want to do this in case our initial task needs access to some facilities it doesn't own, such as a terminal other than the one we are using for input. For example, we may need a printer to schedule the priority of a payroll transaction because of the logical dependency on the success or the failure of one task relative to another. There may be other reasons as well. You might want a task to run (execute) at a given time, or you may want to run your task using different priorities than the ones you have initially requested. The syntax of the START command is shown in Fig. 12-2. Some of the options in this figure were covered earlier; however, we need to elaborate on both the time and the interval options.

INTERVAL(HHMMSS) tells CICS to start the transaction in HH hours MM minutes and SS seconds from the current time. The hours may be from 00 to 99; however, the minutes and seconds should not exceed 59. If you would like to start a task in two days and forty-five minutes, then INTERVAL (484500) should be in your START command.

TIME(HHMMSS) tells CICS to start the transaction at a specific time using 24-hour military time. The following rules must be observed.

If the current time is 060000 (6:00 A.M.) or later, and the time value is less than six hours before the current time, CICS assumes that you mean a time in the past, causing the task to start as soon as possible. This would have the same result as if the interval of zero had been set.

If the current time is less than 060000, and the expiration time is less than the current time, then the time is also considered to be in the past. Note, however, that the time given is never taken to be before midnight of the current day.

In all other cases, CICS assumes that the time is in the future. If you specify a time with an hours component greater than twenty-three, you are specifying a time on a day following the current one. That is, a time of 250000 means 1:00 A.M. on the day following the current one.

If neither the interval nor the time is specified, then CICS defaults to

```
EXEC CICS START
     (INTERVAL(HHMMSS) / TIME(HHMMSS))
     TRANSID(NAME)
     (REQID(NAME))
     (FROM(DATA-AREA))
     LENGTH(DATA-VALUE)(FMH))
     TERMID(NAME)
     (SYSID(NAME))
     (RTRANS(NAME))
     (RTERMID(NAME))
     (QUEUE(NAME))
END-EXEC.
```

Fig. 12-2. Standard format for the START command.

a time of zero. Other options specified in the start command are as follows:

TERMID   is the identifier of the terminal that must be made available to the task being started. This parameter is optional and should only be specified if the transaction requires a terminal.

FROM   contains the area from which the data will be passed to the transaction being started.

LENGTH   is the length of the data being passed (half-word binary) and is required when the from option is present.

RTERMID   specifies an area that can be used in the TERMID option of the START command that may be executed subsequently. (A four-byte area.)

RTRANSID   specifies an area that can be used in the TRANSID option of the START command that may be executed subsequently. (A four-byte area.)

QUEUE   specifies the name of the queue that may be accessed by the transaction that is issuing the RETRIEVE command. (The data area must be eight characters in length.)

Let us now look at some examples. Suppose we would like to start a task in two hours and this task is not associated with any terminals:

```
EXEC CICS START
     TRANSID('SCHD')
     INTERVAL(020000)
     REQID('TASK1')
END-EXEC.
```

Now assume we would like to initiate a task without specifying the request identifier. As we mentioned earlier, under these circumstances CICS will automatically assign one and returns it to the application program in the EIBREQID field (in the exec interface block).

```
EXEC CICS START
TRANSID('SCHD')
TIME(1044500)
TERMID('TRM1')
END-EXEC.
```

Finally, assume we want to start a task associated with a terminal and pass data to it:

```
EXEC CICS START
TRANSID('SCHD')
TIME(194500')
TERMID('TRM1')
REQID(FIELD2)
LENGTH(20)
END-EXEC.
```

12.7 THE RETRIEVE COMMAND

You will use the RETRIEVE command to get access to data that was sent by the START function. Notice the difference between the RETRIEVE and the RECEIVE commands. Both commands can be used to get the initial input to a transaction, but they can't be used interchangeably. RECEIVE must be used in a transaction that is initiated by input from a terminal, while RETRIEVE must be used in a transaction that was started by another transaction. Figure 12-3 shows the format for the RETRIEVE command with a number of available options.

If no more data exists, the ENDDATA exception condition will take place. If an IOERR occurs, you may try to READ one more time by simply reissuing the RETRIEVE command.

Let us illustrate how the RETRIEVE command works along with the START command. Assume that program PAY1 utilizes the START com-

```
EXEC CICS RETRIEVE
[INTO(DATA AREA) / SET(POINTER-REF)]
[LENGTH(DATA AREA)]
[RTRANSID(DATA AREA)]
[RTERMID(DATA AREA)]
[QUEUE(DATA AREA)]
[WAIT]
END-EXEC.
```

INTO	SPECIFIES THE USER AREA INTO WHICH THE RETRIEVED DATA WILL BE WRITTEN.
SET	SPECIFIES THE POINTER REFERENCE TO BE SET TO THE ADDRESS OF THE RETRIEVED DATA.
LENGTH	IN CONJUNCTION WITH THE INTO OPTION, LENGTH SPECIFIESTHE MAXIMUM LENGTH OF THE DATA THAT YOUR PROGRAM IS PREPARED TO HANDLE. IF THE DATA EXCEEDS THE LENGTH, IT IS TRUNCATED, AND THE LENGERR CONDITION WILL OCCUR. ON COMPLETION, LENGTH IS SET TO THE ORIGINAL LENGTH OF THE DATA. WITH THE SET OPTION CICS WILL GET THE LENGTH OF THE DATA SUPPLIED.
RTRANSID	SPECIFIES AN AREA THAT MAY BE USED IN THE TRANSID OPTION OF A START COMMAND THAT MAY BE EXPECTED SUBSEQUENTLY (A FOUR BYTE AREA).
RTERMID	SPECIFIES AN AREA THAT MAY BE USED IN THE TERMID OPTION OF A START COMMAND THAT MAY BE EXECUTED AFTERWARD (ALSO A FOUR BYTE FIELD).
QUEUE	SPECIFIES THE NAME OF THE QUEUE THAT MAY BE ACCESSED BY THE TRANSACTION ISSUING THE RETRIEVED COMMAND. THE DATA AREA MUST BE EIGHT CHARACTERS IN LENGTH.
WAIT	SPECIFIES THAT, IF ALL EXPIRED DATA HAS BEEN RETRIEVED THE TASK IS TO BE PUT INTO A WAIT STATE UNTIL FURTHER EXPIRED DATA RECORDS BECOME AVAILABLE.

Fig. 12-3. Standard format for the RETRIEVE command, with a number of available options.

mand, when a user requests the printing of a report. The START command looks like this.

```
EXEC CICS START
TRANSID('A002')
FROM(PAYTRAN1)
LENGTH(LEN)
TERMID(PRNTS)
END-EXEC.
```

Program PAY1 (TRANSID = A001), will trigger the next program, having the TRANSID of A002, as soon as the printer (PRNTS) is available to be its terminal. Program PAY2, initiated by program PAY1, in turn will issue the following RETRIEVE command in order to RETRIEVE the data passed from the PAY1 program.

```
EXEC CICS RETRIEVE
INTO(PAYTRAN2)
LENGTH(LEN)
END-EXEC.
```

Note that PAYTRAN1 and PAYTRAN2 refer to data areas in the WORKING-STORAGE section of both programs. LEN and LEN1 are used respectively in each program, both having the same length binary fields.

```
77  LEN   PIC  S9(4) COMPUTATIONAL VALUE +200.
77  LEN1  PIC  S9(4) COMPUTATIONAL VALUE +200.
```

As you can see, Interval Control keeps track of both tasks through the invocation of the second task by the first via the TRANSID.

12.8 THE CANCEL COMMAND

In order to cancel a previously issued DELAY, POST, or START command, you may issue the CANCEL command. Remember two facts about the working of the CANCEL command:

1. You may only cancel a DELAY command prior to its expiration.
2. A START command may only be cancelled prior to the expiration of the original command.

You may cancel a task by naming the Request Identifier REQID) of the tasks or via the transaction identifier; for example:

```
EXEC CICS CANCEL
REQID(RIDFR)
END-EXEC.
```

Here we assume that you already have identified your REQID, when you issued your START command. Your START statement could have looked like this:

```
MOVE 'REVERSALS' TO RIDFR
EXEC CICS CANCEL
TRANSID('C008')
INTERVAL(004500)
REQID(RIDFR)
END-EXEC.
```

Another way would be to check and store the contents of the EIBREQID field, which is given in your application program (see the EIBLK EXEC Interface Block) by merely using the DFHEIBLK in the LINKAGE SECTION. The format for the CANCEL command is presented below:

```
EXEC CICS CANCEL
[REQID(NAME)]
[TRANSID(NAME)]
END-EXEC.
```

SUMMARY

The purpose of interval control is to allow a task to be scheduled and executed some time in the future. Such functions are also referred to as time control functions.

When you need the current date or time of the day, you simply query the system via the ASKTIME command. This command is used to update the EIBDATE and the EIBTIME fields in the Execute Interface Block (EIB).

When you wish to delay the processing of a given task, you issue the DELAY command. This command will suspend the processing of the requested (issuing) task until a specified time of the day. Time is specified in terms of military time. For example, 10:00 A.M. would be shown as 100000, or in a full CICS format:

```
EXEC CICS DELAY
TIME (100000)
REQID(TASKA)
END-EXEC.
```

You can use the POST command to attain notification from the system concerning whether or not the time allocated to the task has expired. If you were to issue a DELAY, START, or a new POST command during your current task, it will supercede your last POST command.

A WAIT command is issued to synchronize a task with the completion of an event initiated by the same task or by another. The START command is used to start a task at a specific time. There may be several reasons for starting a task, such as to have access to a terminal we do not own, to arrange different priorities, or to run a task at a predetermined time.

When you need to have access to data that was initiated by the START command, a RETRIEVE statement is issued. The difference between a RETRIEVE and a RECEIVE command is as follows:

A RECEIVE command must be used in a transaction that is initiated by input from a terminal.

A RETRIEVE command must be used in a transaction that is started by another transaction.

A CANCEL command is issued to nullify previously issued DELAY, POST, or START commands. You may only cancel a DELAY command prior to its expiration, and a START command may only be cancelled prior to the expiration of the original command.

QUESTIONS

1. Describe the function of the ASKTIME command.
2. Explain the INTERVAL and the TIME options in the DELAY command.
3. Explain what we mean by INTERVAL(241000) in the START command.
4. What relationship exists between the START and the RETRIEVE commands?
5. Explain the difference between the RETRIEVE and the RECEIVE commands. Can a RECEIVE command be issued in conjunction with a START command?
6. Can you cancel a DELAY command after its expiration date?
7. What does the CANCEL command do?
8. Can you cancel a task via the transaction identifier?

13
Systems Design Under CICS Command: Part 1

HIGHLIGHTS
- Overview
- The Menu Concept
- Table Drive Systems
- The Help Screen

13.1 OVERVIEW

The purpose of this chapter is to review some of the design considerations under CICS/VSAM. It is my intention to review not only what's unique to CICS, but more generically what is unique to interactive processing. Systems design in an on-line real-time environment is most concerned with how the various components of the system fit together, including the transportability of its components.

Fifteen or perhaps twenty years ago, when application programs were developed in a truly batch environment, each program was designed to perform a maximum number of functions. Some times the limit to the number of instructions utilized in the program depended upon the core or the memory size of the system. That is why overlays were frequently used with assembler type languages such as Autocoder or Basic Assembler Language (BAL). For the record, BAL is still preferred over a high-level language by most systems programming staff. Ironically, core or memory size is no longer an issue when using an assembler language. Today, the total number of instructions per program have dramatically shrunk from thousands of lines of codes to a few hundred lines or less. In the past, the application programmer tried to jam dozens of functions into the logic of his program. On-line programs are a great deal more limited. Here the size of the program has to do with efficiency, clarity, response time, and a relatively large list of other considerations.

On-line programs are referred to as tasks or transactions. The terminology is quite correct in the sense that an on-line program should only perform one task at a time and then terminate. Thus, a well-written program should not go beyond several hundred lines, preferably less. This would exclude copy routines such as maps and record layouts brought into the program from the various control tables, such as the DFHAID, the DFHBMSCA, or the DFHEIVAR blocks, most of which are triggered by the system.

One of the most visible symptoms of faulty design may be evident via the response time. We talked briefly about response time earlier. It is an unwritten rule that when the user has to wait more than a few seconds to get results from the on-line system, he or she will be quite vocal about it. A ten-second response time may get the attention of the vice president, and anything beyond that may signal the possible scrapping of the system, all things being equal. Here, we're assuming that the system's configuration is just powerful enough to allow other applications to respond within an acceptable time frame.

Response time is a relative term, and because of its overbearing influence on the success or the failure of the system, we would like to review some of the conditions that may influence response time.

File size is definitely a factor, although with VSAM (using KSDS, as described in chapter 15) you may only have to make one pass at the key. If, however, your installation is still under the Indexed Sequential Access Method, or ISAM, you may run into some serious problems toward the end of the day, as more and more maintenance type operations are being performed against your file. As you probably know by now, ISAM will place the newly added records into an overflow area; they will remain there until the file is reorganized. In the meantime, pointers are constructed by the access method redirecting the path from the prime to the overflow areas.

To further complicate things relative to response time, let us introduce a second problem affecting it. This is the overall user population competing for the valuable resources. The word *resources* is actually a common term for a number of topics encompassing both hardware and software.

First of all, we're talking about the ability of the computer system, namely the hardware, to handle the current load. If, for example, the computer system is already saturated with applications in terms of both CPU cycles and clock time, the systems analyst will have to present suggested changes affecting the current hardware in his impact study. Some upgrading, such as acquiring new and faster direct access devices, different terminals, and satellite printers.

Another factor in estimating response time is the cyclical nature of computer usage. There is a trend by certain user groups to utilize the computer more extensively at one point during the day, even if for a relatively short time. In a university environment, for example, student registration is a highly cyclical event. Unfortunately when it hits, it tends to bring even the more organized and efficient data centers to their knees.

Finally, I believe that response time may also be the direct outcome of how efficiently or inefficiently an application program is coded. It would definitely be worth the analyst's time to audit some of the codes generated by his programmers. When you continually transmit data from the application program to the terminal, make sure you only send the entire map when it is absolutely necessary, otherwise send data only (DATAONLY).

13.2 THE MENU CONCEPT

Menu-driven systems essentially help modularize broad ranges of activities into individual user-oriented procedures. The use of menus actually simplifies the inherent complexities of the total systems design, because they tend to create processing paths for the user to follow. They list options for him, and overall, they provide a high level of organization of functions that would otherwise be difficult to handle.

Menu screens may be triggered a number of ways, based upon selection conditions. Selection conditions may be entered on the menu screen through a code, an acronym, a function key, or a light pen. It is also possible to enter a number of conditions using a single code, while explaining the terminology either right on the menu screen or through the use of help screens.

Let us illustrate the concept, starting with Fig. 13-1.

Level I

The Systems Directory Menu shown in Fig. 13-2 allows the terminal operator to branch to any one of the major functions in the system. This menu is displayed after the operator identifies himself through a password. The password is then checked against a table of authorizations in order to determine if the password is indeed a valid one, and if it is, then, whether or not it is valid in conjunction with a particular code. For example, the system must control what happens if the operator's password is only valid for entering the Position Control subsystem, yet he wants to have access to the entire payroll.

Whatever communications (positive or negative) the system triggers will be displayed in the slot shown as SYSTEMS OR ERROR MESSAGES. Note that once the terminal operator is done using the Systems Menu screen, he will probably not have to return to it until the end of the day, if at all, since logging off procedures normally take place on lower level screens.

Assume now that the terminal operator elected function 3 on the screen, with the proper password, and press the Enter key. (We visualize that the vice president in charge of finance or administration will have an all purpose password that will allow him to view all major functions displayed on the main menu screen.) The terminal operator has invoked the Payroll system, on Level II, as shown in Fig. 13-3.

Level II

At this point, the operator has access to the payroll and will specify to the system the kind of maintenance he'll be performing. Legitimate codes are 01 through 11 and either the character S or the character X. Otherwise an error message will be displayed on the bottom of the screen informing the operator of an undefined code.

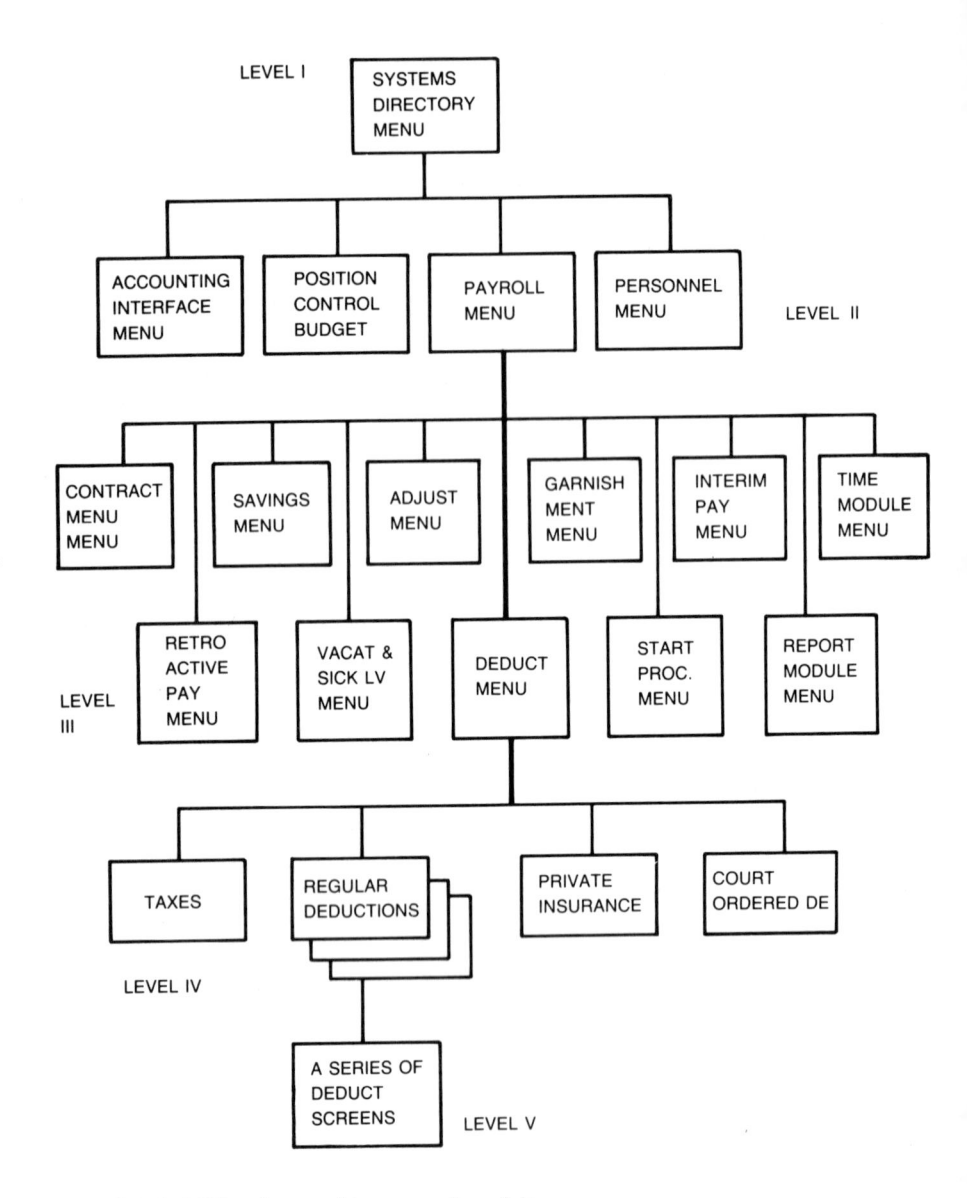

Fig. 13-1. A multilevel menu-driven payroll module.

As you can see, the operator can also sign off here without ever returning to the systems menu screen. Assume now that the operator selected task number 9 in order to enter deduction-related information for new employees. This selection will take him to Level III or to the Deductions menu, which is shown in Fig. 13-4.

172

```
                    SYSTEMS MENU SCREEN


             1.   ACCOUNTING INTERFACE MENU

             2.   POSITION CONTROL MENU

             3.   PAYROL MENU

             4.   PERSONNEL MENU

             5.   SIGN OFF


             _    ENTER SELECTION HERE
            ____  ENTER PASSWORD HERE


        .....RESERVED FOR SYSTEMS OR ERROR MESSAGES.....
```

Fig. 13-2. The general or main menu representing the major functions available in the system.

Level III

The operator moved to Level III, one step short of his destination, which is the Regular Deductions screen. It is possible to enter the social security

```
                    PAYROLL MENU SCREEN

             01   CONTRACT PAY STATUS MENU SCREEN
             02   SAVINGS BONDS MENU
             03   ADJUSTMENTS TO DEDUCTIONS MENU
             04   GARNISHMENT MENU
             05   INTERIM PAY MENU
             06   TIME MODULE MENU
             07   RETROACTIVE SALARY INCREASE MENU
             08   VACATION AND SICK LEAVE MENU
             09   DEDUCTIONS MENU
             10   START PAYROLL PROCESSING
             11   REPORT MODULE


             __   ENTER SELECTION CODE HERE

                  ENTER " S" IF YOU WISH TO RETURN TO THE MAIN
                  SYSTEMS MENU SCREEN.
                  ENTER " X" TO SIGN OFF.


        .....PROGRAMMED SYSTEMS OR ERROR MESSAGES HERE.....
```

Fig. 13-3. Level II functions relating to the payroll module.

```
                    DEDUCTIONS MENU

            1   FEDERAL AND STATE TAXES
            2   REGULAR DEDUCTIONS
            3   PRIVATE INSURANCE
            4   COURT ORDERED DEDUCTIONS


            _   ENTER DEDUCTION SELECTIONS HERE
          ___ __ ___     ENTER EMPLOYEE SOC.SEC.NO.HERE

         _____   ENTER LAST NAME
         _____   ENTER FIRST NAME
            _                   ENTER INITIAL


         "M" WILL RETURN YOU TO THE PAYROLL MENU
         "X" WILL SIGN YOU OFF THE SYSTEM.



         .....PROGRAMMED SYSTEMS OR ERROR MESSAGES HERE.....
```

Fig. 13-4. The deductions menu, showing a number of functions within the deductions module.

number of the employee here, along with the task or the function code. It is also possible to search the file generically, that is, via the last name or the full name, and then visually check to make sure that the employee selection is the correct one. (Look out for common names like John Smith or Dave Jackson).

Note that if you were to enter both the social security number and the name of the employee in question, program logic would prioritize your parameters to determine which entry should be executed and which should be overridden. That is a social security number search would override the employee name search. However, if both name and social security number were omitted, an error condition would prevail.

In order to keep the user from being boxed in, it is still possible to sign off the system at this point or return to the Payroll menu, if required. Also note that the password of a given user may determine the level of access he has. Some users, based on their password, may look at a particular screen without having the ability to modify its contents.

Assume now that our terminal operator enters the next selection code, which is 2. This will take him to Level IV, with the following screen shown in Fig. 13-5.

The purpose of the Regular Deduction screen is to:

1. allow the operator to enter the employee's regular deductions
2. inquire about the employee's regular deductions.

```
                    REGULAR DEDUCTION SCREEN
EMPLOYEE I.D. NUMBER    ___ __ ___
EMPLOYEE NAME           _____,_____ _
EMPLOYEE BANK ACCT.     _____


EMPLOYEE C HECK DISTRIBUTION CODE           _____

     DEDUCTION              CODE    %    AMOUNT      DESCRIPTION
     T.S.A. 1               ____   __   ____.__     _____
     T.S.A. 2               ____   __   ____.__     _____
     DEFERRED COMP.         ____   __   ____.__     _____
     UNION DUES             ____   __   ____.__     _____
     CREDIT UNION           ____   __   ____.__     _____
     ASSOCIATION FEE        ____   __   ____.__     _____
     CHARITY                ____   __   ____.__     _____
     MISCELLANEOUS 1        ____   __   ____.__     _____
     MISCELLANEOUS 2        ____   __   ____.__     _____


ENTER PATH
T=TAXES, P=PRIVATE INSURANCE, C=COURT ORDERED DEDUCTIONS (GARNISHMENT)
M=RETURN TO PAYROLL MENU, X=SIGN OFF.
DEPRESS COMMAND KEY 1 TO UPDATE.


........PROGRAMMED SYSTEMS/ERROR MESSAGES........
```

Fig. 13-5. The details necessary for a payroll deductions screen.

This screen is only concerned with the employee's optional deductions. Note that the terminal operator may process all of his fifteen new employees without ever leaving Level IV (Sublevel V) or the regular deductions screen. Once the information pertaining to the employee is processed and the record is updated (or left in its original state), he may start processing another employee by keying in his or her identification number at the top of the screen.

Add mode is automatically assumed if the ID number of the employee is not on the file. When this situation occurs, the terminal operator will see a screen that has not been filled in.

Update mode is assumed when the employee being processed is already on the file. (Delete essentially has the same mechanism.) If the record already exists all the operator has to do is to key in the employee's ID number (we use identification number and social security number interchangeably) and press the Enter key. This will display the employee's entire deduction segment.

In order to remain on the current screen and process the next employee, the terminal operator will leave the current path function blank. Note that branching to other Level IV screens is possible by merely entering the code T, for taxes, to P, for private insurance, and so on. Also note that Level V is merely a reiteration of Level IV dealing with the second occurrence of the same display screen and on.

Figure 13-5 illustrates the complexities of an on-line system. Although I presented only a one dimensional path (the deduction path from start to finish), you may easily visualize the depth of the system design in terms of screens, application programs, tables, and file structures.

13.3 TABLE-DRIVEN SYSTEMS

A table-driven system, although not purely an on-line innovation, gives the user a great deal of flexibility and organization. Although the concept was slowly developing with the advent of more sophisticated batch systems, ironically, it was the on-line system that became heavily dependent on the concept.

CICS, the software package itself, is essentially a table-driven system in the sense that all major functions, such as storing files, maps, programs, or even the transaction identifier, are systematically arranged in individualized datasets, or tables, accessible to a valid request.

If you have a need to draw upon the record layout of a certain master file, you can be sure that the system will provide you with the latest version of that file.

Tables are normally defined in a standard manner and centrally updated to avoid synchronization problems. Imagine, for a moment, that you work at a place that does not utilize copy statements. You may think of the COPY LIB concept as one of the functions provided by the use of tables. Suppose that instead of using a standard record layout that is available through a copy routine, you will individually have to develop it based on documentation, program specifications, and so on. A numeric field may be specified by one programmer as a binary (computational) field or as a packed (COMP-3) field by another. Or let us assume that through misunderstanding, one of the application programmers utilizes five in place of six positions for specifying a department. Can you imagine the mess that this would create? What if you had to code manually into your program an entire record layout? How susceptible to error would you be?

Many times when changes are made in a table, it may not require the recompilation of a number of source programs. Figures 13-6 through 13-8 illustrate the concept.

Using a department, a job classification, and a salary range table, we require minimum storage in the on-line file. Only eight bytes on the master file will allow us to access both job classification and department descriptions. In terms of space, the savings is quite extensive. If you have a file containing, let's say 35,000 transactions, and if you were to carry a 30-position vendor code in each of the 35,000 records, you'd be giving up over 1,000,000 bytes of storage that may otherwise be placed into a table requiring probably less than 4,000 bytes.

Tables, such as those presented in Figures 6-6 through 6-8 also allow

DEPARTMENT #	DESCRIPTION
1237	ENGINEERING
1240	ACCOUNTING
1388	AUDITING
1391	SUPPLIES
1470	DATA PROCESSING
1481	SALES

Fig. 13-6. A department table.

Fig. 13-7. An individual job description table.

JOB CLASS	JOB DESCRIPTION
0017	ACCOUNTANT III
0038	AUDITOR
0120	PURCHASING AGENT
0121	PROGRAMMER
0210	SR PROGRAMMER
0317	SYSTEMS ANALYST
0328	ACCOUNT REPRE

JOB CLASS	SALARY RANGES MIN/HR	MAX/HR
0017	12.251	23.170
0038	12.011	22.810
0120	09.131	19.118
0121	09.718	19.800
0210	12.100	21.700
0317	12.517	20.917
0328	08.123	14.12

Fig. 13-8. A salary range table.

the user to do complex cross-reference checking. For example, if an employee with job classification 0038, an auditor, is entered into the system with an hourly rate of $22.91, the system will access the job classification table first to verify the rate. According to the job classification table, 0038 may only go as high as $22.81; thus the rate must be investigated, and otherwise resolved. This may involve a decision outside the capacity of the terminal operator.

In addition to saving valuable storage, tables offer the advantages illustrated in the following example: You are to change the title corresponding to department 1237 from ENGINEERING to MECHANICAL ENGINEERING, since the Engineering Department is diversifying into a number of additional areas. If ENGINEERING is stored on each and every one of your records (say up to 200), needless to say that you'll have to change them individually, probably through an application program. With a table-driven system, you'll only have to change the description corresponding to Department 1237 once—no programs to write and not even any JCLs to worry about.

13.4 THE HELP SCREEN

Help Screens provide the user with information as to the options and the overall constraints of the system. Through a series of screen displays, it is a practical and a highly visual way to make a portion of documentation that applies to certain procedures available for the user.

One computer installation, for example, acquired a license to a vendor package that was quite expensive and terribly complex to use. The system came with 12 volumes of documentation, and it was estimated that training the staff would have taken months. This was complicated by the fact that the system had no on-line tutoring capabilities. Every problem, especially in the beginning, had to be researched and resolved either through one of the 12 volumes or else through expensive consulting fees paid to the vendor staff that often came on site to assist from their headquarter some 1400 miles away. A network of help screens probably would have helped considerably.

A help screen is usually invoked when the user has a specific problem in completing a particular task or procedure. By utilizing a command key, the terminal operator will be able to suspend his current activities, look up the answer on the next screen or series of screens, and branch back to the current transaction uninterrupted. The system is designed in such a fashion that when the user is, let's say, on the Garnishment screen, only garnishment related information will be prompted. Figures 13-9 through 13-11 illustrate this concept.

```
                GARNISHMENT DEDUCTION HELP SCREEN

   PAGE 1

   IF YOU WISH TO CONTINUE PLEASE DEPRESS COMMAND KEY 2.
   OTHERWISE DEPRESS THE ENTER KEY TO RETURN TO THE
   GARNISHMENT DEDUCTION SCREEN.

   NAME:  EMPLOYEE'S LAST NAME, FOLLOWED BY A COMMA (,),
          THEN FIRST NAME FOLLOWED BY A SPACE AND INITIAL (I).

   ID NUMBER IS THE EMPLOYEE'S SOCIAL SECURITY NUMBER. IN
      THIS SYSTEM BOTH TERMS, ARE USED INTERCHANGEABLY

   ACTION INDICATOR FOR EACH OF THESE GARNISHMENTS
      DEDUCTION, THERE IS AN ACTION INDICATOR WHICH
      DEFAULTS TO AN N. HOWEVER, THIS INDICATOR MAY HAVE
      A CODE ENTERED BY THE OPERATOR. THESE CODES ARE:

          1)  D   DELETES THE DEDUCTION RECORD
          2)  Y   DEDUCTION IS IN EFFECT
          3)  N   DEDUCTION IS TOPPED, BUT NOT DELETED

   GARNISHMENT AMOUNT:  TOTAL AMOUNT OF COURT ORDER
            FOR GARNISHMENT.......PERCENT(%) LIMIT IS 15
                                   TIME LIMIT 56 DAYS
```

Fig. 13-9. Page one of the help screen on garnishments.

GARNISHMENT DEDUCTION HELP SCREEN

PAGE 2

IF YOU WISH TO CONTINUE PLEASE DEPRESS COMMAND KEY 2.
OTHERWISE DEPRESS THE ENTER KEY TO RETURN TO THE
GARNISHMENT DEDUCTION SCREEN

RECEIVED: DATE ON WHICH THE COURT ORDER IS RECEIVED

START DATE: THE PAY PERIOD ENDING DATE ON WHICH THE
              DEDUCTION IS TO START.
STOP DATE: THE PAY PERIOD ENDING DATE ON WHICH THE
              LAST DEDUCTION WILL BE TAKEN.

Fig. 13-10. Page two of the help screen on garnishments.

Another way of handling help screens is to display only one field at a time and explain it. The particular screen displayed would reflect the location of your cursor at that time. Figure 13-12 illustrates this concept.

From the examples given, you probably visualize by now the important role played by the help screens; however, we must also point out to you the negative aspect of using such a powerful tool—the significant cost

```
              GARNISHMENT DEDUCTIONS

   NAME:          KOWALSKI, CAROL A.
   I.D.NO.    121-70-3988
   ACTION INDICATOR:            N

   GARNISHMENT DOCUMENT NO.   113344755800
   GARNISHMENT AMOUNT:        $ 218.14
   RECEIVE DATA:              01-17-86
   START DATE·                01-22-86
   STOP DATE:                 03-02-86
   STATE AMOUNT:              $ 20.15
   LOCAL AMOUNT               $ 18.00

   TOTAL AMOUNT WITHHELD AS OF TODAY: $ 152.60
   PERCENT(%)                                15
   CREDITOR'S NAME:  THE SEVEN BROS. FAMILY FINANCE CO.

   PATH: T=TAXES, R=REGULAR DEDUCTIONS, P=PRIVATE
   INSURANCE, S=SAVINGS BONDS, C=COURT ORDERED
   DEDUCTIONS , M=PAY MENU, X=SIGN OFF,   PF1= HELP
```

Fig. 13-11. The employee garnishment deduction screen showing employee detail (Level IV) type data.

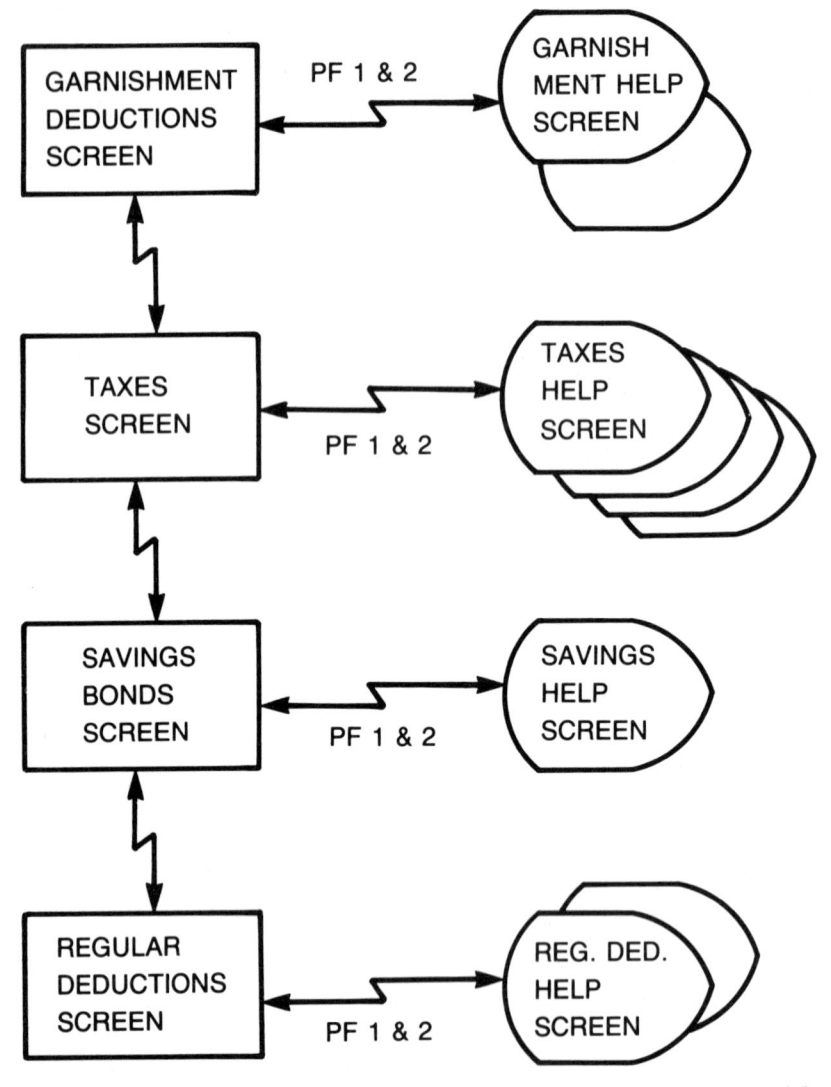

Fig. 13-12. The functional relationship between the invoking, or work screens and the invoked, or help, screens.

in addition to the initial cost of developing your system. An elaborate help screen scheme may add as much as 30 percent to the initial cost of developing the product. When you buy a license to a vendor package, you can be sure your fee will also reflect the additional cost. Small on-line systems (with a total line of codes equal to or less than 5,000) may not require any help functions. However, depending on the complexities of even a small scale system, you might want to provide the user with limited HELP functions.

SUMMARY

Earlier programming techniques utilizing assembler type languages, for example, required extensive overlays because of the limited core or memory size of most systems.

On-line programs are referred to as tasks or transactions. The idea is that on-line programs should only perform a single task and then terminate.

One of the most visible symptoms of faulty design is poor response time. Response time is a relative term dependent on a number of conditions such as:

File size
Access method
The number of users competing for the same resources
Constraint by the current hardware configuration
The way a program is written

Menu-driven systems help modularize broad ranges of activities into individual, user-oriented procedures. The use of menus simplifies the inherent complexities of the total systems design, since they tend to create processing paths with options and alternatives for the user.

The main menu is normally geared to be general, showing limited, high-level definitions. These definitions then become more detailed as they are further broken down via the submenus. Table-driven systems, although not purely an on-line innovation, provide the user with added flexibility and organizational capabilities.

CICS is essentially a table-driven system in the sense that all major functions, such as storing files, maps, programs or even transaction identifiers, are systematically arranged in individual datasets or tables accessible to a valid request. In addition, tables save substantial space and simplify maintenance efforts.

Help screens provide the user with information as to the options and the overall constraints of the system. A Help screen is normally invoked when the user has a specific problem in completing a particular task or procedure. By utilizing a Command key, the terminal operator can suspend his current activities, look up the answer on the next screen or series of screens, and then branch back to the current transaction uninterrupted.

QUESTIONS

1. True or false: Menu driven systems tend to simplify overall maintenance of a given system.
2. What are some of the considerations with regard to designing screen sequences called paths?

3. True or false: Tables are simple to use, but the analyst should minimize their occurrence since they require a great deal of storage facilities, both main and auxiliary.
4. Describe the purpose of using help screens in the system.
5. Which one of the following factors does not affect response time?

   File size
   Overall hardware configuration
   Programming language
   Access method
   The number of users using the system

6. When the terminal operator enters his password on the screen in order to initiate processing, what action will be taken by the systems? Explain.
7. Selections entered on the menu screen may be triggered through the use of . . . (specify three alternatives).

14
Systems Design Under CICS Command: Part 2

HIGHLIGHTS
* **Message Prompting**
* **Creating Paths**
* **Locating Data**
* **Add, Change, and Delete Mechanism**

14.1 MESSAGE PROMPTING

In Chapter 13, we talked about the user help screen. Help screens are normally in need when the terminal operator requires extensive information on what path to follow or what particular code must be entered into the system.

The truth is that a system must be able to continually direct the user as to the status of his inquiries. Message prompting is one of the easiest ways to accomplish that. This method, although not a substitute for the help screens (nor is it as comprehensive as the former), provides the user with vital information. Messages of potential problems or required directions may be displayed on the screen in a number of ways:

1. You may display a message to the user whenever you establish that line(s) of communications on the screen
2. You may also alter the present format of any data element(s) in question. When there is an error condition, you may want to highlight a particular field or fields involved. If your terminal is capable of displaying colors, you may be anxious to develop your own color scheme to remind the user of potential problems or erroneous data entry.

The message prompting capabilities of the system may also be utilized by the user as an extensive tutoring device. Let us illustrate this point. Let's say that you're in the process of entering a new employee on the screen. This screen (Fig. 14-1) contains mandatory and optional fields. The header next to each mandatory field may either be intensified or underscored. If the terminal is capable of displaying colors (such as red, blue, green, or intensified white) the operator may want to rely on them for the purpose of verification. the cursor is initially positioned at the first (high-order) character of the Employee I.D. (or Soc. Sec. Number). Since the operator must add new employees to the file, as part of his standard daily routine, he'll start

```
              EMPLOYEE DEMOGRAPHIC PROFILE

         EMPLOYEE I.D.           ___ __ ___
         JOB CLASS CODE     _____     DEPARTMENT #   _____
         STREET ADDRESS           _____
         CITY                  _____   ZIP CODE  _____
         AREA CODE  ___   TELEPHONE NO.  ___-____
         HOURLY RATE    ___.___        RETIREMENT %     ___
         FATHER'S FULL NAME       _____
         ENTER AN "X" IF YOU WISH TO SIGN OFF.
         FUNCTION KEY 1 WILL UPDATE THE FILE
         FUNCTION KEY 2 WILL RETURN YOU TO THE MAIN MENU

         ENTER CODE HERE  _

            .....SYSTEMS MESSAGE(s)/ERROR.
```

Fig. 14-1. Overview of a simplified employee demographic profile for adding new employees to the permanent pay master file.

with a blank screen. If he isn't sure just how to start the daily processing, he may press the Enter key. (Note that we indicate field lengths on each blank screen through underscoring.) Once the Enter key is used alone one of the following responses may be expected:

1. You may alter the color or the intensity of the Employee ID header.
2. You may decide to change the attribute byte of the cursor in order to make it blink.
3. You may wish to display a message saying "EMPLOYEE ID FIELD IS MANDATORY—RESUBMIT".

Let's say now that the terminal operator is ready to enter the employee's ID, but he accidentally enters it as an alphanumeric field. (We're assuming that there is no numeric lock feature on the keyboard, which is the case most frequently). If he were to press the Enter key at this point, the header next to the employee ID field would be modified, as before, but now in addition to the header, the corresponding field would also be modified either by changing the color of the original entry or simply by highlighting the field. The message on the bottom of the screen would read "EMPLOYEE ID NUMBER MUST BE NUMERIC—RESUBMIT".

To consistently apply the same rules, the job class and the department fields should be treated in a similar fashion to that of the employee's identification field, utilizing the same prompting mechanism. However, let's assume that the operator never presses the Enter key (which is to trigger the transaction) until the entire screen is filled and there are multiple errors to resolve.

The application programmer, of course, may move the cursor to any erroneous field on the screen, but only to the first selected position. (This is done by moving a −1 into the length attribute of the selected field as it is shown on the map). To be more specific about pinpointing an error, the header, corresponding to every erroneous field may be intensified, underscored, or otherwise modified. In the message displayed we want to be able to reflect a number of possibilities. We may specifically refer to the first error on the screen, saying that the job class or department code is missing or not numeric. We may also want to display a more general error message saying that there has been a number of errors during the processing of the transaction and we're now unable to continue.

The main advantage of the message-prompting mechanism is that it reassures the operator that eventually there will be an explanation of whatever problem he is experiencing, and instructions indicating how to resolve that problem.

Now let's look briefly at the optional data elements in the system. These may be classified into two categories:

1. Totally optional, meaning that whatever is entered or not entered in that field will be accepted by the system. Your telephone number may be numeric, or alphanumeric for that matter. If you don't have one that's not going to hinder you from getting paid.
2. Restricted optional fields are those fields that will force you to comply with certain rules and regulations as long as you decided to enter them. For example, zip code may not be a mandatory field. If it isn't, you don't have to enter it. However, if you do enter it, it has to be numeric and of a certain length, or else an error condition will prevail.

If the address field is mandatory, what criterion would you use in order to verify its presence? Would you check to make sure that it hasn't bee entirely left blank? If you check for spaces in the logic of your program, all you have to do is to enter a single character in the address field, and you have created a valid data element.

How do you convey to the user path or function key related information?

There are error conditions triggered by the systems through elaborate cross-reference checks. For example, the terminal operator enters an hourly rate for an employee who is salaried. Once again an error condition prevails.

The question you want to resolve at the time you are designing the system is the amount of initial and the amount of follow up checking you must perform. Can you accept the data at one point in time, having satisfied all the initial rules, only to reject it at the end? The answer is not an easy one. If you want to thoroughly verify your data right at the beginning, you may have to access a number of files initially. If you do that, you may visibly degrade response time. Also, you may not have access to all the information that early. In data processing, like in real life, everything may be the question of trade-offs. You may get all the options you want provided you pay for it—that is, pay for it not just in terms of money, but in terms of opportunity costs, response time, overall efficiency, and so on.

14.2 CREATING PATHS

Pathing is a self-dictating mechanism that allows the user to perform his functions within a given set of constraints. Every screen utilized in the system should have sufficient flexibility so that the user would not have to continually access higher-level screens to perform related functions.

Figure 14-2 shows a higher-level deduction menu screen and paths leading into the taxes, the savings bonds, and the private insurance deduction

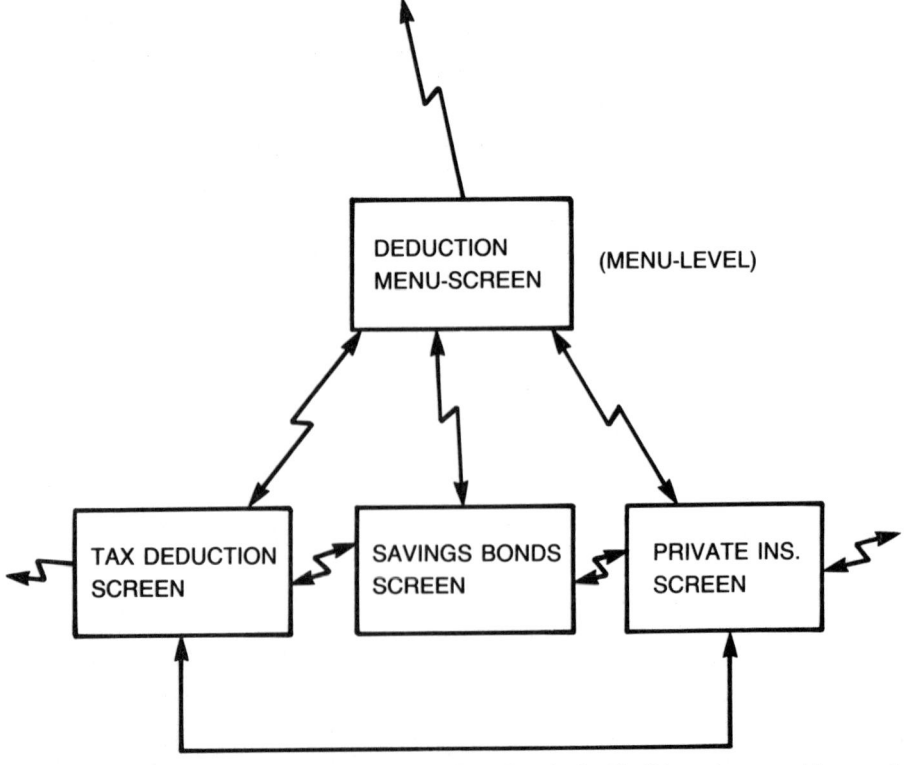

Fig. 14-2. Possible paths working both horizontally and vertically. Flexible systems provide a great deal of horizontal movement so that the operator does not have to jump back to the menu level after each transaction.

screens. Assume you're on the deductions sublevel doing savings bonds deductions for a particular employee; upon completing that task, you'd like to branch to his private insurance module and then subsequently to his taxes without having to jump back to the higher menu-levels. We've seen systems with pathing that would only allow you movement through the menu level. In other words, there was no mechanism set up to jump into the private deductions screen from the savings bonds or from the tax deductions screen.

When the terminal operator must process 150 employees a day in that fashion, the extra step or two may prove to be quite burdensome. There may be, however, situations in which there is no logical-path relationship between certain functions, or when pathing is restricted through a password. When the operator is performing his duties on Sublevel V and is done with his chores, would it make any sense for him to invoke a number of additional screens before he can successfully sign off?

What you need to do is to organize your functions logically and conveniently for the user without sacrificing efficiency or violating a given organizational concept and security. This requires a great deal of in-depth knowledge of the system that can only be attained through an extensive user interface and understanding of similar situations.

14.3 LOCATING DATA

How many times in the past month or two have you relied on an operator's assistance to locate a person or a particular business, and if you didn't have the correct information, such as the name and possibly the address, your chances of attaining the telephone number were pretty dim. Can you find the correct telephone number, for example, for Ron Smith in Chicago without as much as having his address and his initial? How would you trace an item in an inventory without knowing the associated reference number on a file that contains millions of entries?

During the preliminary run of the payroll system, let's say our terminal operator would like to attain some specific data on a number of people resident on the system. The Search Screen in Fig. 14-3 is designed for that purpose.

The first employee, George Q. Calhoun shows two pieces of information. The operator happens to know the person's zip code and his full name. If there is such an employee on file, both the social security number (PAYROLL SSNO ID) and the department code fields will be displayed. If there are more than one George Q Calhoun under 60126, the system will automatically display the first record it encounters on the file, placing a number next to the record count field. The number will indicate to the operator how many other records satisfy the above criteria.

Finally the destination field (DE), the last entry on the screen, will allow the operator to define the path once the search has been successfully completed. In Calhoun's case the terminal operator would like to branch to the employee's deductions screen.

All this is done in inquiry mode by writing key information of those entries in temporary storage. Afterward, by pressing the Enter key, the operator will automatically branch back to the search screen, while setting up the path for the next inquiry, if necessary.

The search to find the required information with regard to William Smith has located the first employee found on the Payroll Master and displayed it on the screen. As you can see in Fig. 14-4, without enough specifics, there were five additional candidates who fit the same criteria.

14.4 ADD, DELETE, AND CHANGE MECHANISMS

We have briefly touched upon the workings of the add mechanism during our discussion on message prompting. When adding a new record to the file, you may define the criteria using the NOTFND option in your HANDLE CONDITION statement. Every field on the file has to be edited to make sure that only the current information is processed. Once the record is edited, you are ready to update the file by writing it. There are two ways you may perform an update:

1. Once all the mandatory fields are entered and they conform to the required edit rules, you have in fact created a valid record on the file.
2. A second way of updating your file is via a positive action on your part.

```
                      SEARCH  SCREEN
       PAYROLL  (SSNO)  I.D.    _____
       NAME  OF  EMPLOYEE       CALHOUN, GEORGE Q._____

       DEPARTMENT  #            _____
       ZIP  CODE                60126

       RECORD  COUNT            __
       DESTINATION(DE)          __
       ----------------------------------------------------
                      SEARCH  SCREEN
       PAYROLL  (SSNO)  I.D.    147-60-9218
       NAME  OF  EMPLOYEE       CALHOUN, GEORGE Q.

       DEPARTMENT  #            12234
       ZIP  CODE                60126

       RECORD  COUNT            01
       DESTINATION              DE
```

Fig. 14-3. The search screen before and after the search.

```
                    SEARCH SCREEN

        PAYROLL (SSNO) I.D.      _____
        NAME OF EMPLOYEE         SMITH WILLIAM

        DEPARTMENT               _____
        ZIP CODE                 ___

        RECORD COUNT             __
        DESTINATION              IN
```

```
                    SEARCH SCREEN

        PAYROLL (SSNO) I.D.      119-56-4533
        NAME OF EMPLOYEE         SMITH, WILLIAM

        DEPARTMENT #             12333
        ZIP CODE                 60123

        RECORD COUNT             05
        DESTINATION              IN
```

Fig. 14-4. The second search screen before and after the search.

A positive action may be triggered by the use of a command key or through the use of an acronym or a code. The message to be displayed may say "RECORD IS READY FOR UPDATE, PRESS PF KEY1." Once you press the command key, the record will be written; otherwise it will not be created.

Changes are normally a great deal less demanding. It would be safe to assume at this point that data elements currently residing on the file are error free to begin with. However, most of the procedures used during the edit cycle will remain applicable for the changes as well. Thus, you may assume that the initial record and its components have been placed on the file earlier, and that they are error free. But as the terminal operator retrieves the existing records to make further modifications to them, he may transform a perfectly legitimate field to an erroneous one.

The delete cycle has the same mechanism as the change cycle. In other words, the record must be in existence before you can delete it. Once the record is retrieved, however, it will not have to comply with any of the current edit criteria. You can delete the record even if you needed to change a zip code from a numeric to an alphanumeric field.

As we indicated earlier under VSAM, (KSDS), a record that's deleted will physically disappear from the file and the space given up will be re-used by the system. Since this is a rather irreversible mechanism, you may want to show extra care in verifying that the deletion of a record is consistent with the user's aim and that it is not merely an exercise in carelessness.

SUMMARY

Messages of potential problems may be displayed on the screen in the following manner:

1. You may display a message to the user whenever you establish line(s) of communications on the screen
2. You may also alter the present format of any data element(s) in question. That is to say that upon an error condition, you may want to highlight a particular field or fields involved. You may also rely on a different color scheme, if your terminal can handle such.

The message prompting capabilities of the system can be utilized by the user as an extensive tutoring device.

Pathing is a self-dictating mechanism that allows the user to perform his functions within a given set of constraints. Even screen utilized in the system should have sufficient flexibility so that the user should not have to continually access higher-level screens to perform related functions.

The ability to locate a specific piece of information in your system is important in order to identify potential problems and expedite the inquiry process.

The add, change and the delete mechanisms require substantially different logic to code. You may, however, think of the delete mechanism as a subset of the change mechanism.

QUESTIONS

1. A simplified way to help inform the user of available choices and codes is done through a mechanism called . . .
2. Describe a *totally* optional field.
3. Describe a *restricted* optional field.
4. Explain two options you may want to rely on in updating a particular file.
5. True or false: upon an error condition, it is reasonable to change the color or the intensity of the field in error. Explain your answer, and state why.
6. Why is it so important to have facilities to locate a particular piece of information?

15

Introduction to VSAM

HIGHLIGHTS
- Overview
- Access methods services
- Security protection
- Cluster definition
- Alternate keys

15.1 OVERVIEW

A brief chapter is insufficient for an in depth presentation of the topic of VSAM, or Virtual Storage Access Method. There have been volumes and volumes written on this subject, both by IBM and by an army of enterprising technical writers. The truth is that the average application programmer assumes minimum responsibility for the overall implementation and maintenance of this software. In fact, strictly from the viewpoint of the programmer, VSAM means added flexibility in allowing him to use certain commands otherwise unavailable.

An access method is the combination of the file organization and the technique utilized to access the data on that file. Virtual Storage Access Method datasets are stored as page size blocks, so that they can be accessed by the system's paging programs.

VSAM datasets may be organized one of three ways:

Entry Sequenced, or ESDS
Key Sequenced, or KSDS
Relative Records or RRDS

Entry-sequenced records are in the physical sequence in which they are entered or loaded into the file. Once you place a record on the file in this fashion, the record will not be moved, lengthened, or shortened. They may be updated (rewritten), provided the length of the record doesn't change. Any new records you wish to add will be added to the end of the file, almost like working with transient datasets. Here VSAM will not create an index. The usual way of retrieving records from an entry-sequenced dataset is to access them sequentially.

Key-Sequenced files are organized logically by a user-defined key field in each record. The file does have an index so that the records on file may be accessed via the key or sequentially, if needed. When the file is created, portions of it can be left empty (free space) to allow for the insertion of new records or for the lengthening of existing ones. Likewise, when a record is deleted or shortened, the space given up by the record can be reused by VSAM for other records.

A Relative-Record dataset is organized like a non-VSAM file. You may access records on that file based on their relative positions. Relative datasets contain record slots that are made up of either data or free space. When you process an RRDS file sequentially, you only process the data portion on that file, skipping the rest (the slots made up of free space). In random mode, however, a slot is accessed even though it contains no data.

Like CICS command language, VSAM offers an entirely new set of terminology. For example, VSAM datasets are referred to as *clusters*. A cluster is made up of two parts: the data part and the indexes. An index functions very much like a table of contents does, pointing to the "page" of the material (which is the file), you wish to read.

Clusters are defined by IBM utility programs, referred to as IDCAMS, which create VSAM storage areas, called *data spaces*, on direct-access devices (such as the IBM 3350 or 3380).

VSAM uses a catalog as a central information point for all VSAM datasets, (clusters, alternate indexes, and as data space). There are two kinds of catalogs:

Master Catalog
User Catalog

While a Master Catalog is required, the User Catalog remains optional. In order for a VSAM dataset to exist, it must be defined in the VSAM catalog. This means that you must enter the DSNAME and other vital statistics about the dataset in the VSAM catalog. Figure 15-1 depicts the catalog relationship.

The unit of information that VSAM transfers between virtual storage and auxiliary storage is referred to as *control interval*. This may contain a single record or a number of records. When a record requires more than one control interval, it's called a *spanned* record. Finally, control intervals are associated together by VSAM into larger groups called *control areas*.

Assume you're processing a key sequenced file and your control area looks like this:

| 05 | 10 | 15 | 20 | 25 | 30 | 35 | 40 | FS | FS |

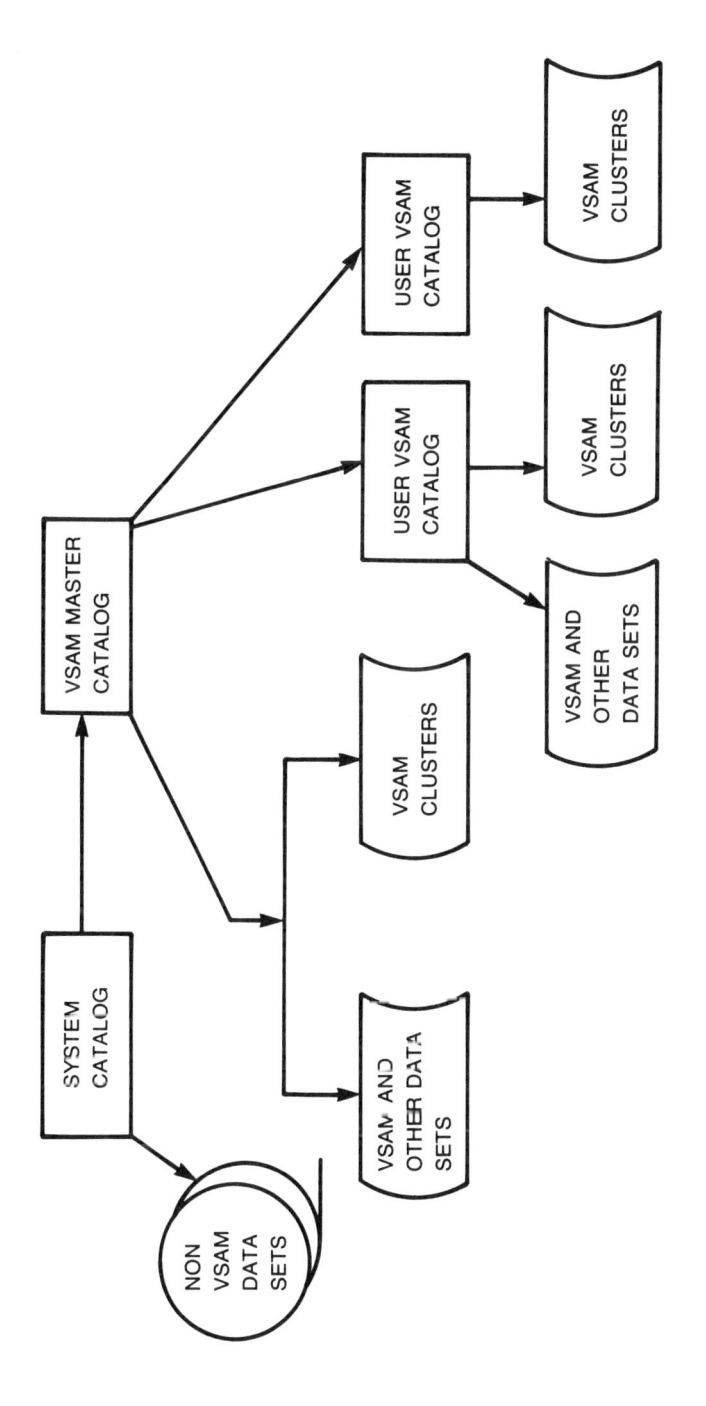

Fig. 15-1. Catalog relationships among the VSAM master catalog and other VSAM and non-VSAM clusters.

where 05 through 40 indicates the key values of the eighth records and FS means free space. Assume now that you want to add two more records with keys 17 and 32 to the file. This is what your control area would look like, as the result.

| 05 | 10 | 15 | 17 | 20 | 25 | 30 | 32 | 35 | 40 |

Although you have no more free space left, assume you're required to add one more record to the file with the key value of 18. This will bring about a *control interval split.* That is to say, if all free space in the control area is full, and you want to insert another record in that control area, VSAM will establish a new control area including all free control intervals:

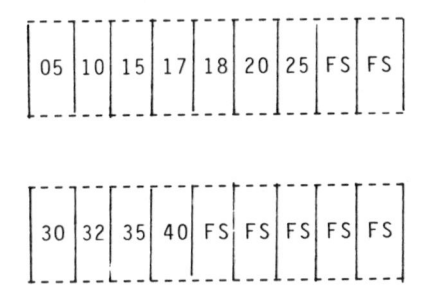

| 05 | 10 | 15 | 17 | 18 | 20 | 25 | FS | FS |

| 30 | 32 | 35 | 40 | FS | FS | FS | FS | FS |

15.2 ACCESS METHODS SERVICES

A multifunction utility program, Access Methods Services, is used to define VSAM datasets and to convert existing indexed sequential or sequential files to VSAM format before the file can be used as input or output to your COBOL program.

Let's review for a moment what steps must be taken using Access Method Services before processing can begin:

- You must define a VSAM catalog. A VSAM catalog is a centralized location for all information about datasets and data space. All VSAM datasets, or clusters, must be defined in the VSAM catalog.
- You must also define the data spaces. Since VSAM does its own resource management, it must have space to allocate to its datasets. This is what we call data space. Essentially, it is accounted for in the VSAM catalog.
- All VSAM clusters must be defined. A VSAM dataset doesn't exist until you define it in the VSAM catalog. Such a dataset will reside in the data space.
- Datasets must be loaded. You may accomplish that through IBM utili-

ties or through your own application program.

VSAM file processing in ANS COBOL is independent of whether the records on file are of fixed length or of variable length format. Records are considered fixed if all records have the same size and no record description contains an OCCURS clause with the DEPENDING ON option. All other records are considered to be of variable length. Note that the RECORDING MODE clause is not used with VSAM files. To refresh your memory, Fig. 15-2 shows both fixed and variable record formats.

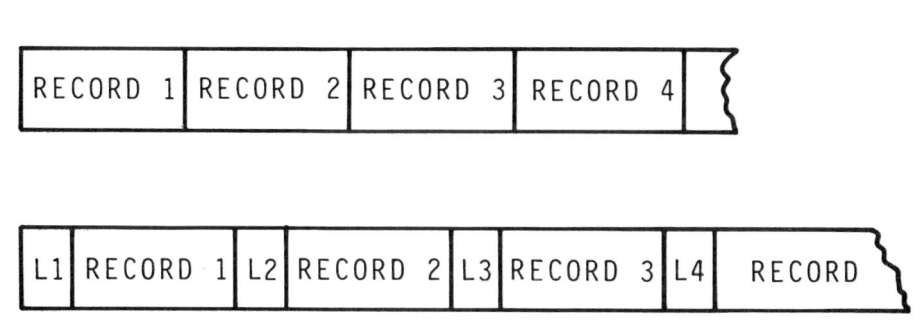

RECORD 1	RECORD 2	RECORD 3	RECORD 4

L1	RECORD 1	L2	RECORD 2	L3	RECORD 3	L4	RECORD

Fig. 15-2. Fixed and variable length record formats, where L represents the actual length of each variable length record.

15.3 SECURITY AND PROTECTION

In order to safeguard the integrity of the data, you can define your own password for clusters and alternate indexes as well as for VSAM indexes. You may also place a password protection on paths and VSAM catalogs. VSAM provides you with a number of password protection schemes:

1. You may have *full access* to the system, which allows you to do just about anything you need to without any restrictions. On this level you may delete an entire VSAM dataset or alter any catalog information including the password.
2. A second-level access, referred to as *control access*, allows you to use what we call *control-interval access*.
3. When you have *update access* to the VSAM datasets, you may update, add, or delete records in the dataset.
4. A *read access* password only allows you to examine both the data and the catalog records, but it doesn't allow you to add new records or modify or delete their contents, nor does it allow you to see password information in the catalog record.

Sometimes, due to system or hardware failure, your data may be destroyed or made inaccessible to you. In order to recover your data from such catastrophe, you may use one or a number of options:

1. You can back up your data. VSAM allows you to do just that via the EXPORT and the REPRO commands.
2. When you preformat the control areas utilizing the RECOVERY command you can identify the last record that was successfully loaded into VSAM before the error occurred. Note that you must be able to identify the last record you successfully loaded, so you may continue from that point on.
3. You may also use the IMPORT command to totally replace VSAM clusters using back-up copies.

There are a number of corrective measures that would require an extensive review. We would like to refer you to the *IBM OS/VS1 Access Methods Services Guide* for an in depth discussion of these topics.

15.4 CLUSTER DEFINITION

As I mentioned earlier, the definition of the cluster and its maintenance is normally within the jurisdiction of those maintaining systems software as opposed to those dealing with applications software. However, we would like to briefly review with you the way you can define and create clusters.

Assume you want to define a Key-Sequenced cluster. (We're also assuming that a VSAM data space exists on volume USER02.)

Let's review Fig. 15-3 statement by statement. Please note that the purpose of this exercise is to show you the additional control language statements necessary to handle VSAM requirements.

Statement 01	This statement is a standard requirement for running a job, and it varies greatly within installations.
Statement 02	This statement will make the catalog available for VFILE1, which is the name of the dataset.
Statement 03	STEP01 will invoke and execute the IBM utility program IDCAMS in order to define the VSAM cluster.
Statement 04	SYSPRINT is required in all access method services job steps. It identifies the output device for systems messages.
Statement 05	This statement defines the incoming data to be placed after this statement. Here incoming data are represented in the form of parameters required to define the cluster.
Statement 06	The DEFINE CLUSTER command builds the CLUSTER entry, a DATA entry, and an INDEX entry to define the key-sequenced cluster

```
01      //VSCLSTR    JOB     (030,4376),LX
02      //JOBCAT     DD      DSNAME=VFILE1,DIS=SHR
03      //STEP01     EXEC    PGM=IDCAMS
04      //SYSPRINT   DD      SYSOUT=A
05      //SYSIN      DD      *
06           DEFINE CLUSTER -
07                  (NAME(CLUSTR) -
08                  VOLUME(USER02)   -
09                  RECORDS(3000 500))   -
10           DATA -
11                  (NAME(KEYDAT) -
12                  KEYS(10 8) -
13                  RECORDSIZE(200 200) -
14                  FREESPACE(10 20) -
15                  BUFFERSIZE(20000)   ) -
16           INDEX -
17                  (NAME(KEYINDX) -
18                  IMBED) -
19           CATALOG (VFILE/PASWRD)
20      /*
```

Fig. 15-3. The definition of a key-sequenced cluster. For the purpose of clarity, lines between VSAM statements have been omitted.

"CLUSTR." Notice the way the parameters are continued after the DEFINE CLUSTER command. The rule is that commands can be continued throughout several records or lines. Each line, except the last, must have a hyphen or a plus sign as the last nonblank character before or at the right margin. The hyphen indicates the continuation of the command or the continuation of the value within that command.

Statement 07   The NAME that specifies that the data component's name is "CLUSTR."

Statement 08   VOLUME specifies that the cluster resides on

197

Statement 09	volume USER02. This statement specifies that the CLUSTER's space allocation is 3,000 records. When the CLUSTER is extended, however, it is expanded in the increment of 500 records at a time. After the space is allocated, VSAM calculates the amount required for the INDEX and subtracts it from the total.
Statement 10	In addition to the parameters specified for the CLUSTR as a whole, the DATA and INDEX subparameters specify values and attributes that apply only to the CLUSTR's DATA or INDEX components. The parameter specified for the DATA component of CLUSTER are:
Statement 11	NAME, which specifies that the name of the DATA component is KEYDAT, and ...
Statement 12	...KEYS, which specify that the length of the key field is 10 bytes, beginning in position eight of each data record.
Statement 13	RECORDSIZE specifies fixed length records of 200 bytes.
Statement 14	FREESPACE specifies that 20 percent of each control interval and 10 percent of each control area will be left free when records are loaded into the cluster. After they are loaded, however, the free space can be used to store new records.
Statement 15	BUFFERSPACE specifies that a minimum of 20,000 bytes must be provided for I/O buffer. A large area for I/O buffers can help to improve access time with certain type of processing.
Statement 16	This statement refers to statement 10.
Statement 17	NAME specifies that the index component's name is KEYINDX.
Statement 18	This statement has to do with the index sequence.
Statement 19	This statement specifies the name of the catalog and its update password. Note that if the catalog were not password protected, this parameter would not be necessary.

Most statements that appear here have been reviewed during the definition of the cluster. The following statements, however, need some clarification.

MASTERPW	This statement specifies the password for the alternate index. UPDATEPW is a password in case you need to update the alternate key.
DEFINE ALTERNATEINDEX	This command builds an alternate index or key; that is, it builds an Alternate Index Entry, a Data Entry, and an Index Entry.
RECORDSIZE	This statement specifies that the alternate-indexed records are of variable length. The average size is defined as 60 characters, with the maximum of 70 characters. (For the KEYS option, see statement 12, Cluster Definition.)
VOLUMES	This statement refers to the area where the alternate index resides, and CYLINDER defines the space allocated to it plus, increments in case they're required.
FILE	This statement defines the DD NAME that specifies the volume of the alternate index for the purpose of mounting.
NONUNIQUEKEY	This statement specifies that the alternate key may not be a unique one.
UPGRADE	This statement specifies that the alternate key value will be upgraded each time the base cluster is open for processing.

15.5 ALTERNATE INDEXES

With these definitions in mind, let us review briefly some of the coding conventions with regard to primary and alternate indexes. In our examples, the primary index is the employee's social security number, and the secondary index is his last name:

When you need to have more than one key to process your VSAM file, the use of alternate indexes will allow you to utilize an alternate key. In fact, you may utilize a number of alternate indexes, as long as you keep in mind the additional cost attached to such a decision. In Fig. 15-4, I show the segment of a record containing one primary key, the employee's social

| 1 2 3 3 5 6 8 7 | 1 2 E 5 6 6 | R W E W 2 4 8 | 6 0 1 2 6 |

Fig. 15-4. A VSAM record with one primary and three secondary keys or indexes.

security number, as well as three alternate indexes, the job class, the sales person's telephone number, and his zip code.

Figure 15-5 shows how coding is done to define one secondary index to VSAM.

```
//ALTKEY   JOB
//STEP01   EXEC   PGM=IDCAMS
//DISKSP   DD     DISP=OLD,UNIT=3330,VOL=SER=VSER04
//SYSPRINT DD     SYSOUT=A
//SYSIN DD *
         DEFINE ALTERNATEINDEX -
         (NAME(ALTXKY) -
         RELATE(ATBCL) -
         MASTERPW(XRTYO) -
         UPDATE(OYTRX) -
         KEYS(5 1) -
         RECORDSIZE(60 70) -
         VOLUMES(VSER04) -
         CYLINDERS(5 1) -
         FILE(       ) -
         NONUNIQUEKEY -
         UPGRADE -
         CATALOG(MCTX/MCCKEY)
/*

WORKING-STORAGE SECTION.
01   LENGTHS.
     05   REC-LEN              PIC S9(4) COMP VALUE +100.
     05   INDEX-LEN            PIC S9(4) COMP VALUE +009.
     05   ALT-INDEX-LEN        PIC S9(4) COMP VALUE +020.
01   DATA-RECORD.
     05   PRIMARY-KEY.
          10   SSN             PIC 9(09).
     05   ADDRESS              PIC X(30).
     05   CITY                 PIC X(15).
     05   STATE                PIC X(02).
     05   ZIP                  PIC X(05).
     05   ALTERNATE-KEY.
          10   LAST-NAME       PIC X(20).
     05   FIRST-NAME           PIC X(15).
     05   MIDDLE-INITIAL       PIC X(01).
     05   FILLER.


PROCEDURE DIVISION.

         READ PRIMARY KEY RANDOMLY
         EXEC CICS READ DATASET(DEMO-FILE)
         RIDFLD(SSN) LENGTH(REC-LEN)
```

```
            INTO(DATA-RECORD)
            END-EXEC.
                         }

            READ ALTERNATE KEY RANDOMLY
            EXEC CICS READ DATASET(DEMO-FILE)
            RIDFLD(LAST-NAME) LENGTH(REC-LEN)
            INTO(DATA-RECORD)
            END-EXEC.
                         }

            START BROWSE ON PRIMARY KEY
            EXEC CICS STARTBR DATASET(DEMO-FILE)
            RIDFLD(SSN) KEY LENGTH(INDEX-LEN)
            END-EXEC.
                         }

            START BROWSE ON ALTERNATE KEY
            EXEC CICS STARTBR DATASET(DEMO-FILE)
            RIDFLD(LAST-NAME) KEY-LENGTH(ALT-INDEX-LEN)
            END-EXEC.
```

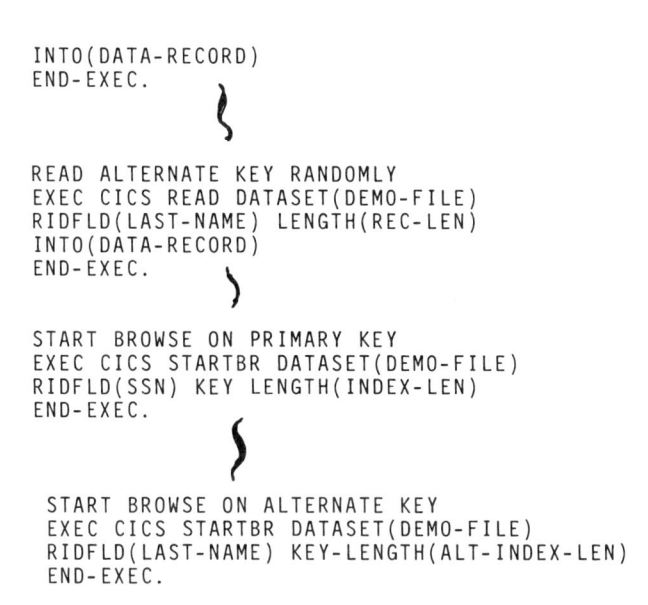

Fig. 15-5. Control statements for building an alternate index.

SUMMARY

VSAM Datasets may be organized one of three ways:

Entry Sequenced, or ESDS
Key Sequenced, or KSDS
Relative Records, or RRDS.

Entry-Sequenced records are in the physical sequence in which they are entered or loaded into the file. Key-Sequenced files are organized logically by a user-defined key field in each record. When a file is created, portions of it may be left empty. Such empty space is often referred to as *free space*. Relative-Record datasets are organized like a Non-VSAM file. You may access records on that file based on their relative positions.

VSAM datasets are referred to as *clusters*, which are made up of two parts: the data part and its indices. Clusters are defined by IBM utility programs referred to as IDCAMS, which create VSAM storage areas called *data spaces* on a direct access device.

VSAM uses catalogs as a central information point for all VSAM datasets (clusters, alternate indices, and as data space).

The unit of information that VSAM transfers between virtual and auxiliary storage is referred to as a Control Interval. Control Intervals may contain a single or a number of records. When a record contains more than one Control Interval it is referred to as a Spanned Record.

A Control Area is made up by a number of Control Intervals. In order to safeguard the integrity of the data, you can define your own password for clusters, alternate indexes, and VSAM indices. VSAM provides you with a number of password protection schemes:

>Full access
>Control access
>Update access
>Read access

When you need more than one key to process your VSAM file, you can utilize an alternate index or key.

QUESTIONS

1. Specify the three ways VSAM datasets may be organized.
2. The unit of information VSAM transfers between virtual and auxiliary storage facilities is called . . . .
3. What is a control interval split?
4. Define the following terms:

   a VSAM catalog
   Data spaces
   A VSAM cluster

5. What is the meaning of a READ access password?
6. What is the nature of the IDCAMS utilities?
7. What do we mean by alternate indexes? Explain under what circumstances would you use them in the system.
8. What is a nonunique key? Is it allowed under KSDS?
9. True or false: CICS command provides a broader choice of options for the application programmer under VSAM than under ISAM or DAM.
10. True or false: the READPREV command is only valid under VSAM?

16
Establishing Addressability

HIGHLIGHTS
- Overview
- Common Work Area
- Miscellaneous Storage Techniques
- The Getmain/Freemain Commands
- The Load/Release Commands
- Locate Versus Move Mode

16.1 OVERVIEW

The purpose of this chapter is to review some of the miscellaneous topics we have not discussed so far. The majority of these topics have to do with obtaining additional storage facilities through establishing addressability. This is done through the BLL cells. In all probability, however, the application programmer will never have to utilize these facilities, since most of it can be easily accomplished either through the use of the communications area available in the LINKAGE SECTION of your program or through temporary storage. But remember, when you use the COMMAREA, you want to use as little of it as possible. The length of such area should be kept at a minimum.

16.2 COMMON WORK AREA (CWA)

The Common Work Area is available to every application program in the system. In order to maintain communications with the CWA, you must define it in the LINKAGE SECTION of your program. As we explained earlier in our discussion on the Communications Area or DFHCOMMAREA, CICS automatically sets up addressability for you—not so with the Common Work Areas.

If you require addressability with this area, you will do it through the Base Locator for Linkage, or BLL, cells. Assume your company stores the header of its five major functional areas in the CWA. These are:

The Marketing and the Sales Reports Module
Accounting and Internal Auditing
Production Related Reporting and Inquiries
Financial Analysis and Statements
Personnel and Payroll Related Inquiries

Every time a report is generated or a screen accessed, we want to display one of the above titles. Review both Figs. 16-1 and 16-2 for further discussion. We have defined an area in Fig. 16-2 following the DFHCOMMAREA in the LINKAGE SECTION called HEADER-ADDRESS. Filler, the first element (binary, numeric), points back to the HEADER-ADDRESS, while APOINTER refers to the CWA-HEADERS area containing the five major functional areas.

Once the EXEC CICS CWA (APOINTER) command is executed, the address of the Common Work Area will be placed into APOINTER for subsequent use. Thus, the header MARKETING or ACCOUNTING will be available for the particular application program.

There is a specific sequence the programmer must observe when utilizing the CWA. Review Fig. 16-3. In this figure, FILLER will refer back to the CWA-BLL-WORK-AREA. (You must always code it following your DFHCOMMAREA statements.) CWA-BLL-ELEMENT1 will point to RECEIVE-FIELD1; CWA-BLL-ELEMENT2 will point to RECEIVE-FIELD2, and so on. Note that right after the CWA-BLL-WORK-AREA related fields, you must define one or a number of corresponding 01 level data elements.

16.3 MISCELLANEOUS STORAGE TECHNIQUES

Let's briefly review three additional storage techniques. These are the CSA, or Common Storage Area, the TCTUA, or Terminal Control Table User Area, and the TWA, or Transaction Work Area. The application programmer may never have to utilize any of the these address commands.

- The CSA simply allows you to have access to certain control blocks addressed by the CSA.
- The TCTUA is used to pass information between the application programs (just like the DFHCOMMAREA), but only if the same terminal is involved.
- The TWA is also used to pass data between programs, but only if it is within the same task.

16.4 THE GETMAIN/FREEMAIN COMMANDS

The purpose of the GETMAIN command is to obtain additional main storage dynamically. Consider the following:

```
EXEC CICS GETMAIN
SET(POINT-TO-BLL)
LENGTH(20)
END-EXEC.
```

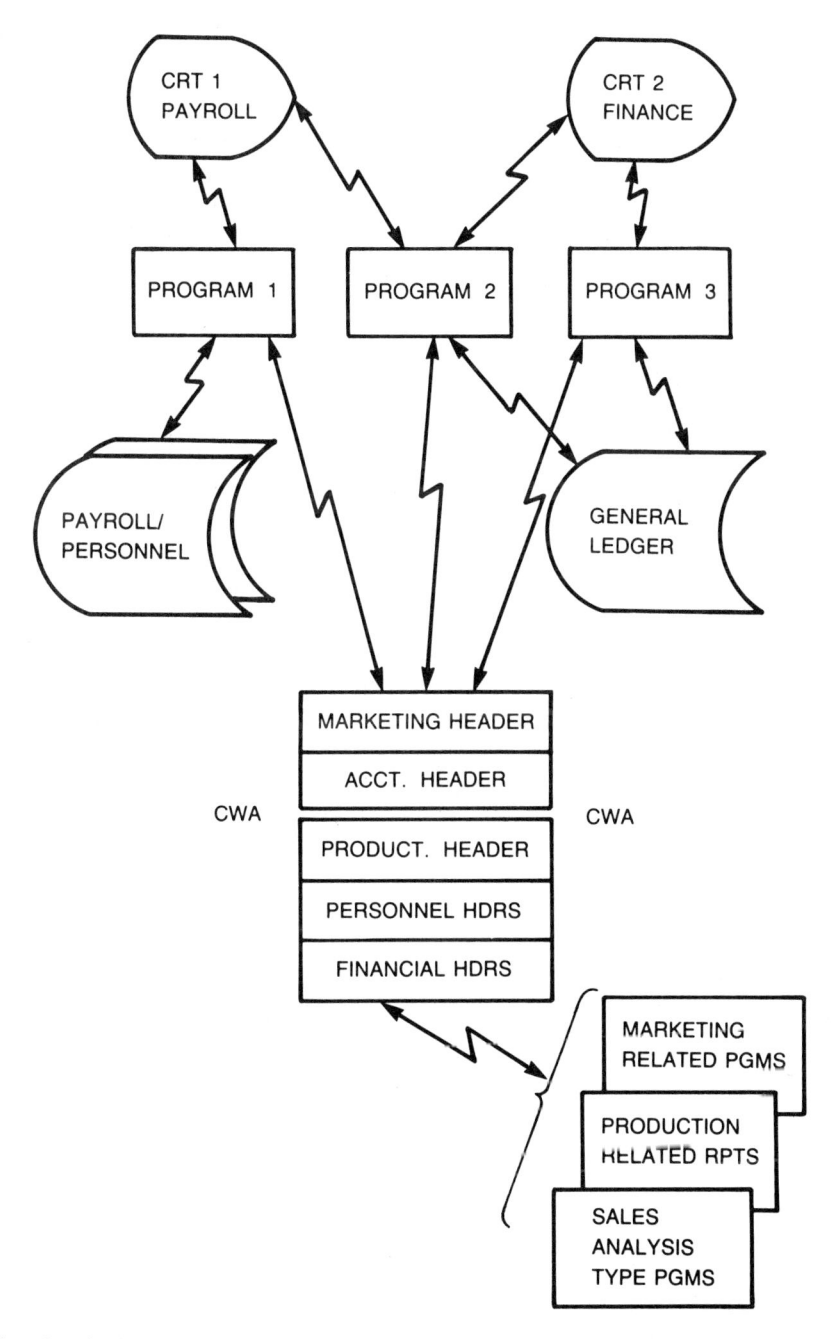

Fig. 16-1. An illustration of how a number of programs utilize a common area via the CWA for constant (seldom changing) data. Typically a header would say "The ABC Company, Quarterly Sales Reports."

```
        LINKAGE   SECTION.
        *
        01   DFHCOMMAREA.
             02   FIRST-BYTE           PIC  X.
             02   REST-OF-DATA         PIC  X(10).
        *
        01   HEADER-ADDRESS.
             02   FILLER               PIC  S9(8)  COMPUTATIONAL.
             02   APOINTER             PIC  S9(8)  COMPUTATIONAL.
        *
        01   CWA-HEADERS.
             02   MARKETING            PIC  X(34).
             02   ACCOUNTING           PIC  X(32).
             02   PRODUCTION           PIC  X(33).
             02   FINANCIAL            PIC  X(33).
             02   PERSONNEL            PIC  X(29).

        ************************************************************


             PROCEDURE  DIVISION.
        *


                  EXEC  CICS  CWA(APOINTER)
                  END-EXEC.
```

Fig. 16-2. The method of making information available in the LINKAGE area. A common work area (CWA) is set up and the pointer concept is utilized. A single statement in the PROCEDURE DIVISION reveals what the program has to do to attain linkage with the CWA.

In this example, CICS obtains a 20-position storage area, placing its address into POINT-TO-BLL in order to establish addressability. The mechanics of this is identical to that of the Common Work Area defined in the prior section, where POINT-TO-BLL is in the LINKAGE SECTION

```
             LINKAGE  SECTION.
        *
        *
        01   DFHCOMMAREA.
        *
        *
        01   CWA-BLL-WORK-AREA.
             02   FILLER               PIC  S9(8)  COMPUTATIONAL.
             02   CWA-BLL-ELEMENT1     PIC  S9(8)  COMPUTATIONAL.
             02   CWA-BLL-ELEMENT2     PIC  S9(8)  COMPUTATIONAL.
             02   CWA-BLL-ELEMENT3     PIC  S9(8)  COMPUTATIONAL.
             02   CWA-BLL-ELEMENT4     PIC  S9(8)  COMPUTATIONAL.
        *
        01   RECEIVE-FIELD1            PIC  X(10).
        01   RECEIVE-FIELD2            PIC  X(12).
        01   RECEIVE-FIELD3            PIC  S9(3)V99.
        01   RECEIVE-FIELD4            PIC  X(03).
```

Fig. 16-3. BLL cell area, which contains data from the common work area. The BLL cell area corresponds to a number of receiving fields.

```
EXEC CICS GETMAIN
    SET(pointer-ref)
    [LENGTH(data value) / FLENGTH(data value)]
    [INITIMG(data value)]
END-EXEC.

Conditions:   LENGERR, NOSTG
```

Fig. 16-4. Standard format for the GETMAIN instruction, including exception conditions.

pointing to the corresponding 01 level field.

The syntax for the GETMAIN command is shown in Fig. 16-4.

Access is established through the SET option, where CICS will place the address of the acquired storage in the pointer reference area.

The LENGTH option specifies the number of bytes being requested. If no space is available, the NOSTG Exception Condition will occur.

The INITIMG option, also known as Initial Image, initializes the acquired storage to the one byte hexadecimal value, normally zeros or spaces. An example is shown in Fig. 16-5.

When processing is complete, you need to release the storage area; otherwise it won't be released until the task is terminated. The FREEMAIN

```
PROCEDURE DIVISION.
EXEC CICS GETMAIN
    SET(POINT-TO-BLL) ◄──────────────┐
    LENGTH(20)                       │
    INITIMG(INITIALIZE-BLANK)        │
END-EXEC.                            │
*                                    │
*                                    │
                                     │
                                     │
                                     │
         DATA DIVISION.              │
         WORKING-STORAGE SECTION.    │
         01  INITIALIZE-BLANK   PIC  X  VALUE SPACES.
         *
         *
         01  BLL-POINTER.
             02  FILLER         PIC  S9(8) COMPUTATIONAL.
          ═══ 02  POINT-T-BLL    PIC  S9(8) COMPUTATIONAL.

       ┌►01  BLL-CORRESPOND-FIELD.
             02  FIELD-1        PIC  X(12).
             02  FIELD-2        PIC  X(05).
             02  FIELD-3        PIC  X(03).
```

Fig. 16-5. The lines emphasize the correspondence between the BLL-POINTER and the BLL-CORRESPOND-FIELD.

command is used to release the storage area:

```
EXEC CICS FREEMAIN
DATA(BLL-CORRESPOND-FIELD)
END-EXEC.
```

Note that there are no exception conditions associated with this command.

16.5 THE LOAD/RELEASE COMMANDS

If an object program in your library is used frequently enough, the LOAD command allows you to load it into main storage and thereby minimize the overhead on the system. This command gives you the ability to load any of the following:

1. A program that is going to be utilized so often that system overhead would be significantly minimized through a one time load.
2. A table.
3. A map.

Figure 16-6 shows the standard format for the LOAD command. PGMIDERR occurs if a program, a table, or a map cannot be found in the PPT or is simply disabled. The SET option essentially works the same way as described in conjunction with the BLL cells. The LENGTH option is used to place the actual length of the loaded module in the specified data area. Finally, the HOLD option is used to retain the module in main storage for use by other tasks. If you don't specify HOLD, CICS will release the area at the end of the task.

You will need to use the RELEASE command in order to delete a module that was previously loaded with the LOAD command from main storage. Figure 16-7 shows a comparison between the LOAD and RELEASE commands.

```
EXEC CICS LOAD
PROGRAM(name)
[SET(pointer ref)]
[LENGTH(data area)]
FLENGTH(data area)
[ENTRY(pointer ref)]
[HOLD]
END-EXEC.

Conditions: PGMIDERR
```

Fig. 16-6. Standard format for the LOAD command.

```
EXEC CICS LOAD              EXEC CICS RELEASE
PROGRAM('TABLEA')           PROGRAM('TABLEA')
SET(TAB-POINTER)            END-exec.
LENGTH(TL-L)
END-EXEC.
```

Fig. 16-7. Comparison between the LOAD and the RELEASE commands.

16.6 LOCATE VERSUS MOVE MODE

When you use storage outside your program, you are considered to be in locate mode. This is so because an area has to be located, and you must establish addressability through *pointer reference*. Note from prior examples that the pointer actually contains the address where the data resides in main storage.

When you use your own storage facilities in your program, you are considered to be in move mode. This is so because all you have to do is to move data in and out of your self-established areas.

SUMMARY

The Common Work Area is defined in the LINKAGE SECTION (ANS COBOL). Unlike in the COMMAREA, CICS does not automatically set up addressability here. Addressability is achieved via the Base Locator for Linkage or BLL cells.

The CSA, or Common Storage Area, will simply allow you to have access to certain control blocks addressed by the CSA.

The TCTUA, or Terminal Control Table User Area, is used to pass information between the application programs just as the DFHCOMMAREA is, but it can be used only if the same terminal is involved.

The TWA, or Transaction Work Area, is also used to pass data between programs, but it can be used only if it is within the same task.

The purpose of the GETMAIN command is to obtain additional Main Storage dynamically; for example:

```
EXEC CICS GETMAIN
SET(POINT-TO-BLI)
LENGTH(ACTUAL-LENGTH)
END-EXEC.
```

Addressability is established via the SET option; CICS will place the address of the acquired storage in the pointer reference area.

The LOAD command allows you to load certain often-used information, such as your object program, into Main Storage.

A RELEASE command is used in order to delete a module from Main Storage that was previously loaded through the LOAD command.

When you use storage outside your program, you are considered to be in locate mode.

When you use your own storage facilities you are considered in move mode. This is so because all you have to do is to move your data in and out of your self-established area.

QUESTIONS

1. Describe the mechanics of the Common Work Area. Under what circumstances would you use it?
2. Define the term TCTUA. What does it mean? Would you ever use it in your program?
3. True or false: the TWA does not pass data between the application programs unless there are at least three separate tasks involved.
4. True or false: the GETMAIN command is used essentially like the CWA module except GETMAIN's addressability is automatically provided by the system, the same way as the DFHCOMMAREA's is.
5. Describe what is meant by locate mode. What are you locating?
6. True or false: the FREEMAIN command is used prior to the GETMAIN command in order to clear required storage areas.

17

Recovery and Debugging

HIGHLIGHTS

- Overview
- The Abend Command
- The Execute Diagnostics Facility
- Command Level Interpreter
- Master Terminal Commands
- Journal Control

17.1 OVERVIEW

The purpose of this chapter is to familiarize you with some of the tools available in testing, monitoring, and debugging your on-line programs. We would like to dedicate a considerable part of this chapter to reviewing the Execute Diagnostics Facility package, or EDF. This interactive debugging aid allows you to review the logic of your application program step by step, alter the execution of each command, and even change the contents of main storage, if necessary.

17.2 THE ABEND COMMAND

The ABEND command is needed in your application program to provide procedures and logic should your program abnormally terminate. CICS command provides you with a handle condition in the following format:

```
EXEC CICS HANDLE ABEND
   (PROGRAM(NAME))
   LABEL(LABEL)
   CANCEL
   RESET)
END-EXEC.
```

In the program option you must specify the name of the program that will receive control if your task abends. Furthermore, you will have to specify the paragraph's name (label) in your statement to indicate where the logic of your program should branch upon the abnormal termination of the task. The cancel option tells CICS that any previously established exits will be cancelled if an abend occurs. Finally, the RESET option will reactivate the exit that was cancelled by a HANDLE ABEND CANCEL command. Figure 17-1 illustrates the functioning of the ABEND command.

LEVEL	NORMAL TERMINATION	ABNORMAL TERMINATION
0	CICS	CICS
1	PROGRAM 1 - LINK	PROGRAM 1 - LINK
2	PROGRAM 2 - XCTL	PROGRAM 2 - XCTL
2	PROGRAM 3 - LINK	PROGRAM 2 - LINK
	...RETURN...	...RETURN...
3	PROGRAM 4 - RETURN	PROGRAM 4 - RETURN

Fig. 17-1. The functioning of the ABEND command.

17.3 THE EXECUTE DIAGNOSTICS FACILITY (EDF)

The EDF mechanism allows you to review the execution of your program, statement by statement, under the control of the Execute Diagnostics Facility software. When you execute your program in this fashion, EDF will intercept each command at the following key points:

- Prior to the point at which the first transaction (program) gets control.
- Before and after the execution of each CICS command. During EDF execution, each command can invoke two status displays.

You may modify the response code before the execution of a command or suppress it all together. Also, at any time (except immediately prior to executing a command), you may turn off EDF, allowing yourself to proceed in a normal manner.

EDF Structure

EDF has a header and a detail section. The header specifies the transaction identifier, the status, the display number, the name of the program, and a task number that is assigned by CICS. The detail shows the command statement as it is used in the application program. Here is an example:

```
EXEC CICS SEND MAP
          ('mapname')
          FROM('........................')
          MAPSET ('mapset')
          TERMINAL
          ERASE
END-EXEC.
```

Following each command the EIB (Execute Interface Block) values are displayed in symbolic form. The contents of any temporary storage queues as well as address locations within the CICS partition are displayed in hexadecimal. Additional information concerning the allocation of Command (Function) keys also appears; for example:

```
Pf4 : Supress Displays
PF8 : Scroll Foward...... etc.
```

Problem Solving Through EDF

Review the screen format presented in Fig. 17-2. In addition, review the source code in Fig. 17-3; it will be referenced during our EDF session. The screen layout presented in Fig. 17-2 (Consolidated American Main Menu) displays nine possible functions, one of which will be selected by the terminal operator. We have, however, removed function five from the table, so that when the operator selects transaction five on the menu screen, EDF will indicate the path the application program will take as the result. The figure numbers shown in Fig. 17-4 show the order in which the steps are performed. Note that steps 17-6 through 17-11 were performed twice due to the fact that the transaction was invoked for the second time after the RETURN command. Because of the repetition, we only show this path once during our EDF session. Reinvocation is indicated by the line connecting Figs. 17-4 through 17-5.

EDF Session Review

To use the EDF software, clear the screen and then enter CEDF, which will invoke the Execute Diagnostics Facility software. Figure 17-5 shows that the transaction identifier MENU was entered. Let us review this first

```
     SCREEN: 1                        ADVANCE TO SCREEN : __
                      CONSOLIDATED AMERICAN
                           Main Menu

                  1. Demographic Maintneance
                  2. Employee Listing
                  3. Sales
                  4. Accounts Payable
                  5. Accounts Receivable
                  6. Vendor Listing
                  7. Security
                  8. Table Maintenance
                  9. Table Display

                  _  ENTER SELECTION



     Password: _____

     XXXXXXXXXXXXXXXXXXXXXXXXXXXXX        PF10: LOGOFF
```
Fig. 17-2. The main menu screen.

```
00001      IDENTIFICATION DIVISION.
00002      PROGRAM-ID. PGMNBR1.
00003      DATE-COMPILED.
00004      ENVIRONMENT DIVISION.
00005      DATA DIVISION.
00006      WORKING-STORAGE SECTION.
00007      01   DFHBMSCA COPY DFHBMSCA.
00008           DFHAID COPY DFHAID.
00009           MAPNAMEI COPY MAPSET.
00010           LASTMAPI COPY LASTSET.
00011      01   SWITCHES.
00012           02   ERR-SW              PIC X(01) VALUE 'N'.
00013           02   XCTL-SWITCH         PIC X(01) VALUE 'N'.
00014           02   UPDATE-SWITCH       PIC X(01) VALUE 'N'.
00015           02   PWRD-OK             PIC X(01) VALUE 'N'.
00016           02   UNP-BRI-MDT         PIC X(01) VALUE 'I'.
00017           02   UNP-NORM-MDT        PIC X(01) VALUE 'A'.
00018           02   XCTL-PROG           PIC X(08) VALUE SPACES.
00019      *
00020      01   999-PASSWORDS.
00021           02   FILLER              PIC X(01).
00022           02   999-KEY             PIC X(06).
00023           02   FILLER              PIC X(43).
00024      *
00025      01   MESSAGES.
00026           02   PWRD-MSG            PIC X(30)
00027                VALUE 'INVALID PASSWORD'.
00028           02   SELECTION-MSG       PIC X(30)
00029                VALUE 'ERRONEOUS SCREEN ENTERED'.
00032           02   ONLY-ONE-MSG        PIC X(30)
00033                VALUE 'SELECT ONE / MENU OR SCREEN'.
00034           02   OUTPUT-MESS         PIC X(30)
00035                VALUE 'PROGRAM ERROR PROCESSING ENDED'.
00036      *
00037      01   CA-COMMON.
00038           02   CA-FIRST-PASS       PIC X(01).
00039           02   CA-PWRD             PIC X(06).
00040      *
00041      01   LEN                      PIC S9(04) COMP VALUE +0.
00042      01   PW-LEN                   PIC S9(04) COMP VALUE +50.
00043      *
00044      LINKAGE SECTION.
00045      01   DFHCOMMAREA.
00046           02   PASS-INFO           PIC X(07).
00047      *
00048      PROCEDURE DIVISION.
00049           EXEC CICS HANDLE AID ANYKEY (TEST-PASSWORD) END-EXEC.
00050           EXEC CICS HANDLE AID PF10 (LOGOFF) END-EXEC.
00051           EXEC CICS HANDLE CONDITION MAPFAIL(RTRN-TO-CICS)
00052                                     ILLOGIC(PROG-ERR)
00053                                     ERROR(PROG-ERR) END-EXEC.
00054      *
00055           IF EIBCALEN GREATER THAN ZERO NEXT SENTENCE
00056               ELSE MOVE 'X' TO CA-FIRST-PASS
00057                  GO TO RTRN-TO-CICS.
00058           MOVE PASS-INFO TO CA-COMMON.
00059           IF CA-FIRST-PASS = 'Y'
00060               GO TO RTRN-TO-CICS.
```

Fig. 17-3. The source code that will be referred to throughout Chapter 17. Continued to page 217.

```
00061 *
00062  RECEIVE-MAP.
00063      EXEC CICS RECEIVE MAP ('MAPNAMEI') MAPSET('MAPSET')
00064                INTO (MAPNAMEI) END-EXEC.
00065 *
00066  TEST-PASSWORD.
00067      MOVE PASSWORDI TO 999-KEY.
00068      EXEC CICS HANDLE CONDITION NOTFND (CHECK-PWRD) END-EXEC.
00069      EXEC CICS UNLOCK DATASET ('PWRD-DD') END-EXEC.
00070      EXEC CICS READ INTO (999-PASSWORDS) DATASET('PWRD-DD')
00071          RIDFLD (999-KEY) LENGTH (PW-LEN) END-EXEC.
00072      MOVE 'Y' TO PWRD-OK.
00073  CHECK-PWRD.
00074      IF PWRD-OK = 'Y' MOVE PASSWORDI TO CA-PWRD
00075         ELSE MOVE PWRD-MSG TO ERR-LINEO
00076         MOVE -1 TO PASSWORDL
00077         MOVE 'Y' TO ERR-SW
00078         GO TO RTRN-TO-CICS.
00079 *
00080  RESET-ATR.
00081      MOVE UNP-NORM-MDT TO ATSA SELECTIONA.
00082      MOVE SPACES TO ERR-LINEO.
00083 *
00084  TEST-SELECTIONS.
00085      IF ATSI = ' ' MOVE 0 TO ATSL.
00086      IF SELECTIONI = ' ' MOVE 0 TO SELECTIONL.
00087      IF ATSL = 0 AND SELECTIONL = 0
00088         GO TO RTRN-TO-CICS.
00089      IF ATSL GREATER THAN 0 AND SELECTION GREATER THAN 0
00090         MOVE UNP-BRI-MDT TO ATSA
00091                             SELECTIONA
00092         MOVE -1 TO ATSL
00093         MOVE ONLY-ONE-MSG TO ERR-LINEO
00094         GO TO RTRN-TO-CICS.
00095 *
00096  SCREEN-SELECT.
00097      IF ATSL GREATER THAN 0 NEXT SENTENCE
00098         ELSE
00099         GO TO MENU-SELECT.
00100      IF ATSI GREATER THAN 1 AND LESS THAN 20 GO TO PASS-CONTROL.
00101      MOVE 'Y' TO ERR-SW.
00102      MOVE -1 TO ATSL.
00103      MOVE UNP-BRI-MDT TO ATSA.
00104      MOVE SCREEN-MSG TO ERR-LINEO.
00105      GO TO RTRN-TO-CICS.
00106 *
00107  MENU-SELECT.
00108      IF SELECTIONL GREATER THAN 0 NEXT SENTENCE
00109         ELSE
00110         GO TO PASS-CONTROL.
00111      IF SELECTIONI GREATER THAN 0 AND NOT GREATER THAN 9
00112         GO TO XCTL-PROGRAM.
00113      IF ERR-SW = 'N'
00114         MOVE 'Y' TO ERR-SW
00115         MOVE SELECTION-MSG TO ERR-LINEO
00116         MOVE -1 TO SELECTIONL.
00117      MOVE UNP-BRI-MDT TO SELECTIONA.
00118      GO TO RTRN-TO-CICS.
00119 *
00120  XCTL-PROGRAM.
```

```
00121          MOVE +07 TO LEN.
00122          MOVE 'Y' TO CA-FIRST-PASS.
00123          IF SELECTIONI = '1'
00124              MOVE 'PGMNBR2' TO XCTL-PROG.
00125          IF SELECTIONI = '2'
00126              MOVE 'PGMNBR3' TO XCTL-PROG.
00127          IF SELECTIONI = '3'
00128              MOVE 'PGMNBR4' TO XCTL-PROG.
00129          IF SELECTIONI = '4'
00130              MOVE 'PGMNBR5' TO XCTL-PROG.
00131          IF SELECTIONI = '5'
00132              MOVE 'PGMNBR6' TO XCTL-PROG.
00133          IF SELECTIONI = '6'
00134              MOVE 'PGMNBR7' TO XCTL-PROG.
00135          IF SELECTIONI = '7'
00136              MOVE 'PGMNBR8' TO XCTL-PROG.
00137          IF SELECTIONI = '8'
00138              MOVE 'PGMNBR9' TO XCTL-PROG.
00139          IF SELECTIONI = '9'
00140              MOVE 'PGMNBR10' TO XCTL-PROG.
00141          EXEC CICS XCTL PROGRAM (XCTL-PROG)
00142              COMMAREA (CA-COMMON) LENGTH (LEN) END-EXEC.
00143 *
00144    RTRN-TO-CICS.
00145          IF (ERR-SW = 'N') AND (CA-FIRST-PASS = 'N')
00146              MOVE -1 TO SELECTIONL.
00147          IF CA-FIRST-PASS = 'Y'
00148              MOVE CA-PWRD TO PASSWORDO.
00149          MOVE +07 TO LEN.
00150          IF CA-FIRST-PASS = 'Y' OR 'X'
00151              MOVE 'N' TO CA-FIRST-PASS
00152              EXEC CICS SEND MAP('MAPNAMEI') MAPSET('MAPSET')
00153                  ERASE END-EXEC
00154          ELSE EXEC CICS SEND MAP('MAPNAMEI') MAPSET('MAPSET')
00155              FROM (MAPNAMEO) CURSOR DATAONLY END-EXEC.
00156          EXEC CICS RETRUN TRANSID ('MENU') COMMAREA (CA-COMMON)
00157              LENGTH (LEN) END-EXEC.
00158 *
00159    PASS-CONTROL.
00160          MOVE 'Y' TO CA-FIRST-PASS.
00161          MOVE +07 TO LEN.
00162          IF ATSI = '02'
00163              MOVE 'PGMNBR2' TO XCTL-PROG.
00164          IF ATSI = '03'
00165              MOVE 'PGMNBR3' TO XCTL-PROG.
00166          IF ATSI = '04'
00167              MOVE 'PGMNBR4' TO XCTL-PROG.
00168          IF ATSI = '05'
00169              MOVE 'PGMNBR5' TO XCTL-PROG.
00170          IF ATSI = '06'
00171              MOVE 'PGMNBR6' TO XCTL-PROG.
00172          IF ATSI = '07'
00173              MOVE 'PGMNBR7' TO XCTL-PROG.
00174          IF ATSI = '08'
00175              MOVE 'PGMNBR8' TO XCTL-PROG.
00176          IF ATSI = '09'
00177              MOVE 'PGMNBR9' TO XCTL-PROG.
00178          IF ATSI = '10'
00179              MOVE 'PGMNBR10' TO XCTL-PROG.
00180          IF ATSI = '11'
```

```
00181                MOVE 'PGMNBR11' TO XCTL-PROG.
00182            IF ATSI = '12'
00183                MOVE 'PGMNBR12' TO XCTL-PROG.
00184            IF ATSI = '13'
00185                MOVE 'PGMNBR13' TO XCTL-PROG.
00186            IF ATSI = '14'
00187                MOVE 'PGMNBR14' TO XCTL-PROG.
00188            IF ATSI = '15'
00189                MOVE 'PGMNBR15' TO XCTL-PROG.
00190            IF ATSI = '16'
00191                MOVE 'PGMNBR16' TO XCTL-PROG.
00192            EXEC CICS XCTL PROGRAM (XCTL-PROG)
00193                 COMMAREA (CA-COMMON) LEN (LEN) END-EXEC.
00194        *
00195        PROG-ERR.
00196            EXEC SEND FROM(OUTPUT-MESS) LENGTH(LEN) ERASE END-EXEC.
00197            EXEC CICS RETURN END-EXEC.
00198            GOBACK.
00199        LOGOFF.
00200            EXEC CICS SEND MAP(LASTMAP') MAPSET('LASTSET')
00201                 ERASE MAPONLY END-EXEC.
00202            EXEC CICS RETURN END-EXEC.
00203            GOBACK.
```

screen in detail so that subsequent screen displays presented in this session will be self-explanatory.

The EIB, or Execute Interface Block, display: This display represents the contents of the EIB in symbolic form. Should your transaction be using the COMMAREA at this time, the contents of it will also be displayed. (Refer to the EIB definition.)

CONTINUE: If you did any modification on the screen, those changes will be reflected on a subsequent display. You may continue the session by pressing the Enter key.

SUPPRESS DISPLAYS: This option will suppress any further displays until one of the stop conditions (PF9) is met.

STOP CONDITIONS: EDF will display a menu screen for your selection needs.

SCROLL BACK/FORWARD: These commands refer to the EIB command display, which may not fit all on one screen.

PREVIOUS DISPLAY: This command causes the display of the previous screen you used immediately before the current one.

NEXT DISPLAY: Once you have invoked the previous screen, this command will allow you to get back to the current display.

USER DISPLAY: This option will trigger the EDF display, that shows what would be on the screen if the transaction were not running under EDF.

SWITCH HEX/CHAR: This command will cause EDF to switch to a hexadecimal display from a character display.

WORKING STORAGE: This command will allow you to see the contents of your working storage on the top of the screen, or other areas in the CICS partition.

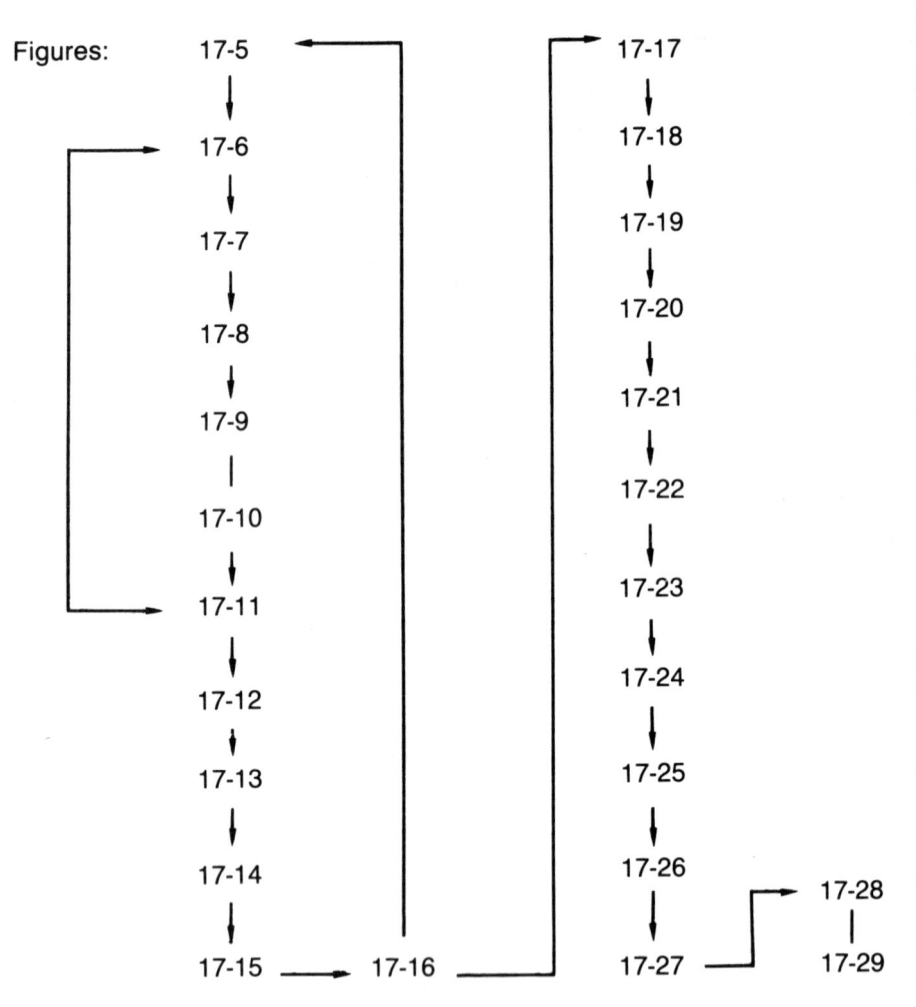

Figures: 17-5 → 17-17
↓ ↓
17-6 17-18
↓ ↓
17-7 17-19
↓ ↓
17-8 17-20
↓ ↓
17-9 17-21
| ↓
17-10 17-22
↓ ↓
17-11 17-23
↓ ↓
17-12 17-24
↓ ↓
17-13 17-25
↓ ↓
17-14 17-26
↓ ↓ → 17-28
17-15 → 17-16 17-27 |
17-29

Fig. 17-4. The figures that illustrate the path the application program will follow because function 5 was removed from the table.

END OF SESSION: Once you are done with your work with EDF, this selection will terminate the transaction.

Figures 17-6 and 17-7 shows the HANDLE AID command prior to and after execution. You may glance at the program listing in Fig. 17-2 and locate that command. Figure 17-7 shows that after executing the HANDLE AID command, the system's response was normal and the program continues.

In Figs. 17-8 and 17-9, another HANDLE AID command is executed, but this one is checking the validity of PF (Command key) 10. (The Handle Aid condition was issued for "anykey.") By now you have probably noticed that CICS will issue two displays for each CICS statement within a major

218

```
TRANSACTION: MENU    PROGRAM: PGMNBR1    TASK NUMBER: 0001323   DISPLAY: 00
STATUS:  PROGRAM INITIATION
    EIETIME    = +0122436
    EIEDATE    = +0086102
    EIBTRNID   = 'MENU'
    EIBTASKN   = +0001323
    EIBTRMID   = 'X101'

    EIBCPOSN   = +00004
    EIBCALEN   = +00000
    EIBAID     = X'7D'                                    AT X'001CC17A'
    EIBFN      = X'0000'                                  AT X'001CC17B'
    EIBRCODE   = X'000000000000'                          AT X'001CC17D'
    EIBDS      = '........'
  + EIBFEQID   = '........'


ENTER:  CONTINUE
PF1 : UNDEFINED            PF2 : SWITCH HEX/CHAR      PF3 : END EDF SESSION
PF4 : SUPPRESS DISPLAYS    PF5 : WORKING STORAGE      PF6 : USER DISPLAY
PF7 : SCROLL BACK          PF8 : SCROLL FORWARD       PF9 : STOP CONDITIONS
PF10: PREVIOUS DISPLAY     PF11: UNDEFINED            PF12: UNDEFINED
```

Fig. 17-5. The initial EDF screen.

```
TRANSACTION: MENU    PROGRAM: PGMNBR1    TASK NUMBER: 0001323    DISPLAY: 00
STATUS:  ABOUT TO EXECUTE COMMAND
EXEC CICS HANDLE AID
     ANYKEY ()



OFFSET:X'00075E'    LINE:00049              EIBFN=X'0206'

ENTER: CONTINUE
PF1  : UNDEFINED           PF2 : SWITCH HEX/CHAR    PF3 : END EDF SESSION
PF4  : SUPPRESS DISPLAYS   PF5 : WORKING STORAGE    PF6 : USER DISPLAY
PF7  : SCROLL BACK         PF8 : SCROLL FORWARD     PF9 : STOP CONDITIONS
PF10 : PREVIOUS DISPLAY    PF11: UNDEFINED          PF12: UNDEFINED
```

Fig. 17-6. The HANDLE AID command prior to execution.

```
TRANSACTION: MENU      PROGRAM: PGMNBR1    TASK NUMBER:  0001323  DISPLAY:  00
STATUS:  COMMAND EXECUTION COMPLETE
EXEC CICS HANDLE AID
ANYKEY ( )



OFFSET:X'000075E'        LINE:00049              EIBFN=X'0206'
RESPONSE: NORMAL                                 EIBRCODE=X'000000000000'

ENTER:  CONTINUE
PF1 : UNDEFINED         PF2 : SWITCH HEX/CHAR    PF3 : END EDF SESSION
PF4 : SUPPRESS DISPLAYS PF5 : WORKING STORAGE    PF6 : USER DISPLAY
PF7 : SCROLL BACK       PF8 : SCROLL FORWARD     PF9 : STOP CONDITIONS
PF10: PREVIOUS DISPLAY  PF11: UNDEFINED          PF12: UNDEFINED
```

Fig. 17-7. The HANDLE AID command after execution.

```
TRANSACTION: MENU     PROGRAM: PGMNBR1     TASK NUMBER: 0001323   DISPLAY: 00
STATUS:   ABOUT TO EXECUTE COMMAND
EXEC CICS HANDLE AID
    PF10 ( )



OFFSET:X'0007A4'        LINE:00050              EIBFN=X'0206'

ENTER: CONTINUE
PF1 : UNDEFINED           PF2 : SWITCH HEX/CHAR    PF3 : END EDF SESSION
PF4 : SUPPRESS DISPLAYS   PF5 : WORKING STORAGE    PF6 : USER DISPLAY
PF7 : SCROLL BACK         PF8 : SCROLL FORWARD     PF9 : STOP CONDITIONS
PF10: PREVIOUS DISPLAY    PF11: UNDEFINED          PF12: UNDEFINED
```

Fig. 17-8. Another HANDLE AID command prior to execution.

```
TRANSACTION: MENU    PROGRAM: PGMNBR1      TASK NUMBER:  0001323  DISPLAY: 00
STATUS:  COMMAND EXECUTION COMPLETE
EXEC CICS HANDLE AID
PF10 ()


OFFSET:X'0007A4'            LINE:00050           EIBFN=X'0206'
RESPONSE: NORMAL                                 EIBRCODE=X'0000000000000'

ENTER: CONTINUE
PF1 : UNDEFINED              PF2 : SWITCH HEX/CHAR      PF3 : END EDF SESSION
PF4 : SUPPRESS DISPLAYS      PF5 : WORKING STORAGE      PF6 : USER DISPLAY
PF7 : SCROLL BACK            PF8 : SCROLL FORWARD       PF9 : STOP CONDITIONS
PF10: PREVIOUS DISPLAY       PF11: UNDEFINED            PF12: ABEND USER TASK
```

Fig. 17-9. The second HANDLE AID command after execution.

command structure, and that Function key 10 in our particular example refers to the application program and will log us off our system.

Figures 17-10 and 17-11 refer to the before and after execution status of the HANDLE CONDITION command. Note that response is still normal, and we are continuing the EDF session. Next, in Fig. 17-12 we are issuing a send map command. Figure 17-13 shows that the system responds by displaying the screen. Figure 17-14 indicates that the map was sent, and that all systems are still go with regards to the transaction. Figure 17-15 indicates that a RETURN command involving TRANSID MENU is about to be sent. It shows program termination (status) in Fig. 17-16. This now continues with the reinvocation of the current transaction (application program). The program is initialized (Fig. 17-17), and continuation of it is requested in Fig. 17-18.

Figure 17-19 picks up from the SEND MAP command. This is followed up by a RECEIVE MAP command presented in Fig. 17-20. Figure 17-21 shows a HANDLE CONDITION that is handling a not-found situation, which is caused by the fact that the transaction corresponding to function five is not in existence. Figure 17-22 shows the completion of the Handle Condition command while an unlock option is specified (Figs. 17-23 and 17-24).

Figures 17-25 and 17-26 read the password file before determining the status of the terminal operator requesting the read. Afterward, Figs. 17-27 and 17-28 will execute an exit routine out of the current transaction. Once branching is complete, the programmer's message will be sent to the terminal (Fig. 17-29) advising the terminal operator that a program error has taken place and processing is ended. Figure 17-30 shows the actual message generated.

17.4 COMMAND LEVEL INTERPRETER (CECI)

The command level interpreter allows you to issue and execute a command without the mechanism of an application program. Thus, you may read a file interactively, let the command execute, and then review the results.

To accomplish this, clear the screen, key in CECI, and press the Enter key. Figure 17-31 shows the display of all valid commands. Assume you selected the READ command. Then, as shown in Fig. 17-32, the full complement of the command is shown. In Fig. 17-33, mandatory input requirements, such as the dataset name, the INTO and LENGTH options, and the key field, are indicated.

Once you have specified to CECI the command that you wish to invoke and pressed the Enter key, the result will be a response by the system (Fig. 17-34) showing that the command was executed successfully. Here we have verified the following:

1. The correct command format (if we weren't thoroughly familiar with it.)
2. The accuracy of data relative to a file or a record key (etc.).

```
TRANSACTION: MENU      PROGRAM: PGMNBR1      TASK NUMBER: 0001323   DISPLAY: 00
STATUS:  ABOUT TO EXECUTE COMMAND
EXEC CICS HANDLE CONDITION
   ERROR ( )
   ILLOGIC ( )
   MAPFAIL ( )




OFFSET:X'0007EA'      LINE:00051              EIBFN=X'0204'

ENTER: CONTINUE
PF1 : UNDEFINED          PF2 : SWITCH HEX/CHAR    PF3 : END EDF SESSION
PF4 : SUPPRESS DISPLAYS  PF5 : WORKING STORAGE    PF6 : USER DISPLAY
PF7 : SCROLL BACK        PF8 : SCROLL FORWARD     PF9 : STOP CONDITIONS
PF10: PREVIOUS DISPLAY   PF11: UNDEFINED          PF12: UNDEFINED
```

Fig. 17-10. The HANDLE CONDITION command prior to execution.

```
TRANSACTION: MENU    PROGRAM: PGMNBR1    TASK NUMBER:  0001323  DISPLAY: 00
STATUS:  COMMAND EXECUTION COMPLETE
EXEC CICS HANDLE CONDITION
   ERROR ()
   ILLOGIC ()
   MAPFAIL ()



OFFSET:X'0007EA'     LINE:00051               EIBFN=X'0204'
RESPONSE: NORMAL                              EIBRCODE=X'000000000000'

ENTER:  CONTINUE
PF1 : UNDEFINED         PF2 : SWITCH HEX/CHAR    PF3 : END EDF SESSION
PF4 : SUPPRESS DISPLAYS PF5 : WORKING STORAGE    PF6 : USER DISPLAY
PF7 : SCROLL BACK       PF8 : SCROLL FORWARD     PF9 : STOP CONDITIONS
PF10: PREVIOUS DISPLAY  PF11: UNDEFINED          PF12: ABEND USER TASK
```

Fig. 17-11. The HANDLE CONDITION command after execution.

```
TRANSACTION: MENU      PROGRAM: PGMNBR1    TASK NUMBER:   0001323  DISPLAY: 00
STATUS:  ABOUT TO EXECUTE COMMAND
EXEC CICS SEND MAP
   MAP ('MAPNAME')
   FROM ('..........................................','....')
   MAPSET ('MAPSET')
   TERMINAL
   ERASE


OFFSET:X'000C62'       LINE:00152              EIBFN=X'1804'

ENTER: CONTINUE
PF1 : UNDEFINED            PF2 : SWITCH HEX/CHAR      PF3 : END EDF SESSSION
PF4 : SUPPRESS DISPLAYS    PF5 : WORKING STORAGE      PF6 : USER DISPLAY
PF7 : SCROLL BACK          PF8 : SCROLL FORWARD       PF9 : STOP CONDITIONS
PF10: PREVIOUS DISPLAY     PF11: UNDEFINED            PF12: ABEND USER TASK
```

Fig. 17-12. A send map command.

```
SCREEN: 1                                    ADVANCE TO SCREEN: ___


                    CONSOLIDATED AMERICAN
                          MAIN MENU

                    1. DEMOGRAPHIC MAINTENANCE
                    2. EMPLOYEE LISTING
                    3. SALES
                    4. ACCOUNTS PAYABLE
                    5. ACCOUNTS RECEIVABLE
                    6. VENDOR LISTING
                    7. SECURITY
                    8. TABLE MAINTENANCE
                    9. TABLE DISPLAY

                    _ ENTER SELECTION


         PASSWORD: ___                       PF10: LOGOFF
```

Fig. 17-13. The display of the screen.

```
TRANSACTION: MENU      PROGRAM: PGMNBR1     TASK NUMBER:  0001323  DISPLAY: 00
STATUS:  COMMAND EXECUTION COMPLETE
EXEC CICS SEND MAP
MAP ('MAPNAME')
FROM (.............................................................)
MAPSET ('MAPSET')
TERMINAL
ERASE


OFFSET:X'000C62'          LINE:00152              EIBFN=X'1804'
RESPONSE: NORMAL                                  EIBRCODE=X'0000000000000'

ENTER:  CONTINUE
PF1 :  UNDEFINED           PF2 : SWITCH HEX/CHAR      PF3 : END EDF SESSION
PF4 :  SUPPRESS DISPLAYS   PF5 : WORKING STORAGE      PF6 : USER DISPLAY
PF7 :  SCROLL BACK         PF8 : SCROLL FORWARD       PF9 : STOP CONDITIONS
PF10:  PREVIOUS DISPLAY    PF11: UNDEFINED            PF12: ABEND USER TASK
```

Fig. 17-14. Screen showing that the map was sent and everything is still normal.

```
TRANSACTION: MENU      PROGRAM: PGMNBR1    TASK NUMBER: 0001323   DISPLAY: 00
STATUS: ABOUT TO EXECUTE COMMAND
 EXEC CICS RETURN
   TRANSID ('MENU')
   COMMAREA ('N......')
   LENGTH (+00007)


 OFFSET:X'000D52'      LINE:00156              EIBFN=X'0E08'

ENTER: CONTINUE
PF1 : UNDEFINED           PF2 : SWITCH HEX/CHAR    PF3 : END EDF SESSION
PF4 : SUPPRESS DISPLAYS   PF5 : WORKING STORAGE    PF6 : USER DISPLAY
PF7 : SCROLL BACK         PF8 : SCROLL FORWARD     PF9 : STOP CONDITIONS
PF10: PREVIOUS DISPLAY    PF11: UNDEFINED          PF12: ABEND USER TASK
```

Fig. 17-15. Screen showing a RETURN command about to be sent.

```
TRANSACTION: MENU    PROGRAM: PGMNBR1    TASK NUMBER: 0001323   DISPLAY: 00
STATUS: PROGRAM TERMINATION

ENTER: CONTINUE
PF1 : UNDEFINED             PF2 : SWITCH HEX/CHAR      PF3 : END EDF SESSION
PF4 : SUPPRESS DISPLAYS     PF5 : WORKING STORAGE      PF6 : USER DISPLAY
PF7 : SCROLL BACK           PF8 : SCROLL FORWARD       PF9 : STOP CONDITIONS
PF10: PREVIOUS DISPLAY      PF11: UNDEFINED            PF12: ABEND USER TASK
```

Fig. 17-16. Screen showing the program-termination status.

```
TRANSACTION: MENU    PROGRAM: PGMNBR1    TASK NUMBER: 0001323   DISPLAY: 00
STATUS:  PROGRAM INITIATION
    COMMAREA   = 'N........'
    EIBTIME    = +0122436
    EIBDATE    = +0086102
    EIBTRNID   = 'MENU'
    EIBTASKN   = +0001323
    EIBTRMID   = 'X101'

    EIBCPOSN   = +01309
    EIBCALEN   = +00007
    EIBAID     = X'7A'                                    AT X'001D53EA'
    EIBFN      = X'0000'                                  AT X'001D53EB'
    EIBRCODE   = X'000000000000'                          AT X'001D53ED'
    EIBDS      = '........'
  + EIBREQID   = '........'

ENTER: CONTINUE
PF1 : UNDEFINED             PF2 : SWITCH HEX/CHAR      PF3 : END EDF SESSION
PF4 : SUPPRESS DISPLAYS     PF5 : WORKING STORAGE      PF6 : USER DISPLAY
PF7 : SCROLL BACK           PF8 : SCROLL FORWARD       PF9 : STOP CONDITIONS
PF10: PREVIOUS DISPLAY      PF11: UNDEFINED            PF12: UNDEFINED
```

Fig. 17-17. The program is initialized.

```
TRANSACTION: MENU                          TASK NUMBER: 0001323  DISPLAY: 00
STATUS: TASK TERMINATION
TO CONTINUE EDF SESSION REPLY YES                        REPLY: ___
ENTER: CONTINUE
PF1 : UNDEFINED            PF2 : SWITCH HEX/CHAR    PF3 : END EDF SESSION
PF4 : SUPPRESS DISPLAYS    PF5 : WORKING STORAGE    PF6 : USER DISPLAY
PF7 : SCROLL BACK          PF8 : SCROLL FORWARD     PF9 : STOP CONDITIONS
PF10: PREVIOUS DISPLAY     PF11: UNDEFINED          PF12: ABEND USER TASK
```

Fig. 17-18. The continuation of the program is requested.

```
TRANSACTION: MENU     PROGRAM: PGMNBR1    TASK NUMBER: 0001323  DISPLAY: 00
STATUS: ABOUT TO EXECUTE COMMAND
EXEC CICS RECEIVE MAP
MAP ('MAPNAME')
INTO ('................................................')
MAPSET ('MAPSET')
TERMINAL



OFFSET:X'0008A4'       LINE:00063              EIBFN=X'1802'

ENTER: CONTINUE
PF1 : UNDEFINED            PF2 : SWITCH HEX/CHAR    PF3 : END EDF SESSION
PF4 : SUPPRESS DISPLAYS    PF5 : WORKING STORAGE    PF6 : USER DISPLAY
PF7 : SCROLL BACK          PF8 : SCROLL FORWARD     PF9 : STOP CONDITIONS
PF10: PREVIOUS DISPLAY     PF11: UNDEFINED          PF12: ABEND USER TASK
```

Fig. 17-19. The results of the send command.

```
TRANSACTION: MENU      PROGRAM: PGMNBR1      TASK NUMBER: 0001323   DISPLAY: 00
STATUS:  COMMAND EXECUTION COMPLETE
EXEC CICS RECEIVE MAP
    MAP ('MAPNAME')
    INTO ('..............5...PASWRD..............'....)
    MAPSET ('MAPSET')
    TERMINAL


OFFSET:X'0008A4'           LINE:00063              EIBFN=X'1802'
RESPONSE: NORMAL                                   EIBRCODE=X'000000000000'

ENTER:  CONTINUE
PF1 : UNDEFINED           PF2 : SWITCH HEX/CHAR     PF3 : END EDF SESSION
PF4 : SUPFRESS DISPLAYS   PF5 : WORKING STORAGE     PF6 : USER DISPLAY
PF7 : SCROLL BACK         PF8 : SCROLL FORWARD      PF9 : STOP CONDITIONS
PF10: PREVIOUS DISPLAY    PF11: UNDEFINED           PF12: ABEND USER TASK
```

Fig. 17-20. The receive map command.

```
TRANSACTION: MENU      PROGRAM: PGMNBR1     TASK NUMBER:  0001323   DISPLAY: 00
STATUS:  ABOUT TO EXECUTE COMMAND
EXEC CICS HANDLE CONDITION
NOTFND ( )




OFFSET:X'0008DA'              LINE:00068              EIBFN=X'0204'


ENTER:  CONTINUE
PF1 : UNDEFINED            PF2 : SWITCH HEX/CHAR     PF3 : END EDF SESSION
PF4 : SUPPRESS DISPLAYS    PF5 : WORKING STORAGE     PF6 : USER DISPLAY
PF7 : SCROLL BACK          PF8 : SCROLL FORWARD      PF9 : STOP CONDITIONS
PF10: PREVIOUS DISPLAY     PF11: UNDEFINED           PF12: UNDEFINED
```

Fig. 17-21. A HANDLE CONDITION handling a not-found condition.

```
TRANSACTION: MENU      PROGRAM: PGMNBR1      TASK NUMBER: 0001323   DISPLAY: 00
STATUS:  COMMAND EXECUTION COMPLETE
EXEC CICS HANDLE CONDITION
NOTFND ( )


OFFSET:X'00083A'         LINE:00068           EIBFN=X'0204'
RESPONSE: NORMAL                              EIBRCODE=X'000000000000'

ENTER:  CONTINUE
PF1 : UNDEFINED            PF2 : SWITCH HEX/CHAR     PF3 : END EDF SESSION
PF4 : SUPPRESS DISPLAYS    PF5 : WORKING STORAGE     PF6 : USER DISPLAY
PF7 : SCROLL BACK          PF8 : SCROLL FORWARD      PF9 : STOP CONDITIONS
PF10: PREVIOUS DISPLAY     PF11: UNDEFINED           PF12: ABEND USER TASK
```

Fig. 17-22. The completion of the HANDLE CONDITION command.

```
TRANSACTION: MENU      PROGRAM: PGMNBR1      TASK NUMBER:  0001323  DISPLAY: 00
STATUS: ABOUT TO EXECUTE COMMAND
 EXEC CICS UNLOCK
      DATASET('PWRDFILE')




OFFSET:X'000938'        LINE:00069                EIBFN=X'060A'


ENTER: CONTINUE
PF1 : UNDEFINED             PF2 : SWITCH HEX/CHAR      PF3 : END EDF SESSION
PF4 : SUPPRESS DISPLAYS     PF5 : WORKING STORAGE      PF6 : USER DISPLAY
PF7 : SCROLL BACK           PF8 : SCROLL FORWARD       PF9 : STOP CONDITIONS
PF10: PREVIOUS DISPLAY      PF11: UNDEFINED            PF12: ABEND USER TASK
```

Fig. 17-23. The specification of an unlock option, part one.

```
TRANSACTION: MENU      PROGRAM: PGMNBR1    TASK NUMBER: 0001323 DISPLAY: 00
STATUS   COMMAND EXECUTION COMPLETE
EXEC CICS UNLOCK
     DATASET('PWRDFILE')




OFFSET:X'000938'          LINE:00069              EIBFN=X'060A'
RESPONSE: NORMAL                                  EIBCODE=X'000000000000'

ENTER:  CONTINUE
PF1 : UNDEFINED            PF2 : SWITCH HEX/CHAR     PF3 : END EDF SESSION
PF4 : SUPPRESS DISPLAYS    PF5 : WORKING STORAGE     PF6 : USER DISPLAY
PF7 : SCROLL BACK          PF8 : SCROLL FORWARD      PF9 : STOP CONDITIONS
PF10: PREVIOUS DISPLAY     PF11: UNDEFINED           PF12: ABEND USER TASK
```

Fig. 17-24. The specification of an unlock option, part two.

```
TRANSACTION: MENU      PROGRAM: PGMNBR1     TASK NUMBER: 0001323   DISPLAY: 00
STATUS:  ABOUT TO EXECUTE COMMAND
EXEC CICS READ
    DATASET('PWRDFILE')
    INTO(' PASSWD................................')
    LENGTH (+00050)
    RIDFLD ('PASSWD')


OFFSET:X'000998'          LINE:00070              EIBFN=X'0602'

ENTER: CONTINUE
PF1 : UNDEFINED             PF2 : SWITCH HEX/CHAR    PF3 : END EDF SESSION
PF4 : SUPPRESS DISPLAYS     PF5 : WORKING STORAGE    PF6 : USER DISPLAY
PF7 : SCROLL BACK           PF8 : SCROLL FORWARD     PF9 : STOP CONDITIONS
PF10: PREVIOUS DISPLAY      PF11: UNDEFINED          PF12: ABEND USER TASK
```

Fig. 17-25. Reading the password file, part one.

```
TRANSACTION: MENU     PROGRAM: PGMNBR1     TASK NUMBER: 0001323  DISPLAY: 00
STATUS:  COMMAND EXECUTION COMPLETE
EXEC CICS READ
     DATASET('PWRDFILE')
     INTO(' PASSWDJOHN DOE                       ')
     LENGTH (+00050)
     RIDFLD ('PASSWD')


OFFSET:X'000998'          LINE:00070          EIBFN=X'0602'
RESPONSE: NORMAL                              EIBRCODE=X'000000000000'

ENTER:  CONTINUE
PF1 : UNDEFINED           PF2 : SWITCH HEX/CHAR     PF3 : END EDF SESSION
PF4 : SUPPRESS DISPLAYS   PF5 : WORKING STORAGE     PF6 : USER DISPLAY
PF7 : SCROLL BACK         PF8 : SCROLL FORWARD      PF9 : STOP CONDITIONS
PF10: PREVIOUS DISPLAY    PF11: UNDEFINED           PF12: ABEND USER TASK
```

Fig. 17-26. Reading the password file, part two.

```
TRANSACTION: MENU      PROGRAM: PGMNBR1      TASK NUMBER: 0001323    DISPLAY: 00
STATUS: ABOUT TO EXECUTE COMMAND
EXEC CICS XCTL
   PROGRAM ('PGMNBR6')
   COMMAREA ('YPASSWD')
   LENGTH (+00007)


OFFSET:X'000BB6'      LINE:00141                 EIBFN=X'0E04'

ENTER: CONTINUE
PF1 : UNDEFINED         PF2 : SWITCH HEX/CHAR     PF3 : END EDF SESSION
PF4 : SUPPRESS DISPLAYS PF5 : WORKING STORAGE     PF6 : USER DISPLAY
PF7 : SCROLL BACK       PF8 : SCROLL FORWARD      PF9 : STOP CONDITIONS
PF10: PREVIOUS DISPLAY  PF11: UNDEFINED           PF12: ABEND USER TASK
```

Fig. 17-27. The exit routine out of the current transaction, part one.

```
TRANSACTION: MENU      PROGRAM: PGMNBR1    TASK NUMBER: 0001323  DISPLAY: 00
STATUS:  COMMAND EXECUTION COMPLETE
  EXEC CICS XCTL
       PROGRAM ('PGMNBR6')
       COMMAREA ('YPASSWD')
       LENGTH  (+00007)




OFFSET:X'000BB6'        LINE:00141              EIBFN=X'0E04'
RESPONSE: PGMIDERR                              EIBRCODE=X'010000000000'

ENTER: CONTINUE
PF1 : UNDEFINED            PF2 : SWITCH HEX/CHAR    PF3 : END EDF SESSION
PF4 : SUPPRESS DISPLAYS    PF5 : WORKING STORAGE    PF6 : USER DISPLAY
PF7 : SCROLL BACK          PF8 : SCROLL FORWARD     PF9 : STOP CONDITIONS
PF10: PREVIOUS DISPLAY     PF11: UNDEFINED          PF12: ABEND USER TASK
```

Fig. 17-28. The exit routine of the current transaction, part two.

```
TRANSACTION: MENU    PROGRAM: PGMNBR1    TASK NUMBER: 0001323  DISPLAY: 00
STATUS: ABOUT TO EXECUTE COMMAND
EXEC CICS SEND
FROM ('PROGRAM ERROR PROCESSING ENDED')
LENGTH (+00030)
ERASE


OFFSET:X'000BB6'         LINE:00141              EIBFN=X'0E04'

ENTER: CONTINUE
PF1 : UNDEFINED           PF2 : SWITCH HEX/CHAR    PF3 : END EDF SESSION
PF4 : SUPPRESS DISPLAYS   PF5 : WORKING STORAGE    PF6 : USER DISPLAY
PF7 : SCROLL BACK         PF8 : SCROLL FORWARD     PF9 : STOP CONDITIONS
PF10: PREVIOUS DISPLAY    PF11: UNDEFINED          PF12: ABEND USER TASK
```

Fig. 17-29. The programmer's message being sent to the terminal.

PROGRAM ERROR PROCESSING ENDED

Fig. 17-30. The actual message generated.

```
STATUS:   ENTER ONE OF THE FOLLOWING

ABEND        ENDBR        PUSH         SYNCPOINT
ADDRESS      ENQ          READ         TRACE
ALLOCATE     ENTER        READNEXT     UNLOCK
ASKTIME      EXTRACT      READPREV     WAIT
ASSIGN       FREE         READQ        WRITE
BIF          FREEMAIN     RECEIVE      WRITEQ
BUILD        GETMAIN      RELEASE      XCTL
CANCEL       HANDLE       RESETBR
CONNECT      IGNORE       RESYNC
CONVERSE     ISSUE        RETRIEVE
DELAY        JOURNAL      RETURN
DELETE       LINK         REWRITE
DELETEQ      LOAD         ROUTE
DEQ          POINT        SEND
DISABLE      POP          START
DUMP         POST         STARTBR
ENABLE       PURGE        SUSPEND

PF:  1 HELP  2 HEX  3 END  4 EIB  5 VAR  6 USER
```

Fig. 17-31. A display of all valid CECI commands.

17.5 MASTER TERMINAL COMMANDS

The CICS Master Terminal Transaction (CSMT) can be used to perform a number of commands with regard to a task or file; it can change the status of a transaction and load the new version of an application program or mapset, among other things.

The following is a list of these functions.

CSMT OPE,DAT,FILEID = ...
Opens the file, making it available to CICS.

CSMT CLO,DAT,FILEID =
Closes the file, making it unavailable to CICS.

CSMT ENA,DAT,FILEID = ...
Enables the file for accessing by CICS.

CSMT DISAB, DAT, FILEID = ...
Disables the file for accessing by CICS.

CSMT DAT,INQ,FILEID = ...
Displays file status related information.

243

```
STATUS:   COMMAND  SYNTAX  CHECK
EXEC CICS   READ
     DATASET()                                                              NAME=
     [ SYSID() ]
     SET() / INTO()
     [ LENGTH() ]
     RIDFLD()
     [ KEYLENGTH() [ GENERIC ] ]
     [ SEGSET() / SEGSETALL ]
     [ RBA / RRN / DEBREC / DEBKEY ]
     [ GTEQ / EQUAL ]
     [ UPDATE ]

MESSAGES: 2 SEVERE,   0 ERROR,   13 WARNING,   0 INFORMATORY.
PF1: 1 HELP 2 HEX 3 END 4 EIB 5 VAR 6 USER 7 SBH 8 SFH 9 MSG 10 SB 11 SF
```

Fig. 17-32. The full complement of the command.

```
READ DATASET('DDNAME') INTO (&REC) LENGTH(+70) RIDFLD(331231234)
STATUS: ABOUT TO EXECUTE COMMAND                                            NAME=
EXEC CICS   READ
     DATASET ( 'DDNAME' )
     [ SYSID() ]
     SET() / INTO()
     [ LENGTH( +00070 ) ]
     RIDFLD( '331231234' )
     [ KEYLENGTH() [ GENERIC ] ]
     [ SEGSET() / SEGSETALL ]
     [ RBA / RRN / DEBREC / DEBKEY ]
     [ GTEQ / EQUAL ]
     [ UPDATE ]

PF1: 1 HELP 2 HEX 3 END 4 EIB 5 VAR 6 USER 7 SBH 8 SFH 9 MSG 10 SB 11 SF
```

Fig. 17-33. The mandatory input requirements.

```
READ DATASET('DDNAME') INTO (&REC) LENGTH(+70) RIDFLD(331231234)
STATUS:  COMMAND EXECUTION COMPLETE                        NAME=
EXEC C=CS  READ
DATASET ( DDNAME' )
[ SYSID( ) ]
SET( ) / INTO( '331231234JOHN DOE       ELMHURST      IL  '...' )
[ LENGTH( +00070 ) ]
RIDFLE( '331231234' )
[ KEYLENGTH( ) [ GENERIC ] ]
[ SEGSET( ) / SEGSETALL ]
[ RBA / RRN / DEBREC / DEBKEY ]
[ GTEQ / EQUAL ]
[ UPDATE ]
RESPONSE: NORMAL                          ERIBRCODE=X'000000000000'
PF1: 1 HELP 2 HEX 3 END 4 EIB 5 VAR 6 USER 7 SBH 8 SFH 9 MSG 10 SB 11 SF
```

Fig. 17-34. The display that shows that the command was executed successfully.

CSMT NEW,PGRMID = ...
Loads new version of map or program.

CSMT TRMNAT, TERMID = ...
Aborts a task via the terminal I.D.

CSMT ENA,SIN,TRNACT,TRANID = ...
Enables a transaction.

CSMT DISAB,SIN,TRNACT,TRANID = ...
Disables a transaction.

CSMT SIN,PRO,INQ,PGRMID = ...
Displays program-status related data.

CSMT ENA,SIN,PRO,PGRMID = ...
Enables an application program.

CSMT DISAB,SIN,PRO,PGRMID = ...
Disables an application program.

17.6 JOURNAL CONTROL

A journal is a special purpose sequential dataset used in order to reconstruct a file. Journal files are identified by the journal file numbers 2 through 99, the first being reserved for the system log and the rest for the user journal.

Journal files are variable length, meaning that the application programmer must supply both the data and length. Standard format for the JOURNAL command is shown in Fig. 17-35.

On the next page are explanations of the statements used.

```
EXEC CICS JOURNAL
    JFILEID(DATA-VALUE)
    JTYPEID(DATA-VALUE)
    FROM(DATA-VALUE)
    LENGTH(DATA-VALUE)
    (PREFIX(DATA-AREA))
    (PFXLENF(DATA-VALUE))
    (WAIT)
    (REQID(DATA-AREA)
    (STARTID(DATA-AREA))
    (STARTIO)
    END-EXEC.
```

Fig. 17-35. The standard format for the JOURNAL command.

JFILEID   This binary half-word field specifies the journal dataset to receive the data. Data values may range between 2 and 99.
JTYPEID   This statement specifies a two-character identifier for the journal record. It is used to put multiple record types on a single journal.
FROM   This statement specifies the user data to be included in the journal record.
PREFIX   This statement specifies the user prefix data for the journal record.
PFXLENF   This statement specifies the length of the user prefix.
WAIT   This command allows the application programmer to request synchronous journal output. When you use the WAIT option, the requesting task will wait until the output is completed. This ensures that the journal record is written before processing continues.
STARTID   This statement tells the system that the journal output operation should start immediately.
REQID   A unique identifier for the record is returned by CICS within this field, so that the record may be referenced at a later time.

Please note that setting up and utilizing journal control pertains to the software department in most installations. Thus, some of the options (for example, JTYPEID and PREFIX) are normally referenced through predefined standards.

The WAIT command specifies to wait until the journal data is physically written to the device. The format for the WAIT command is as follows:

```
EXEC CICS WAIT JOURNAL
     JFILEID(DATA-VALUE)
     (REQID(DATA-VALUE))
     (STARTIO)
END-EXEC.
```

SUMMARY

The ABEND command is required in your application program to provide procedures and logic should your program abnormally terminate. The Execute Diagnostics Facility (EDF) allows you to review the execution of your program, statement by statement, under the control of the Execute Diagnostics Facility software.

The Command Level Interpreter, or CECI, allows you to issue and execute a command without the mechanism of an application program. Thus you may READ a file interactively, let the command execute, and then review the result.

The CICS Master Terminal Transaction (CSMT) can be used to perform a number of commands, such as opening and closing files, enabling and disabling transactions, loading maps, aborting transactions, and displaying file-status information.

A Journal is a special purpose sequential dataset used in order to reconstruct a file. Journal Files are identified by the Journal File Numbers ranging from 2 through 99. Journal Files are variable length records, meaning that the programmer analyst must supply both the length and the data.

QUESTIONS

1. True or false: the EXEC CICS HANDLE ABEND condition is used to force an abnormal termination during the execution of a CICS transaction in order to help the programmer debug his system.
2. Define the function of the Execute Diagnostics Facility software package.
3. Define the function of the Command Level Interpreter.
4. Describe the following terms:

    Journal File
    SyncPoint

5. What are the following commands used for?

    CSMT NEW,PGRMID = ...
    CSMT DAT,INQ,FILEID = ...

Glossary

Glossary

abend—Means the abnormal termination of a task due to error.

add mode—The mode in which a new record is added to a dataset that doesn't already contain the record.

application program—In an on-line environment represents duration of a transaction cycle. On-line programs, as opposed to their batch counterparts are short and highly specialized.

attribute byte—That portion of a field that can alter its own characteristics. For example, you can protect a field by modifying the attribute byte. You can highlight or intensify such field, underscore it, or introduce a color scheme, if your terminals have the required hardware facilities. You use the attribute bytes in connection with map related datasets.

automatic task initiation—This feature is designed to trigger a task automatically. The trigger level is usually set by the systems programmer via a set of entries made into the Destination Control Table.

basic mapping support—A feature that comes into play as a link between the application program and the terminal control functions to provide device and format independence. It is a tool that allows the application programmer to design screen layouts in batch mode or interactively.

batch processing—A type of processing in which the result is not immediately available. Rather, it requires turn-around time, which may affect the timely status of the information presented.

BLL—Stands for Base Locator for Linkage and it provides addressability to the programmer when storage space is required outside his own program area.

browsing—The browse mechanism consists of a number of CICS commands. It is designed to allow for sequential processing in an otherwise purely interactive environment.

BTAM—The Basic Telecommunications Access Method, which is provided by the terminal control program in order to establish a communications link between your application program and the terminal.

CECI—The Command Level Interpreter, an interactive tool designed to help you structure and execute your commands without relying on a program.

CICS—The Customer Information Control System, an IBM telecommunications monitor providing the user with on-line facilities.

COBOL (ANS)—The standardized Common Business Oriented Language for developing applications.

Common Work Area—A storage area within the system available to every application program. In order to maintain communications with the CWA, you must define it in the LINKAGE-SECTION.

conversational—A mode that results when you use the CONVERSE command in your CICS program. The overall effect of this is like issuing a SEND MAP command followed by a WAIT TERMINAL instruction and a RECEIVE TERMINAL command. All that is accomplished without ever issuing a RETURN TRANSID statement.

data spaces—VSAM clusters or datasets on a direct access device.

delete mode—This mode requires the existence of a valid record on the file. Once the record is retrieved, it will not have to comply with any current edit criteria.

destination control table—CICS requires the entry into the Destination Control Table pertinent information with regard to Transient Data Sets, including the definition of the name and the trigger level.

DFHCOMMAREA—This area stores and relays messages between two or more transactions as long as transmission is successive. If data is not passed during the current transaction cycle, it will be destroyed at the end of the task.

DFHEIBLK block—This block contains a number of useful functions available for the programmer, including the EIBCALEN, which allows you to check the total length of the communications area. It also contains cursor positions, task numbers, and attention identifiers.

dynamic area—This area contains a number of storage facilities, such as the Terminal Control Area, the Transaction Work Area, the Execute Interface Block, and application programs.

EDF—The Execute Diagnostics Facility is a comprehensive, interactive IBM package. The purpose of this software is to perform trouble shooting, to find logical problems during the execution of an on-line transaction.

ESDS—Entry-Sequenced records within the VSAM structure. These records are in the physical sequence in which they were entered or loaded into the file. The usual way of retrieving records from an ESDS file is to access them sequentially.

FCT—File Control Table.

File Control Table—One of a number of internal CICS tables, the File Control Table, or FCT, must be entered for every file utilized in the system.

fourth generation languages—Languages that are quick to interface with on-line systems, but overall don't seem to have the power for handling more complex assignments. At best they are great inquiry-type languages.

function keys—These keys allow the terminal operator to invoke a number of different programmable procedures, such as paging, updating, and branching to various other parts of the system.

generic key—Generic search is a method used to locate an individual record based on a partially defined key.

help screens—Help screens are invoked when the user has a specific problem in completing a particular task or procedure. By utilizing a Command key, the terminal operator will be able to suspend his current activities, attain the answer, and branch back to his current screen uninterrupted.

inquiry—A method of accessing a given file or database to review the contents without any attempt to modify them.

ISAM—The Indexed Sequential Access Method, ISAM, creates three distinct areas on disk: the index, the prime area, and the overflow area. Additions are placed into the overflow area, causing a great deal of sluggishness as the volume increases and prompts periodic file reorganization.

journaling—This technique provides the application programmer with vital data concerning his job should it terminate abnormally.

KSDS—Key Sequenced files are organized logically by a user-defined key in each record.

LINK—The LINK SECTION allows the programmer to branch out of his

253

current transaction, perform parts of another application program, and then branch back to complete the current cycle. It is reminiscent of a PERFORM statement in batch environment.

locate mode—When you use storage areas outside your program, you are considered to be in locate mode. This is so because an area has to be located, and you must establish addressability through pointer reference.

Logical Unit of Work—Usually when you have a long, complex program you may want to split it into logically separate segments called *Logical Units of Work*. This can be accomplished through the SYNCPOINT command. When your program abnormally terminates, SYNCPOINT tells CICS that certain segments, or Logical Units of Work, will have to be backed out.

maps—Screen layouts created through Basic Mapping Support; MAPS are logically arranged into mapsets and are referred to in the application program via a number of CICS commands (SEND, RECEIVE, etc.)

menu-driven systems—A general system design philosophy wherein certain levels of responsibilities are established in handling the job. Menu-driven systems provide the user with a comprehensive method of performance.

move mode—When you use your own storage facilities in your program, you are considered to be in move mode. This is so, because all you have to do is to move data in and out of your self-established area.

nucleus—The area that contains a number of internal tables and control programs, such as the Program Control program, the Task Control program, and the Trace Control program.

on-line systems—Those systems in which processing is usually instantaneous and is normally triggered outside the computer room, typically by a user. On-line systems, through telecommunications monitors such as CICS, are able to access, inquire about, and update information on a second's notice.

paging—A technique used to move back and forth through various screen displays. This can be accomplished a number of ways. In our presentation, we recommended that you utilize temporary storage queues.

pointer reference—The name of any BLL cell.

Processing Control Table—This table contains two basic pieces of information. It carries the transaction identifier, or TRANSID, and the name of the program that is matched against the entry in the Processing Program Table, or PPT.

response time—The lapse of time from when a request is initiated at the terminal until the system responds to that request. It is normally contingent of a number of factors, such as file size, access method, number of users competing for the same resources, and how well the system is conceived and implemented.

RETURN—A command required in pseudo-conversational programming when the same transaction has to be reinvoked a number of times.

RRDS—The Relative Record Data Set is organized like a non-VSAM file. You may access the records on that file based on their relative positions.

SDF—The Screen Development Facility is an interactive IBM screen-painting technique that allows you to develop your maps interactively and efficiently.

security—CICS provides security on a multilevel basis. These are password protection and a full range of access through terminals, from limited to unrestricted access. In addition, VSAM also provides comparable file security.

suspense file—This file is designed to monitor changes and utilize data that will become fully authorized some time in the future.

syncpoints—Syncpoints are programmer-requested checkpoints used to simplify recovery procedures.

tables—Tables and table-driven systems, although not purely on-line innovations, give the user a great deal of flexibility and organization. It also saves both time and money because maintenance is vastly simplified, and it is relatively easy to make the system work.

task—When related to transactions and transaction processing, *task* is the internal execution of a transaction for a given user or user group.

TCT—Terminal Control Table.

temporary storage and transient data—CICS provides the application programmer with two types of temporary storage facilities. These are main and auxiliary areas. Main storage is normally used when the data is to be retained for only a short period of time. Auxiliary storage is of a more permanent nature, ranging from a few transaction cycles to as much as a day. Transient Data Control allows the user some sequential, batch processing type capabilities. In fact Transient Data Control provides for direct interface between the on-line system and a number of batch programs.

terminal—A device that is utilized by the operator for sending and receiving information over a communications channel.

transaction—The processing of a single request, such as updating a file or reading a record.

TRANSID—The Transaction Identifier is a four-character (max) identification code that enables the terminal operator to invoke and execute a transaction.

trigger level—The trigger level determines the accumulation of the total number of records before the start of printing. Trigger level is defined in the Destination Control Table as part of the requirements for transient data.

Index

A
ABEND, 211
abnormal termination (abend), 13, 19
absolute time of day, 159
ACCUM, 94
ADD, 188
addressability
  common work area (CWA) in, 203
  GETMAIN/FREEMAIN commands for, 204
  LOAD/RELEASE command and, 208
  locate vs. move mode, 209
  miscellaneous storage techniques for, 204
  overview of, 203
advance to screen entry, 144
ALARM, 94
alternate indexes
  control statements to build, 200
  VSAM, 199
ANS COBOL, 31
application program services, 19
ASKTIME command, 159
asynchronous transaction processing, 149
attribute bytes, 52, 79
attribute character chart, 54-56
attribute definition chart, 54
attribute functions, 56
autocoder, 169
automatic task initiation (ATI), 151

B
base locator, 21
basic assembler language (BAL), 169
basic mapping support (BMS), 14, 26
batch printing
  procedural flow for, 155
  mechanism for, 154
batch programming, 99
BLL cell area, 206
browsing, 115
BTAM, 12

C
CANCEL, 165
case study I
  counter part of program in, 123
  HANDLE AID and HANDLE CONDITION paragraphs in, 126
  highlights of, 119
  logical flow of, 121
  PARA-1 part of code in, 124
  preparing to return to CICS in, 126
  PROCEDURE DIVISION on-line program of, 122

257

READNEXT and READ-TO-SCREEN paragraphs in, 125
  screen generated by SDS module in, 123
  screen layout for, 119
  START BROWSE and NEXT BROWSE code in, 124
case study II
  logical flow of, 137
  overview of, 135
  program for, 139-143
  SDF map for, 146
CHANGE, 188
CICS commands
  logical relations: LINK, XCTL and RETURN, 32
  overview of, 27
  restrictions of, 31
  statement structure of, 30
CICS/DOS/VS, 11
CICS/OS/VS, 11
CICSPARS, 22
cluster definition, 196, 201
COBOL, 27
command being executed, 242
command level interpreter (CECI), 224
common work area (CWA), 203, 205
communications area (COM), 46
  code for information altering within, 49
  DFHEIBLK block in data division of, 48
condition codes, 106
control access, 195
control areas, 192
control interval, 192
control-interval access, 195
conversational coding, 97
CONVERSE, 96, 97
copy book, 74
CTLCHAR, 95
CURSOR, 94
Customer Information Control System (CICS)
  application program services of, 19
  data communications in, 14
  data management functions in, 16
  monitoring functions of, 22
  overview of, 11
  systems services for, 20
  table entries of, 22

D

DAM, 12, 13
DATA, 97
data communications, 14
data entry, 3

data management, 16
data spaces, 201
DATAONLY, 94
debugging, 211
DELAY, 160
DELETE, 110, 188, 157
DELETEQ, 132
design considerations, 3
DEST, 96
destination control, 13, 151
DFHEIBLK, 48
directory, 22
display block, 5
display of screen command, 228
DSECT, 79
dump control, 20
dynamic transaction backout (DTB), 19

E

ENDBR, 116
entry sequenced dataset, 201
ERASE, 94
ERASEUP, 95
execute interface program, 27
execution diagnostics facility (EDF), 20
  initial screen for, 219
  problem solving through, 213
  session review of, 213
  structure of, 212
exit routine, 240-241
expiration time, 159
extrapartition, 149
  destination queue for, 150

F

field analysis report, 74
fields, 52
file control, 22, 23, 24
file control commands
  DELETE command in, 110
  ENDBR command, 116
  file browse command in, 112
  overview of, 103
  READ command in, 104
  READNEXT command, 113
  READPREV command, 114
  RESETBR command, 117
  REWRITE command in, 109
  STARTBR or start browse command in, 112
  WRITE command, 108
file control table, 115
flowchart, 73
fourth generation languages, 7
free space, 201
FREEKB, 95
FROM, 93

258

full access, 195

G
generic deletion, 111
generic key, 105
generic search, 3
GETMAIN/FREEMAIN commands
  for addressability, 204
go to statement, 33
green card, 80

H
HANDLE AID command, 126
  after execution, 221, 223
  prior to execution, 220, 222
HANDLE commands, 126
  application program for, 45
  ignore condition, 46
  logical steps performed by, 44
  use of handle aid and handle condition, 42
HANDLE CONDITION command, 107, 126
  after execution, 226
  completed, 235
  prior to execution, 225
help screen, 7
help screens vs. work screens, 180
HONEOM, 95

I
immediate synchronization points (syndpoints), 19
inquiry language, 7, 8
interactive systems
  design consideration using menu concept, 3
  generic search in, 3
  inquiry and fourth generation languages in, 7
  on-line data entry in, 3
  on-line vs. batch processing in, 1
  response time in, 2
  suspense file in, 3
  workings of, 1-9
interval control, 21
  ASKTIME command, 159
  CANCEL command in, 165
  DELAY command in, 160
  overview of, 159
  POST command in, 160
  RETRIEVE command in, 164
  START command in, 162
  WAIT command in, 161
intialized program, 231
intrapartition, 149
  destination queue, 150, 151
ISAM, 12, 13, 58

J
journal control module, 13, 246

K
key sequenced dataset, 201

L
L40, 95
L64, 95
L80, 95
LENGTH, 93
level interpreter, 20
LINK, 32
  overview of, 33
linkage cell (BLL), 21
linking, 33
LOAD/RELEASE command, 208
locate mode, 209
logical units of work, 19

M
main storage, 127
maintenance code, 60
map editor, 65
map sets, 74
MAPONLY, 94
maps, 15, 27, 51, 74, 229
  attribute bytes, 52
  creation, 51
  generation of, 57
  overview of, 51
  physical, 51
  symbolic, 51
  unformatted, 71
MAPSET, 93
mapsets, 51
master catalog, 192
master terminal commands (CSMT), 243
  full complement of, 244
  mandatory input requirements of, 244
  successful execution of, 245
MAXLENGTH, 96
menu, 5
  screen, 3
  sub-, 6
menu concept, 3
  level I and II, 171
  level III, 173
  multilevel payroll module, 172
modified data tag (MDT), 53
move mode, 99, 209
multitasking, 19, 21, 25
MVS, 11
MVS/XA, 11

N
NEXT BROWSE, 124

259

nondisplay map field, 100
nonprocedural language, 7
not-found condition, 234
NOTRUNCATE, 97

O

optional field
　restricted, 190
　totally, 190
OS/VS1, 11

P

PAGING, 93
password file, 195
　reading the, 238-239
paths, 186
payroll, 7
performance analysis, 23
physical map, 74
pointer reference, 209
POST, 160
PROCEDURE DIVISIONS, 97, 122
processing control, 24
processing errors, 106
processing program table, 22, 25
program control, 21, 22
program initialization, 231
program processing table, 58
promotional line, 119
properties, 52

Q

queues, 127

R

read access, 195
READ command, 104
READNEXT, 113, 125
READ-TO-SCREEN, 125
READPREV, 114
READQ, 130, 155
RECEIVE MAP, 98, 99, 233
recovery, 211
recovery and debugging
　ABEND command in, 211
　command level interpreter (CECI) in, 224
　execution diagnostics facility (EDF) in, 212
　journal control in, 246
　master terminal commands (CSMT) in, 243
　overview of, 211
　source code for, 214-217
relative records dataset, 201
REQID, 94
RESETBR, 117
RETRIEVE, 164
RETURN command, 32

prior to execution, 230
REWRITE, 109

S

scratch pad facility, 16, 130
screen definition facility (SDF), 20, 57, 62
　application structure screen for, 72
　COBOL DSECT screen for, 79
　field analysis report I-IX, 82-90
　field attribute definition screen for, 69
　field identification screen for, 67
　field names screen for, 75
　flowchart representation of, 73
　full-screen naming screen for, 70
　input pictures screen for, 76
　map characteristics screen for, 66
　map identification screen for, 64
　map status report screen for, 81
　master selection screen for, 63
　output pictures screen for, 77
　unformatted map screen for, 78
screen display, 27
SEND command
　after execution, 232
SEND MAP, 93, 227
SLRII, 22
sowing key assignments, 40
spanned record, 192
START, 162
STARTBR, 112, 124
storage control, 21
suspense file, 3
symbolic map, 74
synchronous transaction processing, 149
syncpoints, 20, 25
syndpoints, 19
system services, 20
systems design under CICS command (Part I), 171
　help screen for, 178
　menu concept of, 171
　overview of, 169
　table driven systems for, 176
systems design under CICS command (Part II)
　ADD, DELETE, and CHANGE, 188
　creating paths with, 186
　locating data with, 187
　message prompting with, 183
systems network architecture (SNA), 15, 17
systems services
　interval control, 21
　program control, 21

260

storage control, 21
task control, 21

T

table maintenance screen, 57
table-driven systems, 176
task, 16, 25
task control, 21
TCAM, 12
telecommunications line, 14
temporary storage
  DELETEQ TS command, 132
  overview of, 127
  possible queue standardizations for, 128
  queues for, 127
  READQ TS command, 130
  WRITEQ command in, 129
  WRITEQ TS command for, 128
TERMINAL, 93
terminal control commands
  converse command in, 96
  miscellaneous commands for, 98
  RECEIVE MAP command for, 98
  SEND MAP command of, 93
trace control, 13, 20
transaction, 16, 25
transaction identifier (TRANSID), 16
transient data control, 13, 18, 154
  automatic task initiation (ATI) in, 151
  DELETE command for, 157
  destination control table in, 151
  exception condition codes for, 156
  overview of, 149
  READQ TD command, 155

WRITEQ TD command in, 152
transient data set, 150

U

unformatted maps, 71
unlock option, specifications for, 236-237
update access, 195
updating file, 107, 108
user catalog, 192

V

virtual telecommunications access method (VTAM), 152
VM/370, 11
VSAM, 12, 58
  access methods services for, 194
  alternate indexes to, 199
  catalog relationships in, 193
  cluster definition in, 196
  introduction to, 191
  security and protection of, 195
VSE, 11
VTAM, 12

W

WAIT, 94, 161
work screens vs. help screens, 180
write control character (WCC), structural detail of, 95
WRITE, 108
WRITEQ, 129, 152

X

XCFL, 32
XCTL, 33